# THE
# FRUGAL
# YOUTH
# CYBRARIAN

## Bargain Computing for Kids

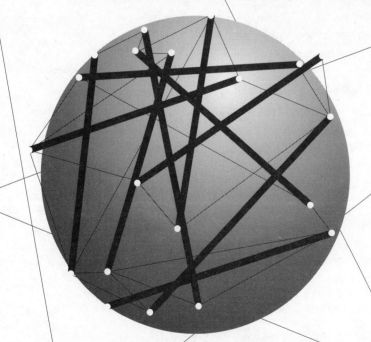

# Calvin Ross

## American Library Association
### Chicago and London
### 1997

...suring the reliability of information
...akes no warranty, express or implied,
...nformation, and does not assume and
...erson for any loss or damage caused by
errors or omissions ...

Trademarked names appear in the text of this book. Rather than identify or insert a trademark symbol at the appearance of each name, the author and the American Library Association state that the names are used for editorial purposes exclusively, to the ultimate benefit of the owners of the trademarks. There is absolutely no intention of infringement on the rights of the trademark owners.

Project editor: David M. Epstein

Cover design: Richmond Jones

Composition by Calvin Ross in Bauhaus and Palm Springs using Aldus Pagemaker 5.0 on a homebuilt IBM-compatible 486-DX120 PC

Printed on 50-pound Thor offset, a pH-neutral stock, and bound in 10-point coated cover stock by McNaughton & Gunn

The paper used in this publication meets the minimum requirements of American National Standard for Information Sciences—Permanence of Paper for Printed Library Materials, ANSI Z39.48-1992. ∞

**Library of Congress Cataloging-in-Publication Data**

Ross, Calvin.
    The frugal youth cybrarian : bargain computing for kids / by Calvin Ross.
        p.    cm.
    Includes indexes.
    ISBN 0-8389-0694-X (alk. paper)
    1. Children's libraries—Collection development.  2. School libraries—Collection development.  3. Libraries—Special collections—Shareware (Computer software).  4. Libraries—Special collections—Free computer software.  5. Education—Data processing.  I. Title.
Z718.1.R677    1997
025.2'187625—DC20                  96-45724

Printed in the United States of America.

01  00  99  98  97       5  4  3  2  1

# Contents

# Introduction

Those of us in the world of information services and education are living through some very exciting times. The revolution known, rather too compactly, as the Information Age has changed the nature of the library and the librarian very dramatically. Nothing demonstrates this more than the current struggle to find a coherent, comprehensive new title to take the place of the apparently antiquated term, *librarian*. In various e-mail discussion groups I have been participating in, the search is ongoing. Today's librarian is now variously described as media specialist, library media specialist, information specialist, library information center director, library information specialist, learning resources specialist, teacher-librarian, and my personal favorite (because it sounds so exotic), cybrarian.

Unfortunately, another profound movement accompanies the Information Age: the slow and steady erosion of public funding of libraries and education. Not every library and school in every county in every state is experiencing the simultaneity of technological explosion and budget crunch in the same way; but the vast majority are, to varying degrees, making decisions on very vital issues that will shape the near- and far-term destinies of their library media centers and the accompanying media distribution services.

Because of the too-often-high price tags of software and reference resources, libraries and schools are having to make decisions that are self-limiting at best. In today's environment, frustration abounds. We want to do well, but how do we do it? The use of the Internet seems clearly imperative. Its vast, ever-expanding resources are tantalizing in their diversity and ingenuity, but how can we afford them? And if we can afford them, how do we manage them or utilize them when our constantly evolving roles place demands on our time (and in some cases, our expertise) which preclude us from reaching first base in this brand new ball game? To extend the baseball metaphor a bit, we're at the plate and we just want to get on base. Some of us have the power and resources to smack a double up the alley; others of us will have to content ourselves with reaching first base with a bunt or a walk. Once on base, we have a chance to work our way home.

That is what *The Frugal Youth Cybrarian* is all about: finding our way home. There are many ways to score; sometimes the craftiest are the most satisfying.

*The Frugal Youth Cybrarian* hopes to help by introducing you to the many resources available in the online world, all at bargain prices compared to what's on the retail shelf or in the catalogs. As you read this book, I would hope more than anything to hear you say, "I didn't know that was out there!" You'll find pointers to unexplored areas of cyberspace and windows into areas you've never accessed. In turn, those who depend on you will find creative avenues to learning and growing.

I wrote this book for library staff whose job is connecting kids to the world of information available by computer. In public libraries, this would be the responsibility of the youth librarian and technology staff. However, in certain schools and districts, a number of people are given this role. Some of you just happen to be the smartest or most experienced with computers in your school. You're given a little stipend and a title such as technology coordinator or computer mentor. Maybe you're a math teacher and you've been given the job of managing the computer lab because, well, nobody else stepped forward. Many school districts have had the foresight to appoint a technology director to develop and coordinate a cohesive districtwide plan. All of you who don this hat have had your hands full and all too often you are given scant time and resources.

## Shareware and Freeware

At the heart of *The Frugal Youth Cybrarian* is the phenomenon of shareware and freeware. I hope to direct you to the most creative and helpful software products available online and save you the hours it would take to find them yourselves. I also seek to flatten the learning curve for understanding how to harvest other innovative software in the online world. In the future you'll be able to go out into cyberspace knowing how and where to search for just what you require. With the low cost of shareware and freeware, you'll be able to provide software to the schools, districts, libraries, and counties you serve while helping them all to stay within their budgets!

When I began to investigate the use of shareware and freeware in libraries and schools, I expected to find these wonderful resources already widely at play. I was a bit shocked to find their use almost non-existent! Yet, the more I interviewed teachers, librarians, and curriculum directors, the more I realized why these resources have not received widespread use. The very bureaucratic organization of educational institutions (and I don't mean this derisively) tends, not surprisingly, to departmentalize and compartmentalize the various functions into rather strict organizational roles. For software and other media, this tends to make educational purchasing strictly a retail matter. Discovering the value of shareware and freeware is understandably difficult and rare in this environment. This mainstreaming of media purchasing is very natural and not altogether unreasonable. It just doesn't encourage innovation.

I'll explain later in greater depth, but for now suffice it to say that shareware and freeware differ in no way from retail software offered by stores, catalogs, or textbook companies except that this segment of the industry chooses to market itself online. Except that shareware and freeware are only visible to those who actively search for them, this marketing strategy has the advantage of requiring no packaging or advertising, thus substantially reducing prices. This has no effect on the quality of the best of shareware. In fact, the very nature of shareware has allowed it to produce some of the most creative and expertly targeted products around today. Is it any wonder that Netscape, the strongest emerging company in the computer world recently, is using the shareware approach to introduce and deliver its new products and versions?

I would be less than candid if I did not tell you that, due to low or nonexistent capitalization costs, many marginally effective shareware and freeware programs make their way around the online world too. This should in no way discourage you from using the best of them; for the very chance-taking encouraged by this marketing strategy allows the creativity that blossoms into the superb products to be found. The purpose of this book is to guide you to the flowers among the weeds.

## The Range of Solutions

When I began writing this book, the focus was bargain software for kids. This remains at the heart of it. However, the more I researched the needs of libraries and schools, the more needs I found. Librarians, administrators, and teachers need more than a new, creative math game or a bang-up geography tutorial. You all need tools, tools, and more tools to fulfill the expanding demands of your jobs. In this rich, new world of multimedia computing, you need desktop publishing programs and utilities, graphics viewers, paint and photo retouching applications, clip art, presentation materials, animations, sounds, templates, fonts, and the myriad objects that enhance computer-driven document production. You need cataloging and bar-coding tools. You need classroom, school management and accounting programs. You need worksheet, word-puzzle, and test generators. So much needs to be accomplished every working day, and anything that helps with this awesome workload means more time spent delivering information and learning to library users and students.

The beauty of shareware and freeware is that they can so directly target a need. A math teacher in Ann Arbor, Michigan, who understands programming and knows how time-consuming it is to create math worksheets, decides to put together a program that can generate unlimited, random worksheets, and *voilà*, it's out in the online world as freeware. You'll find many such gems in *The Frugal Youth Cybrarian*, saving yourself the endless hours of searching Internet sites. After you become adept, you'll soon be sleuthing out your own jewels.

One of the largest and fastest-evolving resources in the history of the world is at our fingertips: the Internet. The World Wide Web, which might be described as the greatest and most provocative communal project yet devised to share information, is host to so many resources it boggles the mind. Many of you are already comfortably surfing around this intriguing world to find the many treasures that await you. Others have found it disconcertingly difficult to navigate. Since so much of this book requires using the Internet, I'll sort it out for you. Then I'll point you to the many great sites for librarians and educators.

I listened to the desires of teachers and librarians and found out what kinds of resources are most in demand. I've put together a list of today's most valuable sites on the World Wide Web for librarians, media specialists, and teachers. There are lesson plans, field trips, and resources of all kinds for enlivening the classroom, as well as links to curriculum tools for history, science, math, astronomy, art, music, culture, health, and more. There are mailing lists and listservs you can join to stay abreast of your subject area and share ideas with like-minded souls via e-mail. As with shareware and freeware, by the time you've meandered through the Web sites in this list, you'll have begun to find the links to links upon links that make the World Wide Web so exciting. As new Web sites pop up, you'll have the tools to locate them.

An important area where you'll be served by this book is in security and protection. So many of you voiced concerns with protecting the programs on your computers and in your labs. I've hunted down some very effective security programs for locking kids out of places on your hard disks where they shouldn't go. Many of you worry, too, about downloading resources from the online world because of the dangers of infection by computer viruses. In this book, you'll find the latest, most popular and effective shareware programs for viral protection, and I list the online sites for staying current with emerging threats. The existence of viruses doesn't need to knock you off your game.

Though the Internet currently dominates the online world, the commercial online services and bulletin board systems that preceded it in popularity are still of great value, especially as large repositories of shareware and freeware. I'll show you how to use them to your advantage.

In addition to all the Internet offers, CD-ROMs are storehouses of information. Many feature multimedia presentation. I not only make recommendations for standard library reference CD-ROMs, but also provide strategies for low-cost acquisition of many CD-ROMs that deepen and enrich the existing resources of your libraries and classrooms.

Finally, I'll spend a little time on ways to lower the cost of acquiring the hardware our libraries and schools need to continue this technological revolution.

In creating *The Frugal Youth Cybrarian*, I've taken quite a journey of discovery. Without leaving my computer workstation, I've been to Taiwan, Israel, the Netherlands, Austria, Singapore, Germany, Finland, Japan, France, Australia, Uruguay, Hong Kong, Canada, Spain, Belgium, China, Britain, and scores of FTP and World Wide Web sites across the United States. I've talked by e-mail with hundreds of librarians and educators who have pointed the way both to the needs of today's media specialist and to the resources to fulfill those needs. As you travel through these pages, I sincerely hope you find it to be a trip well taken.

# PART ONE

# Bargain-Hunting Strategies

# Chapter One

# Crafty Solutions to the Budget Conundrum

## Declining Budgets

We live in a most remarkable time. What has correctly been called the American Century is coming to an end in the midst of a total reexamination of just what the United States of America is all about as we approach the twenty-first century. The Industrial Age, which powered the American rise to world dominance, is rapidly receding into the mists of history as the new epoch, the Information Age, is yet to be fully understood in its ramifications or potential.

Many of us remember watching the news reports in disbelief on October 4, 1957, when the Soviet Union launched Sputnik I and moved ahead of the United States in the space race. That event has receded in significance, but it drove American education and funding for the next two decades.

The national debt, the great legacy of the Cold War, is a burden that places great downward pressure on nearly every sphere of public life, including education. It is deeply ironic that our rivalry with the Soviet

Union not only fueled the rise in support of public education but has also contributed to its decline.

From this recent past comes the reality for library services and education today: As technological possibilities expand, our school and library budgets decline. With the growth of global competition, never before have we been more in need of strong public education. Yet never before have we been more in the mood to abandon it. Education budgets at federal, state, and local levels continue to decline in real dollars nearly everywhere. In its tumultuous budget battles, Congress has shown increasing determination to undermine education funding. As of this writing, Congress is embroiled in an epic struggle that threatens education more than ever. When this fighting subsides, funding for some key programs may be restored, but nothing in Washington bodes well for the foreseeable future.

Granted, these kinds of threats are nothing new; neither are declining budgets. But to get a genuine feeling for what educators have been experiencing in the past decade, I recently spent a few months listening to librarians and teachers all over the country. Time after time, they spoke of a decade of stagnant or declining budgets. All across the United States, these are the kinds of comments I heard again and again:

"The block grants came in the form of Chapter 2 funds administered by the state and could be spent in ways other than library funding so, naturally, our funds decreased from about $10,000 a year for books to about $3,500."

"My district receives about half of what it got ten years ago from these federal programs. Since these funds have historically been spent for library books in our district, this has severely impacted book collections."

"My budget is exactly the same as it was ten years ago, which means of course that my buying power is less than one-half. I buy fewer books. I don't replace worn-out classics like the *Berenstain Bears* often enough. I keep reference purchases to a minimum. I buy few professional books...I spend more on supplies because the cost has skyrocketed and computers require more kinds of extra supplies than previous technologies.

Disks, paper, notebooks for the documentation, etc. In addition to the regular budget, we have lost money from federal funding."

"My library budget has decreased 30 percent in the last six years alone! Have I noticed a pattern? I would have to characterize it as a steady general erosion."

"Over the past several years our budget has increased very slightly, about 5 percent at a time, though not every year. One year in the last five there was a slight decrease. All this despite the fact that our computer software needs have greatly increased our nonbook expenditures. Therefore we are spending noticeably less on books, though not willingly or happily."

"I have been a 9–12 librarian since 1974 and my budget allocation from the district has not changed in over fourteen years."

"Decrease in budget, due to declining enrollment. About 10 percent per year for Media Center. Yes, it has affected my choices. Due to information technology more of the budget is spent on CD-ROM resources for reference and subscription services. Less and less is spent on materials for books, other than reference books or encyclopedias."

And the comments go on and on, with roughly the same trend common to all. There were, not surprisingly, perhaps one out of ten whose budgets had risen, but those fortunate few expressed that the increases came from hard-fought battles and they urged all to fight the good fight. In most cases, as with the comments above, the erosion of funding continues unabated, with the added pressure of continuing inflation in book prices further contributing to the strain.

I was struck to find that librarians and teachers commonly responded by buying fewer and fewer books. Notice, too, how these resources are being redirected to technology such as computers, networking, and software. Here is the dichotomy at the heart of the struggle in our public and school libraries. And this is why I hope, with this book, to help you lower your technology costs. Computers should not supplant books; they should supplement them. But perhaps, just as the industrial base of America must surely give way to service industries as we move from a resource-rich society to an information-rich one, so must the libraries of the future be shaped to reflect the new realities. Nevertheless, as America struggles to maintain that all-important balance required of a self-sustaining, self-invigorating economy, so must today's libraries and schools work to incorporate what the new technologies offer without sacrificing those resources of the past that continue to hold their value.

## The Promise of Computers

I, like Captain Picard of the Starship *Enterprise*, have a warm spot in my heart for the good, solid book that one can hold in one's hands and open to an inspiring, dog-eared passage. When I stand with my well-worn copy of *Great Expectations* by Charles Dickens in one hand and the latest, greatest CD-ROM in the other, I am not confused as to which one moves me or tugs at my heartstrings. But neither is Captain Picard confused as to what directs his craft where no man has gone before: It's the computer. It, as much as anything, is leading us into the future.

A decade ago, the personal computer was a nifty timesaver when it came to word processing and crunching numbers, but its expanding capabilities have grown at such a rate that today it places an astounding set of resources at one's fingertips. Individuals of many stripes now run companies from their home offices. Documents and publications that once required a skillful layout artist and professional printer are now easily and quickly produced without the added expense. Educational and reference materials for children that were inconceivable ten years ago are now available at the click of a mouse.

Many components have contributed to this expansion of horizons. Affordable infinite-color monitors needed to be produced. Hard-drive capacity needed to increase, as did the speed of microprocessors. CD-ROM hardware had to be developed and improved. Lastly, the software developers had to create the programs and applications needed and organize the content to be harvested. This has all been accomplished with lightning speed. Every day, prices fall on hitherto unaffordable hardware and software. Everything is becoming more and more affordable while media are becoming better and better. I shudder with delight (and not a little dizziness) at the thought of what will be happening in six months, a year or two, even five years hence.

Still, the overall expense of it is daunting. When libraries can't afford new books and cut back on operating hours just to stay within shrinking budgets, who cares if there's a revolution going on out on the Information Superhighway? When school districts can't replace the textbooks in their classrooms or afford to build badly needed new schools, how can they sink thousands of dollars into the new tools required to utilize the newest computer media or link up to the Internet?

## The Expense of Computers

Throughout the past decade, schools and libraries have, in fact, worked hard to bring the computer into the classroom. Apple Corporation, in its marketing wisdom coupled with a generosity of spirit, helped to bring its computers into thousands of schools across the country. Where IBM and other companies would not, Apple guaranteed technical support and maintenance services and thus achieved hegemony in computer-based education across the nation. This early lead has, unfortunately, led to a major quandary for many schools and districts: what to do with the thousands of obsolete Apple computers, such as the model IIe, that fill the computer labs (or the storage rooms) everywhere. Though their early lead in the education world has led to an obsolescence problem for Apple machines, many middle and high schools that favored the IBM-compatible computer now face the same dilemma.

In fact, there are ways to utilize some of these obsolete machines, if one taps into the plethora of shareware and freeware available online. We may need to continue buying new machines, but so many of the old machines can still be of value when tagged with the right software.

In this way we can offer more resources for learning by making use of what we already have while we expand in other directions with our new equipment.

For most libraries and schools, the reasons for bringing the new technology to bear on today's challenges are far too compelling to ignore. The ongoing move to automation taking place across the nation has led to efficiency and convenience that will ultimately prove to be quite cost-saving. Where hundreds of square feet were formerly needed to house the tons of newspapers and periodicals for library customers, the electronic resources are too brilliant in their ease of use, compactness, and scope of material to eschew. Even microfiche systems now look bulky, awkward, and inefficient compared with today's CD-ROM technology. Nowadays, a year of *New York Times* articles can fit on one compact disc. The searchability of this new medium far outstrips that of the old. A patron pops a disc into a CD-ROM drive (or accesses it from a CD-ROM tower), opens the program, types in a topic, and in seconds dozens of related articles are at his fingertips waiting to be perused and printed. Research that once took a week now may take one afternoon. This is truly an information revolution.

A similar revolution is taking place in our schools. Many of the basic skills can be reinforced by the power of the computer and the innovative software being produced for it. Few would argue against the notion that people teach people best. A machine can never be the guiding hand that a teacher offers to his or her students. When a child says, "I don't get it," a computer can't know the child well enough to say, "Okay, let's look at it this way." A computer can't look into the depth of the human character and mirror it back in all its richness and frailty so that we can understand the meaning of human history. Still, from my experience, basic skills such as math, spelling, reading, geography, and the like can be reinforced extremely well by using computers, offering more time to teachers to add the character and richness that flesh out the deeper meaning. The ways that computers bring information sources into the classroom are also a great boon to the student-teacher experience.

# The Shareware Solution

The part of this expanding set of resources that this book hopes to introduce to librarians and educators is the creative and innovative software known as shareware and freeware. There are thousands of independent programmers, often librarians and educators themselves, who have spent their days designing low-cost programs specifically targeted to the needs of libraries and schools. I will explain shareware in greater detail later in the book, but for now it's important to state that these resources, marketed online out in cyberspace, are often missed in this overly commercial world. You won't find these programs in the catalogs; you won't hear the textbook representatives touting them; there are many reasons why you'll never hear of them until you become educated about the online world. However, the only way to tap into this expanding horizon is to jump off into cyberspace and go trolling. To save you time, I've done a lot of that trolling for you.

Shareware and freeware are hardly the only new resources out on the online services and the Internet. The World Wide Web, easily the most popular and accessible resource of the Internet, is growing at such an incredible rate and is becoming such a powerful resource tool that I've made it a secondary emphasis of this volume. Information is being digitized and made available to the people around the world by this web of computers straddling the globe. It's easy to become mesmerized by a new medium, but it is my fervent belief that the single most profound movement in the human sphere today (other than trying to feed the teeming masses, but that's another story) is the linking up of cultures around the world via the huge windows opened by the World Wide Web. Due to its interactive and visual nature, the Web may far outstrip television and even the telephone in its ability to bring the world together into that "global village" envisioned by Marshall McLuhan so many years ago. He was right for reasons he could not have predicted. We can see it and profit and grow by it. Not only may we open the windows of the World Wide Web, but we may also participate further by opening our own windows for the world to look back and see who we are and what we have to offer.

Though the Web is becoming more commercial as the underwriting of it transfers from government agencies to a commercial consortium, I am continually struck by how the notion of sharing permeates the World Wide Web experience. If I want something, I go browsing around the Web and more often than not return with more than what I went looking for. Not only that, but I come away from the experience feeling moved by the generosity of others and proud to be a part of the human race. This feeling, shared by so many around the world, is a powerful teaching tool in and of itself. We strive to instill in our students the love of knowledge and the dignity and understanding to use this knowledge in ways that further the human experience. We wish to help our charges break out of the parochialism which often marginalizes others' concerns and values while isolating ourselves from the larger society and its diverse members. The World Wide Web breaks down these barriers and exposes us to a larger vision of the world. What a great thing it is for children to be able to experience from an early age this vast, ongoing sharing fest! The medium does half our work for us. This aspect of the medium is worth its weight in gold, notwithstanding the information delivery and learning which were the original goal.

So here we have had a quick overview of the expanding horizons of computers and the online world that now extend to the far reaches of the globe. We are also painfully aware of the budgetary problems libraries and schools face when deciding how to allocate scant resources. Everyone wants to expand services using the new technologies, but how can it be done in the prevailing atmosphere of funding decline? It takes dedication, innovation, and hard work, but it can and must be done.

## Reconciling Rising Expectations and Fiscal Reality

It's all too common for bureaucratic institutions, of which public libraries and school systems are prime examples, to be constrained by organizational pressures and chains of command. It is the exceptional situation when an individual librarian or teacher feels empowered to make his or her own choices, even when those choices would be superior to the organization's decisions and be innovative at a time when innovation is most required.

It's also a general rule that the further up the chain of command one goes, the less innovation and inspiration one finds. Fortunately, this is untrue is many cases, but sadly for many counties and school districts, not in all. It then falls to the visionary down in the ranks to apply upward pressure for change, always a dicey proposition.

It would be unfair not to point out that the further toward the top of the organizational chart you are, the more people you are obliged to help; your resources then tend to become diluted, making it harder and harder to please everyone. So there is reason to be understanding of everyone's plight when trying to break out of molds that are as self-limiting as those most librarians and educators find themselves stuck in today.

I hope, then, that the kind of advice I am offering can be heard not only by those in the trenches but by those in the command bunker as well. The basis of the advice, thus, is this: Break out of the mold when it comes to software and reference material acquisition. Don't be as rigid about how you obtain it as you may have been in the past. Learn to be crafty, innovative, and creative, even if it means a little sweat and extra work. It may be the only way to expand the services you wish to provide in the library or obtain the tools necessary to make our classrooms (and the future members of society that they prepare) ready for the opportunities of the twenty-first century.

The same goes for hardware. There are some crafty ways to obtain new hardware, as well as for deploying aging hardware to tasks suitable to it. Not all of the old stuff needs to be consigned to the trash heap. There are many programs which do quite nicely on some otherwise obsolete gear. Learning where this can work takes a little self-education, but it's well worth it when you see how much it can yield.

There are four major threads to follow:

1.  Shareware and freeware are wonderful, low-cost programs that can fill needs in administrative offices, libraries, labs, and classrooms.

2. Buying all our reference CD-ROMs and educational CD-ROMs through normal channels will eat up budgets quickly. Learn to shop the way America shops, by bargain-hunting every step of the way. Thousands of dollars can be saved.
3. Not using aging equipment appropriately is a major failure to utilize resources to the best of our ability. If our equipment is, in fact, outdated, we must learn how to get more and better equipment without busting the budget. This means learning not to overbuy. We must learn to buy the most powerful equipment whose cost has plummeted but whose usefulness is only marginally diminished. Many have found it wise to stagger district purchases so that every piece of hardware does not become ancient at the same time. Leasing hardware may also be a cost-effective option for some.
4. Learn to harvest the World Wide Web for all the software treasures it possesses and all the diverse resources it offers. Being well-connected to the Web can expand reference resources and provide new learning and publishing tools without putting undue strain on funding sources.

## New Library Services

Due to technological advances, both public and school libraries have recently expanded their roles in providing services. Public libraries everywhere are installing media centers with the many new reference and multimedia tools coming onto the market. You can play additional roles, in both the adult media rooms and in the children's wing, by providing learning centers that supplement the public education system. These tools can be in the form of CD-ROM multimedia programs as well as the more utilitarian software. The use of shareware and freeware can provide hours of learning activities for all ages. These low-cost software programs can help libraries branch out into offering desktop publishing and word-processing services they hitherto couldn't have dreamed of affording. In this way, libraries can expand their services without feeling too much strain on existing budgets.

Those of you in school libraries can do very much the same. Many of you already host the site of your schools' computer labs; you can expand the versatility of your offerings by utilizing shareware and freeware desktop publishing and graphics applications. You can help students improve the final product of their writing and publishing by making available to them the vast resources of graphics, fonts, clip art, and animation available on the World Wide Web (many such sites for these goodies are in this book's Web listings). Finally, you can respond to individual teachers from various departments by making certain types of shareware and freeware programs available.

I don't need to tell you how many teachers rely on library media specialists to point the way to new computer resources. Sometimes the only technology consultant available in school districts will be the librarians. You can help not only by making shareware, freeware, and Internet resources available to the many who seek your guidance, but also by doing a little motivational work. In many cases, teachers won't innovate in their use of computers without a little (or a huge) push from you. If you're feeling a real time crunch, just sharing this book with them may get them started on the road to self-sufficiency in the use of the marvelous resources of the Internet and the online world.

Just as our real or imagined struggle with the Soviet Union inspired our drive toward better public education back in the fifties, we have our own new "foes" to motivate us. The most popular one is "global competition." Whether this new view of our economic relationship with the rest of the world is overstated or overused by politicians and the media is open to serious question; that the nature of business and competition is changing as we move toward the close of the century is not. Maybe we need a bogeyman to inspire us to take action. Maybe global competition will be the force behind our efforts to prepare our children for the world of tomorrow. It's always good to know why we do what we do.

I prefer a more positive view of the forces at play. We don't need foes, real or imagined. We live in an exciting world where boundaries to new experience are being broken down every day. Bridges are being

13

built everywhere to openly share the world's repositories of information and innovation. Due to our technological ingenuity, we have never had greater resources available to us on so many fronts: in education, medicine, business, entertainment, and science. We can use these marvelous new tools to do wonderful things in the coming century. If, because of tight budgets, we have to be a little crafty, a little resourceful, to realize the benefits of the Information Age more fully, well then, let's do so. We can't afford not to.

# Chapter Two

# Shareware and Freeware for Libraries and Schools

The most clearly recognizable word anywhere in the world is Coca-Cola. Whether it should be so is moot. The most recognizable symbol or logo of all time is most certainly the Coca-Cola logo. Imagine, if you will, a world in which Coca-Cola had never been tasted, a world in which the Coca-Cola logo had never been seen. If you stumbled across a bottle of Coca-Cola in a café in, say, the Outback of Australia, would it be any less appealing a beverage than in the real world in all its fame and glory? Probably so. We can't undo one hundred years of marketing. We drink Coke because it's Coke, not just because it's a tasty, bubbly drink.

It's the same with software. The big names in the world of software such as Microsoft, Corel, Adobe, Novell, Lotus, and the like have established reputations that are hard to match. Of course, this has very much to do with the fact that they make good, reliable products that allow us to use our personal computers in completing the tasks we set for ourselves. Is computer software any less useful because it doesn't carry a famous logo or is put out by a company that is unknown to us? Naturally, my answer is no.

## What is Shareware?

Shareware (and its cost-free companion, freeware) is very much like that no-name bottle of brown soda in the Australian Outback. It's the real thing, it just hasn't marketed itself indelibly into our consciousness. Simply put, shareware is software marketed by its producers by placing it online for us to discover, sometimes by pure chance and other times by very purposeful searching. By using this marketing technique, shareware producers can offer their creations at a fraction of the cost of most software programs. They can also afford to target small segments of computer users. They don't need to gain a certain level of market share to justify their research and development and subsequent marketing expenses. They simply develop a program and launch it out into cyberspace, where it cruises around on its own looking for customers. This process is highly democratic in that useful, well-designed programs are downloaded by the thousands while the duds float around until system operators delete them out of their misery. Harvesting the best of shareware is mostly a process of separating the wheat from the chaff. Much of this task I have done for you, and the results are found in my extensive shareware listings in this book.

One of the wonderful aspects of shareware is that it is often created to fill a niche that commercial software ignores. For example, a program that generates random math worksheets has very little chance of succeeding as a retail product, but may be created by an amateur programmer in the education field solely to benefit his or her peers in the profession. This type of program is often offered as freeware; if a small fee is requested, it is often sought only to recoup expenses or to provide funds for further creations.

If you think this is a small segment of the computer software industry, think again. There are literally thousands upon thousands of shareware programs available at FTP and World Wide Web sites around the world, from the U.S. to Israel to Hong Kong. Thousands of people have dedicated their energies, often for no reward, to spreading this huge resource to the masses of computer users lucky enough to have become acquainted with the concept. I am one such lucky fellow. I have been using shareware for years. I never could have afforded to help in my son's education to the extent that I have without it. I've used many other shareware programs in managing my various enterprises, and I've received hours of enjoyment on my computer listening to music and exploring digital composition, all because of shareware and freeware.

Though I had already written a parents' guide to educational shareware, I hadn't considered one for libraries and schools until I had a conversation with the local K–6 curriculum director. She told me that they had just introduced a new set of math textbooks to the district. I asked her if the textbooks had accompanying software and she replied, "Yes, but as the districtwide license for only one of the programs in their software package was $16,000, we decided not to go with any of it." I was shocked! Then I thought of how much shareware could be purchased for $16,000, and I had to get the word out concerning this tremendous resource.

## Tools for Learners, Educators, and Librarians

In the online world you can find some of the best programs for assisting in education as exist anywhere, whether it be on the retail shelves of software dealers or in the catalogs of educational materials providers. This is especially true in the area of learning and reinforcing basic skills. There are brilliant programs in math, reading, spelling, phonics, geography, and social studies. There are a host of applications for student desktop publishing and electronic book creation. There are advanced graphing programs for higher mathematics. There are innumerable useful tools for the K–12 classroom. The heart of this book is chiefly dedicated to finding programs and resources for patrons of libraries and students in schools, but I've gone much further than that.

Knowing that these programs would best be directed to students and teachers through the hands of librarians, I decided also to look for those things that could be helpful to librarians themselves. I was not disappointed. There are many fine cataloging shareware programs available which can easily help you automate small to medium-sized collections. Some even include bar-coding options. For those that didn't, I searched for and found bar-code-generating programs. I've found a few programs which can build MARC records, print spine label sets, cards, lists, and so on. There are also a number of programs which streamline research projects and allow for easy organization of research materials. Since librarians have a continuing need for desktop publishing and presentation graphics, I looked far and wide and found many useful tools to assist in the librarian's own productivity.

Realizing how the time-consuming tasks of preparing teaching materials and lesson plans burden teachers today, I looked for tools for creating classroom activities. I found word-search puzzle generators, crossword puzzle creators, and many pencil-and-paper activity makers. In the listings you will find math worksheet and test generators. I even found a program that creates not only math homework and tests but also provides a clear, effective, interactive tutorial for solving the various algorithms in ways that clearly demonstrate them. I've also been able to provide a number of desktop lesson planners and helpful tools such as automated gradebooks.

In addition to programs for teachers that increase productivity, I've located many programs that enrich their lesson plans or support their teaching. For example, many teachers encourage students to keep journals and therefore are always on the lookout for journal topics. Out there online, I've found programs that contain hundreds of proverbs, give teachers a constant source of today-in-history information, provide online grammar and style guides, give students story-starting ideas, and interactively teach the rudiments of effective essay writing. There are a variety of spelling and grammar checkers and aids that work with a variety of programs and platforms. From my investigations of teachers' needs I've learned that teachers have many unconventional ways of developing their students, so you'll find in my listings some offbeat inclusions such as genealogy programs to help us understand our cultural diversity.

I didn't know what I would find to help administrators, but again I was not disappointed. There are useful scheduling tools and what-not, but I was especially elated to find a shareware package capable of administering an entire school, keeping all student records, inventory-ing the school band's equipment, and providing for the accounting and billing needs in the event that the school was a private institution. This program, called SchoolWrite, even tracks all students' immunization and disciplinary records.

I describe here my exciting journey of discovery for one purpose: to demonstrate the endless resources you'll find once you become adept at searching the online world to fulfill your own particular needs. The world of shareware and freeware is diverse, and not nearly as obscure or as difficult to find as a solitary outpost in the Australian Outback. Truth be told, the sources of shareware are right under your noses, if you have a computer, modem, and adequate Internet access. Even membership in one of the major online services such as America Online or CompuServe is more than adequate to harvest ample amounts of shareware.

## What's "The Deal" on Shareware?

One thing I continually stress is the low-cost nature of shareware and freeware. Freeware is shareware that is free, obviously, so you can't beat that. It's amazing how much freeware is out there for educators. People get generous when they're helping kids. The cost of educational shareware is equally generous. The prices range, generally speaking, from $5 to $29, with a few programs asking for a bit more. I've found the median price to be about $15. Sometimes the price does compare with commercial software, but there are ways that even relatively expensive shareware programs hold advantages over retail software.

An important consideration is the site license. Where many commercial software producers offer very little discounting in their site licensing or district licensing, the shareware producers offer substantial breaks. For example, MathHomework costs $24 for an individual user and $79 for a site license. That's a great break! That example is very true to the pattern I've discovered everywhere.

Also, one can rarely hope to negotiate with a commercial software company—the price is the price. But the independent shareware producers, who always include their addresses so you can register and pay for their products and often include their e-mail addresses, are usually prepared to negotiate price if you have a compelling case or are asking for licensing for an entire district or county. They're more than happy to give you a break if you want to install their programs on a large number of machines; as entrepreneurs, they're more likely to be creating policy than following it. The independent shareware producer hasn't created educational programs to make it difficult for you to obtain and use them, quite the opposite. They're ready to enable you rather than deprive you.

How, then, is shareware paid for? The euphemism used by shareware producers is "registration," which is as appropriate a term as any. In most cases, one registers a program by sending a check to the appropriate address listed in the accompanying documentation. There are other ways, however. A very convenient one, for those who are members of major online services such as America Online and CompuServe, is called online registration. You simply go to the shareware registration forum, choose the program you want to register, click okay, and you'll be charged on your next billing statement. Of course, this is only available if the shareware provider is using this facility. After registration, you will be mailed disks of the program along with more complete documentation. For those in a hurry, some shareware producers will send the complete program to you as an attachment to an e-mail message. I've done this in the past with excellent results.

Registration of shareware does not, however, have to be done right away and perhaps this is the most compelling feature of shareware: the opportunity to try before you buy. After downloading a program, you are encouraged by the author to try it out before paying a penny. Many authors don't put an exact time limit on the trial period, but a common time limit is thirty days. If you don't like the program, you delete it from your hard disk. If you find you'll be using it, pay for it. It's that simple.

I suggest you follow the guidelines and register shareware according to the author's wishes. If, however, the author places no specific time limit, feel free to test-drive the program for as long as it takes you to discover its value before deciding. That is in line with the author's intentions. Some authors or producers provide extra incentives to register by circulating "demo" versions or versions otherwise limited or "crippled." That is, the program you download for trial is not as complete or functional as the version you'll receive upon registration. I don't like this strategy and tend to register programs more often when I am able to test a fully functional version before paying for it. Yet you'll find that most of the limited versions let you discover enough of their value to make a wise purchasing decision. Also consider this: What major commercial software providers allow you to try before you buy? There are very few.

## Keeping Up

The beauty of shareware (and freeware, too) is that it's a living, breathing, growing thing. It's constantly regenerating its supply. With the development of newer and faster toys in the computing world, shareware programs get more sophisticated and diverse every day. The growth of the World Wide Web encourages shareware producers to become even more productive as the means of distribution become more sophisticated and efficient, enabling computer users to locate shareware more easily than ever before. When I first started searching for shareware, the Internet was a well-kept secret and was rarely heard of outside the walls of research facilities on college campuses or the defense establishment. I used to spend hours on local bulletin board systems combing their file menus for a decent educational program for

21

my son or an accounting program to help me run my businesses. Those BBSs have no doubt retained their value for local users, but the vast majority of us can now streamline our searches using the powerful search engines of the World Wide Web. It's amazing the way the Web has accommodated the independent programmer. Shareware clearinghouses and libraries are springing up all over the Web with the sole purpose of helping us tap into this fabulously rich resource. The Virtual Software Library, c l net's shareware.com, The Shareware Links, and Jumbo!, just to name a few, provide easy means to locate and download shareware products for users' particular needs. Also amazing is the number of private citizens or members of foundations who have generously established Web sites to make their own contribution to society by organizing and evaluating shareware targeted to specific groups of users. There are many examples of these in my WWW listings.

## The Virus Risk

Aside from the caveat concerning dud shareware, there is one other cautionary note. Many people are alarmed at the idea of downloading files because of their fear of computer viruses doing harm to their computer systems. This is especially worrisome for those using networks. Although this fear is somewhat overplayed, there is reason to be cautious. Here are some basic guidelines. The major online services such as CompuServe, America Online, Prodigy, GEnie, and Microsoft Network always scan the files they offer for known viruses, and they are always on guard for the next big scare; they guarantee that the best efforts are being made to protect the consumer. These major online services also provide Internet access but warn their users that they cannot be responsible for the products and data downloaded from the Internet via their services. We can be relatively sure that major clearinghouse sites for shareware and freeware are constantly on the lookout for viruses, but no guarantee exists. So a good rule to follow is to feel comfortable with materials downloaded from the major online service providers but to consider safeguards for anything downloaded from the Net. There are many antiviral scanning programs, available both commercially and as shareware, which can be used to catch most viruses (the natural exceptions being the newest, latest, and greatest unknown virus). Many of these scanning programs can be downloaded for free or minimal cost. I've listed the best of them in the shareware listings and have included descriptions of the pertinent sites in the World Wide Web listings. Use them if you're nervous about infecting your system. However, please remember these three points: One, it is virtually unheard of for viruses to be placed in educational shareware; two, viruses are extremely rare in general; and, three, a life spent in fear of unpredictable disaster is a life held captive. Still, take the precautions you deem necessary. My advice is heartfelt but given without any guarantees. In seven years of downloading educational or other shareware, I've never encountered any problems with computer viruses; however, in heavily trafficked libraries and schools, computer viruses are known to make the rounds in very much the same way as their biological counterparts. You will be happy to know that you can feel completely safe with the programs listed in this book, for I've downloaded and tested all of them with never a virus invading any of the three computers used.

## Fun with Shareware

In addition to the shareware for libraries, schools, and administrative offices I've listed in this book, and the antiviral programs I've just talked about, there are myriad other programs that can be of benefit. Shareware and freeware developers have created unbelievably diverse kinds of programs and utilities. There are biorhythm charting programs, tarot card readers, accounting and invoicing applications, nutrition and health programs, paper airplane construction kits, database programs of every conceivable variety, cooking and recipe programs, music composition and replay programs, real estate and investment tracking programs, as well as programs to calculate loan payments and amortization, to name a few. If you can think of a need to be fulfilled with shareware, a developer has thought of it, too, and done his or her best to fill that need. Don't hesitate, once you've gotten the hang of searching for and locating shareware, to look for programs to suit your own particular needs. They're probably out there and no doubt affordable.

Much of the educational shareware available online is so entertaining that it makes learning wonderful fun. I've watched children spend hour upon hour of indisputable glee while learning all of the multiplication tables before the age of six! I've seen them giggle with excitement as they learn to add and subtract four-digit numbers, and watched them thrill to the crackle of robot-fired lasers while absorbing the concepts of division, fractions, percents and so forth. I've smiled to witness the feelings of accomplishment with arcade-style spelling and vocabulary-building games. Yet I've talked with teachers and read e-mail from listservs only to discover that some frown on this as frivolity. I demur, if you don't mind; learning can be as fun as you want it to be. But for those who want stricter, straighter methods to employ in their libraries or classrooms, I've included in my listings a number of more straightforward, less "giddy" programs. I don't see the harm in having fun while learning, but others do make valid points when they say that learning should be its own reward, and that constant stimulation and rewards for mastering what is itself already precious and valuable is to obscure the meaning of the skill being mastered. Perhaps, though, we should not judge a program's real value by its seemingly frivolous style but by its effectiveness as a teaching tool. A child's imagination and *joie de vivre* may, in the end, be beneficiaries of this joyous approach to learning and growing.

I do want to stress, however, that I, like many educators, don't value shoot 'em up-style, overly competitive games that in any way promote violence. Aside from their disruptiveness in both lab and classroom settings, some of them tend to be aimed more at boys than girls. No such programs are included in this collection. I have chosen some lively educational "games" and some are competitive in that they are scored; care has been taken that each selection have intrinsic educational value without offering deleterious subliminal stimulation.

In the end, I pray that you find in the world of shareware the wonderful, effective, entertaining, productive, and utilitarian tools that I've discovered to my own great satisfaction. I pray equally that your libraries, labs, classrooms, and offices all hum a little brighter and that all shall profit by it.

## What to Do with It

The uses of shareware and freeware programs and resources are varied, but can be placed into a few simple classifications:

### Public Libraries

Shareware and freeware can be used to provide learning games and educational activities in the children's library. Typing and keyboarding programs can help patrons improve skills that better enable them to benefit from the media center in the library or at work or school. Word processing programs and multimedia presentation and document creators will be popular tools for creative projects for school, work, and both public and private life. Templates, graphics, clip art, fonts, and assorted utilities which assist users in incorporating art and illustrations in their presentations and documents will enrich the value of the media center. Financial programs that can, for example, allow users to calculate loan interest rates and amortization schedules can help homeowners and prospective buyers to know more about what they're getting into. Reference works such as online style guides, spell checkers, and grammar checkers can help users with their word processing and project development. Resumé software can assist job seekers in obtaining work. In addition to use by patrons, the above shareware programs and resources can be very useful for librarians in the production of signs, banners, flyers, brochures, and other publications to promote and publicize their services or to help organize library use and flow.

## Secondary School Libraries and Computer Labs

Shareware and freeware tagged to the curriculum of the school can be of use in the computer labs and media centers of high schools and middle schools. Instructors from various departments might like to have directories or folders with programs helpful to each subject area, such as mathematics, English, social studies, history, and foreign languages, where shareware and freeware programs and reference works for each discipline can be placed. Even more so than in public libraries, the document and presentation programs and the utilities, such as graphics viewers, graphics catalogers, templates, paint and coloring programs, and so on, which support them can encourage students to create top-notch presentations for their school projects. Typing programs, resumé programs and tutorials, English style guides, spell checkers, and grammar checkers can help students in their present and future lives. As in public libraries, these shareware resources can be useful for librarians, administrators, and teachers in the production of signs, banners, flyers, and brochures to publicize services and special programs.

## Elementary School Libraries, Computer Labs and Classrooms

Shareware and freeware programs, properly tagged to the curriculum, can be made available anywhere in the school where they can be of service. Whether in the library, computer lab, or classroom, the electronic book creators, multimedia document makers, and presentation programs can help students with their creative projects. Typing programs and other computer training programs can nurture and improve the children's keyboarding skills. Basic skills programs and games in areas such as math, reading, spelling, phonics, geography, etc., should be made available in both labs and individual classrooms.

## Library Staff, Faculty, and Administration

Book-cataloging programs, bar-coding programs, and various utilities useful to libraries can be placed in the staff computers. Whether on staff computers or student-accessible computers, librarians will want to be able to use the programs associated with document or presentation creation. School administrators will want to use the administration programs and may also want document and presentation shareware put on their office computers; accounting shareware programs can be helpful in managing funds. Teachers will want access to the student-activity makers, lesson-plan aids, test and worksheet generators; they will also want access to document and presentation programs. Teachers with computers in their classrooms will want these close at hand. Those without may have to content themselves with a trip to the computer lab or media center.

Not every library or school situation is the same. Each of you will have your own ideas how best to use your computers and facilities. The most important thing of all is that you do take advantage of the many wonderful shareware and freeware programs available everywhere in the online world. It's out there waiting for you.

# Chapter Three

# Where to Find Shareware

The Internet will be a natural place to start your search for shareware and freeware. If you subscribe to a commercial online service, you'll have easy access to a rich variety of programs. Finally, the old online workhorses, the bulletin board systems (BBSs), still have much to offer, and they shouldn't be ignored. What follows is a tour of the online world, especially those parts of proven value to you, with an emphasis on finding shareware and the various tools you'll need to harvest it.

## The Internet

The Internet is the grandest network of them all, and thus the scariest. I myself was afraid of the Internet at first; I bought guides and read countless articles in magazines, all virtually to no avail. I didn't relax about the Internet until I jumped headlong into that greatest of black holes, only to discover that I had landed in a place that was not all that unfamiliar. There is nothing to fear but fear itself when it comes to the Internet and it bears repeating: You can't break the Internet. You just get out of where you are and try again.

What is the Internet? Without getting wordy, it is a vast link-up of thousands of computers throughout the world, a network of networks, all interconnected, all accessible through Internet service providers. The Internet used to be maintained by a confederation of government agencies and various universities for the purpose of streamlining research, especially in defense. Now it is commercial interests that are the driving force of the Internet. The change in stewardship hasn't as yet led to any major changes, especially for tangential users like you and me.

Nobody actually owns the Internet. Each of the various networks has its own governing body. The Internet Society (ISOC), a volunteer organization, perhaps comes closest to "running" the Internet. The ISOC's various committees and task groups cooperatively establish protocols and address technological issues.

The Internet offers various resources distributed by different network protocols (i.e., software rules for communicating over a network). These resources are described here in their order of importance from our perspective.

## World Wide Web

The World Wide Web (WWW) is exactly that—a web of files residing on computers throughout the world which offer documents which a visitor can view interactively. The documents on Web servers, often referred to as home pages, are written in a scripting language known as HyperText Markup Language (HTML). Users access the World Wide Web through software called a browser. The first of the browsers was Mosaic, developed at the National Center for Supercomputing Applications (NCSA) at the University of Illinois at Urbana-Champaign. Now there are several in the field, with Netscape Navigator and Microsoft's Internet Explorer slugging it out for market dominance. Browser

29

software reads the HTML documents and displays the content graphically on the user's computer. Content may consist of text, graphics, and with rapidly developing technology, sound and video as well. Linking is one of the most powerful features of the Web as a communications medium. With HTML, icons, images, or text can be linked to documents residing on servers around the world. The user will recognize links by underlined, colored text or when the mouse's pointer becomes a finger when moved over an icon or image. You can save files from the Web onto your hard drive or print them. By selecting "view source" in a pull-down menu, you can also see the HTML code. World Wide Web sites are different from FTP sites (where most files and software reside), but they also have software you can download. Web pages often offer links to FTP and gopher sites for efficient downloading of files and shareware programs, and most browsers allow direct access to FTP and gopher.

The World Wide Web is an incredibly diverse set of resources from the ridiculous to the sublime. Almost anyone who is a member of an Internet service provider which offers a Web site option can have a Web page if he or she desires. Many people of various arcane interests have built Web pages for mere self-aggrandizement. This is not necessarily a bad thing. Those who are interested in a particular subject will naturally gravitate toward these obscure home pages. Occasionally, you'll end up with one of these pages in a search results list, but you can quickly backtrack to more relevant ground.

The World Wide Web is not only a very creative place, but it also offers some incredible resources. As an example, WebMuseum is nothing less than majestic. WebMuseum is a WWW home page in France (which is "mirrored" to different sites around the world, allowing you to go to the nearest home page in order to allow faster accessing) where you can view many of the most famous paintings in the history of the world, from Da Vinci's *Mona Lisa* to Van Gogh's *Sunflowers*. If you wish, you can save them to disk and build up your own computer fine art collection. Fabulous! As far as librarians and academics are concerned, there could hardly be a better site than the Internet Public Library at the University of Michigan. It is no less than a digital stroll through a warm, friendly library with a wealth of information. Read more about it in its entry in my Web sites listings.

The Web is expanding and evolving at such an incredible rate that it would be ludicrous and not a little deceitful to pretend that I can relate to you in a book what the Web will be like in only a few months after that book is printed. But I can tell you this: If it's not on the Web now, it will be. If you can't do something on the Web now, you soon will be able to do so. That, of course, is a bit of hyperbole, but it makes the point. The Web is so interactive that the possibilities are awesome. Here is an example that will help show the potential for growth. Not long ago, there was virtually no way to have anything happen in what is called "real time." The Web was a static place where pages were created at a fixed time and later viewed or interacted with by a future viewer. Now, Federal Express has arranged for patrons who have packages in transit to access their Web site to track the movement of a package. By entering the required information, patrons can find out just where their packages are at any given moment. This is real interactivity in real time. It's very exciting. Online banking is already becoming available. Real-time video chat and conferencing will be more and more widespread. The possibilities are extensive for online education and classes. Each day, new plug-ins become available to add capabilities, such as real-time streaming audio and animation, to Web browsers. What the future has in store is up to the imagination.

All major online services and Internet providers offer access to the World Wide Web, but you may need to acquire the browser separately. The major browsers are available for download from many sites. It is more and more common, though, for Internet service providers, including the commercial online services, to offer a Web browser free of charge when you join. I got a version of Mosaic free from CompuServe, all set up to use with CompuServe; Prodigy offered me its free, high-quality Web browser when I joined. America Online and Microsoft Network do the same. You won't have any trouble getting ready to go onto the Web if you're a member (even if only a free trial member, by the way) of a commercial online service. By the way, an image-viewing program also comes with the Web browser so that all the images can be automatically viewed when you select them. Once you're on the Web you can find the sites for downloading current versions of state-of-the-art Web browsers such as Netscape Navigator and Microsoft Internet

Explorer, and with a modicum of work you can configure them to work with any Internet service provider.

> *Note*: The graphic images which are popular on the Web and in the online world in general are stored in formats known as GIF and JPEG files. GIFs are 256-color images and JPEGs are 16.7-million-color images; they are stored in compressed form so that they deliver more detail than their comparatively small sizes would indicate. The GIF is usually the smaller file, so it is eminently practical. The JPEG is larger, but its so-called infinite color produces higher quality images. The file extensions are, naturally, .gif and .jpg.

The ever-expanding World Wide Web is, at present, unparalleled in its cultural diversity and usefulness in education and information resources. Beyond the cultural arena, there are scores of home pages aimed at providing educational resources, many of them tailored to specific interests and age groups. Resources for libraries, schools and teachers abound. Extensive examples of these resources are in the World Wide Web listings at the end of the book.

Here's an example of browsing the Web. Let's say you're a member of Prodigy, which offers very easy access. You merely click on the Web button, which in turn takes you to the Web menu. Click on "Browse the Web" and Prodigy's Web browser automatically turns itself on, then takes you to Prodigy's home page. One of the clickable blue texts says "WWW search engines." Clicking on that, you move to a page full of different search options, one of my favorites being WebCrawler. In the WebCrawler's key word box, you might type "european art." In a few seconds, you'll be given a list of documents. You'll see WebMuseum there. Select the WebMuseum nearest you (you can, of course, select the WebMuseum in Paris just for the fun of being linked to France, but after the thrill is gone, be practical and choose a mirror site near you for speed and courtesy). Once the WebMuseum is loaded, click around for a while to see all the choices on the various pages. You'll find one page which lists many of the famous painters in world history. You could, for example, click on Da Vinci. You could then download *Mona*

*Lisa* in JPEG format for viewing via the graphic viewer automatically provided with the rest of the Prodigy software. If you want to save *Mona Lisa* to disk, click on "Files" on the menu bar, choose "Save," give the file a name (e.g., Monalisa.jpg) and click "OK." Easy, huh? All of a sudden, you're an art collector. If you're a teacher, you can take your students on a tour of famous art of the world. If you're a librarian, you can advise patrons on ways of accessing the great art and artists of the world.

The above example holds virtually true, except for variations in the particulars, for any of you accessing the World Wide Web via any of the online services, including America Online and CompuServe.

Those of you who will access the Internet via an ISP (Internet service provider) will go at it a different way, but it'll be just as simple. The software package will come with an automated installation and sign-up procedure which you will follow step by step. Once everything is installed, it'll just be a matter of clicking on an icon for automated logon and you're connected. Once you become adept, you'll know how to set up new Web browsers that you may later choose to install and use.

World Wide Web pages are actually document files on various host servers, each with its own unique Web address. The address lookup function built into your web browser is known as an URL, or Universal Resource Locator. HyperText Transport Protocol (HTTP) is the command that takes you to the specified location. Just type the address of the document you wish to view into the URL line and press enter. That should connect you to the host server where the WWW page resides. The address of a WWW page will look something like <http://louvre.fr.m.pichont.html> but don't worry about the confusing addressing system. Eventually, you'll start to understand the code after looking at it for a while, but whether you do so or not isn't all that important. You'll be browsing the Web looking for cool stuff using the search tools and standard English, so it won't matter what the Internet addresses are for the WWW pages you visit. Once you find a Web document you know you'll want to revisit, you can add it to the "Hot List" or "Bookmarks" menu item which all Web browsers have, so you can go to that document with the click of a mouse or press of a button without having to type in the strange address.

# FTP

This stands for File Transfer Protocol, which basically means an agreed-upon system for transferring files. An FTP site is virtually identical to the directory or folder structure of a hard drive and is organized into a root directory and various subdirectories, just as your hard drive is. A good way to look at FTP is that it makes a one-to-one connection between your hard drive and another computer's, allowing you to copy its files. All you need to do is log onto an FTP site, navigate through the various subdirectories until you find the one which has files of interest to you, and then download the ones you want. Once you get past the first uneasiness (or thrill) of being connected to a site in Finland or Uruguay or Germany, you'll quickly realize that it's the same as being connected to a local BBS or World Wide Web site; the only difference is how you log on. You need to give a user name (most sites accept "anonymous") and a password (most sites accept your e-mail address). Online services such as CompuServe streamline this logging-on process by automating it for you. Popular Web browsers do the same. It's all getting so simple.

Here's an example of FTP-ing: At a prompt, type <ftp://oak.oakland.edu> and press enter. Soon you'll be connected to Oakland University's FTP site in Rochester, Michigan. Then, you enter your user name and password as explained above. Next, you are granted access. By clicking on the various subdirectories, you can move, for instance, to the SimTel/win3/educate/ subdirectory. Here, you'll find one of the best collections of Windows educational programs I've yet found on the Internet. In the SimTel/dos/educate/ subdirectory are DOS-based educational programs which are, again, pretty useful. Select and download the files you want! At <ftp://wuarchive.wustl.edu/> you'll find loads of Macintosh shareware and freeware. There's something for everybody with FTP.

If you get lost or confused, don't panic. Just exit and try again.

Most online services have a list of recommended or popular FTP sites to visit. Also, there are a lot of guides, such as The Internet Yellow Pages, with which you can locate good educational sites. Another way to find great FTP sites is by posting messages to "all" on BBSs or in appropriate forums on CompuServe, America Online, or other services, asking members to offer their suggestions. If you are a member of an e-mail discussion group, post a message asking for favorite FTP sites. Soon people with interests similar to yours will message you back with their hot tips. Online people love to connect and share. With a little effort, you can soon have a list of favorite FTP sites. I've provided many good sites in the FTP listings.

Remember, the key to using FTP is thinking of sites as being organized like directories and subdirectories on your hard disk. And don't think of yourself as an intruder. The universities, colleges, and companies that maintain these sites do it so they can be used, and the public is invited. That's what's so great about the Internet.

If you know the name of the file you're looking for, one of the best ways to locate it is by using Archie, the FTP search tool developed at McGill University in Canada. Archie routinely goes out to Internet servers and indexes their files in order to compile a single, searchable database. A very good Archie search form can be found at <http://hoohoo.ncsa.uiuc.edu/archie.html>. I typed "sm_math.zip," a shareware file I haven't been able to find through any of the Web shareware sites, and located it at a French FTP site!

Other good Archie gateways and forms can be found by typing "archie" into a search engine like Yahoo or WebCrawler.

## Gopher

In the simplest of terms, gopher is a system whereby you "go fer" data resources by navigating menus. The system was developed at the University of Minnesota years ago and there are now a number of gopher servers at various locations around the world. The rest of the story, though interesting to some, is unnecessary for using gopher to access tremendous stores of Internet resources.

Gopher can be accessed by special client software and a TCP/IP connection or by those with a shell account with an Internet service provider; those of you who have such software or accounts most certainly know already how to access gopher. For the rest of us, the simplest and most common way of accessing gopher today is the all-purpose Web browser such as Netscape Navigator. The address format is <gopher://> plus the particulars of the address.

Those of you familiar with FTP will see the similarity between its menu system and gopher's, which are not unlike the tree structure of a hard drive. At gopher sites around the world you'll find various resources including text, graphics, fonts, software, and the like, just as you do at Web and FTP sites. Each of these different Internet systems have grown up alongside each other and naturally have some duplication of resources. But the gopher navigation system can streamline the search for resources and will lead you to some great finds. So don't hesitate to follow gopher links or use your browser to go to recommended gopher addresses. Once you get used to gophering, you'll find "gopherspace" to be inhabited by some of the largest collections of data and resources anywhere in the world.

One shouldn't spend much time in gopherspace before becoming familiar with Veronica, short for Very Easy Rodent-Oriented Net-wide Index to Computerized Archives. It is a very powerful tool for searching known gopher servers for topics by keyword. It was developed at the University of Nevada at Reno. You'll find a powerful Veronica there at <gopher://veronica.scs.unr.edu/11/veronica>. I typed in "scarlet letter" and, in seconds, got thirty-four related entries, including full e-text versions of the novel and articles of scholarly criticism. Use Veronica just as you would any keyword search engine. If you're doubtful, the above UNR site has full documentation and advice on how to profit best from a Veronica search.

## Telnet

Telnet is a protocol and software utility that allows terminal emulation so that you can log onto a remote computer's programs and databases. Access to servers via telnet is available only with a proper password, though some servers allow users to log on as "anonymous" guests. Telnet is particularly helpful to libraries and schools in that it allows remote users to conduct searches of large databases with such content as educational journals, magazines, and even Shakespeare's plays. A couple of major servers are free of charge, such as CARL and

ERIC. I've used these to search for documents and magazine articles for use by some of my students in their term papers, so these resources can be of great value, especially to your high-school- and college-age patrons. There are also database providers such as DIALOG and OCLC which charge a fee.

Many commercial online services and Internet service providers offer access to telnet services, and many libraries maintain accounts with various telnet services. My local library has such accounts and even has a phone number which I can call using my basic communications program, so I don't even need to leave home. I log on more or less as one would to a BBS; from a menu, I can choose to do a word, title, or author search in the catalog of my library and I can even place books on hold for my later use. From this same menu, I can access CARL and ERIC. Any documents which I find useful I can print by pressing the "print screen" key on my keyboard, printing each screenful as I scroll through the document.

Another feature of telnet is that it allows members of certain networks to access their servers when they're away from home, in order to download their e-mail and stay in touch with home base. College students can log on to telnet servers at their school to access computers and their programs, or even if they just want to check out their grades.

## USENET

USENET is a system for conducting online discussions via messaging. A collection of users who converse via messages on a specific subject are referred to as a newsgroup. Some of the earliest newsgroups were dedicated to libraries and schools, and can be found under the group area k12.* (where * is a wild card for various extensions), with names such as k12.library, k12.news, and k12.ed.* (e.g., k12.ed.art, k12.ed.math, etc.). Professionals upload messages that are organized in "threads," i.e., messages grouped by identical subject headings. Ideas are shared back and forth. But it isn't like e-mail where you can send messages to individuals; one can only message the group as a whole. Also, anybody in the world with access to newsgroups can read your messages, so consider that before including your e-mail address!

There are literally thousands of newsgroups dedicated to the discussion of anything under the sun. Naturally, those of you who enjoy participating in these online discussions will find much value doing so. USENET's inherent usefulness is in being able to tap into a huge body of resources and opinion. If this type of resource development and sharing appeals to you, by all means join a newsgroup and start talking. Be prepared, though, to not like every answer you hear. Good luck.

*Note*: I have to issue a warning about the content of many USENET groups. USENET, more than any other area of the Internet, is where users are likely to find pornography (graphic images can be embedded in messages) and offensive or obscene speech. This is a potentially dangerous area for students and young patrons. Make USENET available to your young users only under strict guidelines. Many choose not to make it available at all. For communicating, there are many discussion groups accessible via listservs; this may be a preferable way of participating in discussions, trading ideas, and gathering valuable information.

## E-mail, Discussion Groups, and Listservs

One of the most revolutionary aspects of the Internet is the powerful new way to communicate called e-mail (electronic mail). E-mail allows us to communicate within minutes instead of days. Beyond the advantages this provides to personal communication, this has been a great boon to business and education. Large telecommunication projects are being facilitated by e-mail, foundations conduct research projects via e-mail, and many university activities are so coordinated. Many World Wide Web sites incorporate e-mail to allow for rapid communication. Throughout the Web you will find many mentoring programs and features such as "Ask an Expert," which rely heavily on e-mail.

The online services all provide easy messaging and e-mail service and have built-in offline readers in their communications software. Internet service providers also facilitate e-mail and almost all of their software packages come with an offline mail reader-composer, such as

Eudora. Netscape Navigator has an excellent built-in mail reader. All of the offline readers provided with Internet packages are of excellent quality and are easy to use, though some have better features than others.

Two valuable uses of e-mail are the special interest discussion groups for professionals and electronic correspondence between students. There is a variety of listservs managing discussion groups on topics of interest for librarians and educators, and I have included a number of Web pages with extensive listings of these discussion groups in the Web page listings in this book. Some of these sites offer tutorials on the somewhat confusing procedures for joining discussion groups. A very good discussion group Web site is the Liszt Directory of E-Mail Discussion Groups at <http://www.liszt.com/>. It offers a search engine to locate listservs by name or topic. The resultant list tells you how to get the information needed to join each mailing list. Two very good discussion groups worth mentioning are both handled at Syracuse University: LM_NET for library media specialists and K12admin for, obviously, kindergarten through twelfth-grade school administrators. Another is Ednet, dedicated to the use of technology in education.

In addition to managing the exchange of e-mail messages between members, listservs also distribute electronic journals (commonly known as e-journals or e-texts), which are moderated online magazines usually dedicated to a specific area of research.

The discussions in these groups are lively and helpful. Many members are ready to share their expertise and advice with those who pose questions. In most cases, the groups are very friendly, though messages occasionally prompt "flaming," which is hostile or inappropriately unfriendly e-mail responses. Flaming is a basic violation of what is known as *netiquette*, the communication rules of the road on the Information Superhighway. There's no reason for these occasionally rude communications, but they do pop up. Most members of discussion groups frown on this kind of rudeness and generally rally around those who have been mistreated. The managers of the mailing lists, called "owners," are quick to send out private messages counseling more courteous use of the list. The overall value of being in a discussion group is so great as to overwhelm the occasional discomfort of getting flamed. It's one of the reasons offline readers have a handy delete button.

"Keypals" are the electronic equivalent of the penpals of yester-year. Students of all ages in countries across the world maintain correspondence with each other, leading to a warm and wonderful intercultural sharing. This is one of the truly great by-products of the Internet. The borders between countries are falling and in this arena the children are leading the way. Yet correspondence between keypals is not simply a matter of kids writing to other kids. These correspondences are often organized by teachers and librarians into projects for gathering information of all kinds from around the world.

There are World Wide Web sources for locating keypals in countries around the globe. Once again, they are mentioned in the WWW listings. Additionally, there are at least two e-mail discussion groups maintained to help connect keypals; type "keypals" into the keyword search line of Liszt and you'll get information on joining these lists.

A final thought: Those of you who are seeking the kind of information a discussion group provides but cannot afford the time such participation takes may find it more effective to access a discussion group's archives to search for the information you are seeking. Many such archives exist. For example, LM_NET archives are located at the AskEric gopher at Syracuse University. You'll find the address in the Web site listings, where you'll also find Web sites with links to other discussion group archives.

So there you have it, the quick guide to using the Internet. Sure, there's much more to the Internet than I've mentioned, but for the purposes of librarians and educators, I opened only the doors into cyberspace which are easily accessible and highly profitable in terms of delivering resources, programs, and files. Happy surfing!

## Getting Your Connection

Many of you will be provided an Internet connection under a district, county, or state program. Those of you in remote or underdeveloped areas may need to choose your own Internet service provider (ISP) until a large entity takes charge.

At present, there is an ever-growing number of Internet providers. Many services have developed their own Internet software. Many will use a well-known browser like Netscape Navigator or Microsoft Internet Explorer, and most will offer you a complete package with a browser, mail reader, and graphics viewer. For those wishing to choose their own software, Netscape Navigator is free to educators and librarians and can be downloaded from Netscape's Web site included in this book's Web listings. Currently, Microsoft is offering Internet Explorer free to all from its Web site, also included in the listings.

To help you choose an Internet service provider, it's wise to look in the current issue of magazines like *Netguide, Wired, Windows, PC, or Internet World*. They're all filled with advertisements for ISPs, each with free trial offers. Feel free to try these offers, one by one if you wish, until you've found a reliable service. Some ISPs, NetCom for one, offer special programs and rates for libraries and schools. Don't hesitate to inquire about such programs.

Finally, don't worry about installation and setup of software provided by ISPs. Assuming you have a working modem, setup is highly automated and guided by easy-to-follow, step-by-step instructions.

## Commercial Online Services

Though large libraries and schools would naturally require a full Internet account with no hourly limitations, smaller ones may prefer the friendliness and convenience of an online service. All of these online services now provide access to the Internet so, in a sense, you get the best of both worlds. The advantage of the online service, though, is that there are many services provided in-house; additionally, they have superior member help services and provide easily accessed chat facilities, e-mail services, and product support. Until you're ready to fly solo on the Internet, it may be smart to use an online service as your gateway. Even if you've got full Internet access, which is so valuable to patrons and students, I know a number of librarians and teachers who also maintain an account with a major online service for their own personal affairs and communications. Because online services, especially CompuServe and America Online, maintain large and easily searched stocks of shareware and freeware, I highly recommend that crafty librarians and teachers hold an account if only for accessing that resource.

I've found that spending about $20 a month to subscribe to a major online service pays for itself in more ways than one. As a member of CompuServe and America Online, I have access to newspapers and weekly news magazines; I can read stories hot off the wires of the Associated Press and Reuters. With a few clicks, I can be viewing weather satellite photos less than an hour old. On CompuServe, to which I've subscribed the longest, *U.S. News and World Report* and *Time* magazines are available online at no extra charge (the cover and full-color photos and charts are easily viewed). I can obtain fixes, patches and refinements for many of my software programs in the various forums or software libraries managed by numerous software companies such as Microsoft, Adobe, Netscape, Novell, or Corel. I've often saved hours of time on the telephone waiting for my turn on a tech support queue by getting my questions answered by e-mail at these same software forums. And, of course, many shareware and freeware programs you might spend hours searching for on the Internet or local BBSs can be found in minutes using the great search functions these online services provide.

Each of the major online services has many of the same resources, though they differ enough to warrant careful examination before choosing one to subscribe to on a long-term basis. Not all of them have the same ease of access or operation and each has its particular quirks and style. I'll try to steer you in the right direction.

Of course, for libraries and schools, each offers a lot of different files and shareware, in fact more than many will ever use. All have online encyclopedias and atlases. These aren't quite as good as the CD-ROM versions, but they have the advantage of being updated frequently and, more important for some of you, don't require the investment in the multimedia hardware. For small libraries and schools, an online service might be all you need, at least for the time being. It does serve as a great introduction to cyberspace.

There is one limitation which could preclude the use of the services by patrons: the hourly charge after the first five hours. Especially in schools, the hourly limit is used up quickly and abuse of an online service can quickly build up sizable charges. Either a strict AUP (Acceptable Use Policy) must be implemented or use of the online services should be restricted to librarians for the purposes of locating shareware, getting tech support, or managing e-mail. If you should want to make access available to patrons, I recommend having online services available at no more than one workstation and that the access be carefully monitored.

Before I talk about each of the services, I offer a brief but important disclaimer. The commercial online industry is one of the fastest-growing, most competitive businesses in America today. What is true about each service as we go to press may have changed before you pick up this book. They're changing almost daily, inevitably for the better, as each service tries to offer the subscriber more, more, more for less, less, less. You'll have to make your own decision based on your own experience with each service, but many of the things I have to say about the services will be more or less true in most significant respects.

The best thing of all about these services is that, with the market so competitive right now, they're always offering free trial subscriptions to introduce themselves to new potential users. So the good news is you'll be able to try them all for free for one month and make an informed decision about which serves your purposes best.

The trick is to find these free offers, but that's not very difficult if you know where to look. (I include the most recent free-offer 800 numbers following this paragraph.) Chances are one or more free offers came with your modem or communications software, or with some of the software bundled with your computer if you bought it new. The other simple way to get these free trials is to peruse the computer magazines, especially the magazines about the online world such as *Wired*, *Internet World*, or *NetGuide*. Either pick up a copy at the store, or if your library subscribes to these magazines, go through the latest editions and jot down the 800 numbers in the ads for each online service. They'll all be happy to mail you a trial offer and the free software to access the service.

Here are 800 numbers for free trial offers:

CompuServe—800-848-8990
America Online—800-827-6364
Prodigy—800-PRODIGY
GEnie—800-638-9636

Each service usually offers a free month plus free hours to allow you to try out the various services they provide. This process of trying out services can take months and, by the time you've chosen a permanent service, you've enjoyed yourself and maybe already discovered and downloaded dozens of programs recommended in this book, all without spending a penny. You can then settle into using the service that best suits your needs.

Now let's look at these services.

Since I have a very specific goal in mind for you, I'll be rating the services and editorializing a bit, but please keep in mind the previous disclaimer. I'll present the services in the order of their current desirability and usefulness.

## CompuServe

This is my favorite service because it offers the widest variety of services with the least amount of phony flash. The monthly fee is $9.95. CompuServe has a vast array of resources which can be utilized free for the first five hours, after which each additional hour will cost you $2.95. (Actually, all the major online services charge almost exactly the same rates now.) CompuServe has dozens of special interest forums, which can best be described as mini-BBSs accessed from the mother service, and each of these forums offer software libraries, message sections, and live online chat rooms where you can visit with people of similar interests. Its news and weather services are excellent and they provide online magazines such as *U.S. News and World Report* and *Time*. There are more than 200,000 files available from CompuServe and the collection of educational shareware and freeware is great. Now that CompuServe has an excellent global search function, searching for files can be done with the same ease as America Online. It has wonderful encyclopedias, health libraries, extensive searchable databases, and a vast collection of digital graphics.

CompuServe's latest communications software for Windows 95, Windows 3.1x, Windows NT, and Macintosh, called CompuServe 3.0, is state-of-the-art and easy to use. Multimedia components such as high-performance graphics rendering, and a sound and movie player are provided or integrated into the software. With its online multitasking, you can chat and download a file at the same time, and a "To Do" list enables you to queue up and set off multiple tasks in a background session. With its new Internet strategy, CompuServe offers access at a very fair, affordable price. CompuServe 3.0 offers a new integrated Web browser from Microsoft, Internet Explorer version 3.0. The popular Netscape Browser version 2.0.2 is also available for download. Or, you may easily use any browser of your choice.

## America Online

This service is so close to CompuServe in quality that I have to call it a tie for first. As I write this, America Online (AOL) has improved its news service with more up-to-date news and very slick color photos linked to many of the stories. Like CompuServe, AOL has thousands of shareware, freeware, graphic, music, and text files all linked to special interest forums. It may, in fact, be of superior value to K–12 educators because of its extensive collection of Macintosh educational programs and its Mac Education Forum. Finding programs and files is easy, because AOL has a great global search function accessible from the menu bar and a great time-saving download manager which allows you to select and mark files from multiple forums via global search, then to download them in a queue with automatic disconnect. Also, AOL has achieved a form of multitasking where you can access news or forums, or search for more files while you're downloading others. This saves money and time, and now that its news services are getting so slick, maybe America Online is the one for you. AOL's list of searchable databases is awesome, with everything from *Compton's Interactive Encyclopedia* to health care to wine ratings. Its new user-interface soft-

45

ware program for Windows, AOL 3.0 (the Macintosh version will be available by press time), makes everything available with one click of the mouse. It has e-mail, live chat rooms, online magazines, and a complete, easy-to-use, integrated Internet connection. The AOL 3.0 Web browser embraces existing standards with support for most of HTML 3.2, Netscape Extensions, and Secure Sockets Layer (SSL). AOL 3.0 accurately renders "Netscape enhanced" and other visually-compelling Web pages. Free monthly trials are widely available.

## GEnie

GEnie offers everything that CompuServe and America Online offer, but just doesn't do it as well. It has considerably fewer files to choose from, and the last time I looked, its Internet connections weren't quite up to speed. If, for some reason, GEnie is the only service with a local access number in your area, don't despair. Competition is causing all the online services to get better and cheaper all the time, so you can be quite content to stay with GEnie until CompuServe and AOL get access numbers in your area.

## Prodigy

Prodigy was a limited service until just recently, when it decided to add shareware libraries. With that addition, it's catching up with the other online services, though Prodigy has actually been out in front in selected areas. There are certain services which Prodigy provides that keep it in the running, not the least of which is Homework Helper. HH is a set of resources including maps, encyclopedias, and newspaper and magazine databases, with a good, fast search tool to locate multiple articles on any given topic. You can download pertinent articles, then print them out. So this would be a great help to users from junior high school through college. Another good feature is its online games for kids. They're fun, educational, and challenging, but rather costly. Also, Prodigy's interface program is pretty slick and getting better all the time, especially since Prodigy upgrades your software automatically when you log on, assuming there's an upgrade you haven't received yet, of course. Prodigy has a news service with linked photos, and its many special interest BBSs are great messaging centers and places to network with like-minded people. Prodigy was the first to have a great Internet connection with easily accessible search tools, but FTP is only available via the World Wide Web. Its recent addition of shareware libraries has raised it to the level of a competitive service, but its supply of shareware and freeware will be limited until it builds up its stock. Macintosh shareware, for example, is virtually nonexistent on Prodigy. It is aggressively courting customers and free trial offers are easy to find. It's definitely worth trying out.

## Microsoft Network

It's tough to evaluate the Microsoft Network (MSN) because it's so new and surrounded with so much hoopla. It has a seamless integration with Windows 95, though at present it is much slower than the other services, primarily because it is so integrated and freely accesses and uses Windows swap files for downloading and caching news stories and Internet Web pages. All that swapping to hard disk takes time, though having sixteen megabytes or more of memory mitigates the problem considerably. It's still very young as of this writing, so the shareware libraries aren't very full, though that will change rapidly with time. MSN has access to *Microsoft Encarta Encyclopedia*, but otherwise its searchable databases are far less in number than those of the established leaders, CompuServe and AOL. I am a little put off by MSN's commercialism, but I suspect that will be the wave of the future, with the other services getting into the act with online ads and more ties to product brand names.

In recent months, Microsoft has reevaluated its positioning of MSN and now offers MSN in two distinct ways. While MSN remains a commercial online service offering its usual package including Internet connectivity, Microsoft has also begun to offer for-fee access to MSN via the World Wide Web to those who already have an Internet connection. Microsoft continues to bundle a free-trial offer of MSN with its Windows 95 software packages. Regardless of which approach you chose, there's still a free trial attached, so give it a look.

47

# Evaluating and Exploring Online Services

There are a number of regional and national online services which are debuting all the time and it's fun to try them out. Once again, shop the ads for the free trials. There's no reason to pay for a first month if every service offers a free trial.

I've given you some guidelines for choosing a service, but each library's or school's needs are different and an online service which doesn't appeal to me may be just the one for you. CompuServe is newsy and I love news. Prodigy is obviously a family-oriented service with a lot of fun online games. America Online is targeted very well to the twenty-somethings who love e-mailing *Time* magazine. GEnie is a "we try harder" service which may grow into a competitor. Microsoft Network is a hard call because of its uncertain future. I have to recommend CompuServe and America Online at this time because of all the readily available shareware, resource tools, and top-flight Internet connections. If you can afford several services, well, you'll have it all.

> *Note*: A critical factor for choosing an online service is the existence of a local access number. Some smaller, more remote towns might not have a local, free-of-charge access number for one or more of the online services, which really dampens your enthusiasm for one service or another. You may have an access number, but the speed of the connection may be too slow. These factors may decide for you which service(s) you will choose.

Once you're online with one of the services, whether permanently or during a trial period, the first thing you should do is acquaint yourself with the overall service. Each service has a member center or help area, and they're always ready to help you learn how to use their service. Take some time to get comfortable. Experiment with using the commands and the tools for navigating around. I know from my own experience that accessing services and finding where you want to go can be a very confusing affair in the beginning, but today's software interfaces are getting pretty user-friendly. And remember, you can't break any of these services. So go for it.

Areas of an online service to explore:

1. Software libraries (especially educational and those with library utilities)
2. Online reference resources (encyclopedia, thesaurus, medical references)
3. Online games (especially educational)
4. Internet connections—FTP, World Wide Web
5. E-mail
6. Classified ad sections (these contain real bargains in hardware and software)

Whether you have to enter an area to access software libraries (on Prodigy and Microsoft Network, for example) or you're able to do a global search from the main menu (as on America Online and CompuServe), the key to finding shareware programs is the same. When you are at a "search files" or "search software libraries" dialogue box, simply leave the file name blank and enter words to define your search criteria in the "key words" box. For example, you might enter "mac educational game," "windows educational game," or "dos educational game." After a few seconds, you'll get a list of files meeting your criterion, with descriptions to help you evaluate each program's usefulness. You can then mark those files which sound good to you for download. There you have it!

## Bulletin Board Systems

My original favorite for getting educational programs is where I started in cyberspace years ago: the local Bulletin Board System, or BBS. There are literally thousands of these BBSs across the nation, and no doubt there are several right in your local calling area. These are mostly run by hobbyists, though many are run by local computer stores as a way to attract customers. By and large, these BBSs are very friendly places and most of them are free of charge! A few of them ask for small donations and some of the better ones ask for a subscription price of something like $12 a year to help pay for their operating costs. Given all you can get for such a small fee, this is one of the great bargains in the world.

A BBS is a computer which has been set up in such a way that a remote computer like yours can call up and log on. Once you log on for the first time, you can join the BBS and gain member access status. As a member, you can post and read messages and send electronic mail via the networks that a particular BBS is connected to. You'll find that many BBSs have a local classified ads message section—it's a great place to find bargains. Most important, there is a selection on the main menu of the BBS called "Files Menu." This is where to find what you're looking for.

Before I tell you how to log on, you need to know a few things. First, BBSs are almost without exception very friendly places. A BBS is run by a "sysop," short for system operator. He or she is glad you've come to visit, so if you're having a problem joining, accessing files, or using any area of the BBS, just go to the messages area and post a message to the sysop (it's often a menu choice all by itself) asking for guidance. The next time you log on, a message will likely be waiting for you with everything you will need to access and use the board to your best advantage. They want to help you—it's why they've put a BBS together in the first place.

Also, not every BBS gives you full access from the day you join. Some will limit your messaging capabilities while others might limit or prevent your downloading of files until you've either proven yourself in some way or paid the small fee to join. Again, each BBS is different, so follow the prompts and guidelines of each BBS. If joining involves a fee, it makes sense to peruse the files in the educational or games area even if you don't have downloading privileges, because you'll know quickly whether a particular BBS has enough educational resources to warrant joining permanently. There are usually plenty of BBSs around, so don't join one unless you're sure it has what you want, especially if they're asking for a fee. Some BBSs have very particular slants aimed at different types of users. What you'll be looking for are family-oriented BBSs which are stocked with a good selection of shareware and freeware. What you are not looking for are the so-called adult, political or life-style BBSs which serve a specific interest group.

One of the best ways to find out about the BBSs in your area is to obtain local computer shopping magazines that are widely available at computer stores. In my area we have *Micro Times* and *Computer Currents*. These are free shopping guides, but they also have large listings of BBSs in the area, with descriptions of what each BBS has to offer. No doubt your area has such a guide as well. If not, asking around among the salespeople and techies at the local computer shops will usually elicit the phone numbers of favorite BBSs. Tell them you're especially looking for educational programs. Computer buffs love to share their favorite online sites. BBSs often offer lists of other BBSs in the local area, so once you're online your knowledge of the online world will start to feed itself.

## Using BBSs

So you've found a few numbers and you're ready to fly out into cyberspace! An important thing to remember before you do is that you can't break a BBS. If things get messed up, find the "good-bye" menu item, log off, and try again. If you can't find "good-bye," it's okay to find the "hang-up" command in your communications program and just bail out. It's not considered good manners, but there are times while you're learning when it's necessary. Don't worry. When you become adept, you can respect the etiquette. If you're earnest, sysops are forgiving. And they're not Big Brother. Usually there's nobody watching. So go out there and have fun.

Here's how logging on works:

1. Buy and install a modem if one didn't come with your computer.
2. Install the communications program which came with the modem, or, if you're a PC user, use Terminal, the communications program that comes with Windows 3.1 (it's called HyperTerminal in Windows 95).
3. Configure the communications program to work with your modem. Both the modem and the "comm" program have information in their manuals on how to do this.

4. Chose the terminal emulation you'll use. This is ordinarily ANSI or one of the generic emulations such as TTY. This has to do with the way the text is displayed on your screen.
5. Enter the phone number of the BBS you wish to connect with and press "dial."
6. When the BBS answers, you'll be prompted to give your name. When the BBS doesn't recognize your name, you'll be prompted to enter information in order to join the BBS.
7. The BBS will often have a callback verification system in which it hangs up, then calls you back via computer to verify that it's your phone number you've given. Usually this will qualify you to become a full member, though different BBSs have different policies. Follow the policy of each BBS.
8. Once you're a member (or at least granted full or partial access), follow the menu prompts of the BBS, which usually require typing a highlighted letter and pressing enter. This can lead to the Files Menu, which is the place where all the goodies are.

The Files Menu is organized a bit differently on each BBS but generally follows a similar structure. All BBSs have a standard "search for files" selection on the Files Menu. Most of them allow you to search by a number of parameters, although "search by key word" is usually the most productive. Type in, for example, "educational, game" and you'll get a list of files to choose from. This searching is faster than perusing all the categories but does leave you open to missing some great stuff. So if you have the time, fully check out the available online stock in the categories of interest, beginning with the educational shareware.

Some small BBSs won't have a separate category for educational shareware but you can usually find some in the "Games" area. When you've reached a particular category from the files menu, select "list files." Check out the list of file names and the accompanying descriptions. One can't always tell from the name or description whether a program or game is useful; there's always a chance that a program isn't well designed or effective for your target group. The way to find out is to download a program that looks good and check it out. If you like it, you keep it. If you don't, that's what the "delete" command is for!

While you're visiting a BBS, don't hesitate to surf through categories not directly of interest to libraries and schools. You're bound to find useful programs you hadn't considered in your search.

Once you find a file you think will be useful, download it. I suggest using the transfer protocol, ZMODEM. It's fastest and most reliable. (A transfer protocol is a standard method for your computer and the remote computer to talk to each other while transferring files, to make sure everything is going smoothly. The protocols are built into your communications program.)

After you've gotten used to one BBS, try another one. In fact, try every single one in your calling area. You might want to spend a little money and try some outside your calling area, especially if you're not in a large metropolis, or if the nearest Mac Users Group BBS isn't in your town. I wait until after 11 p.m. to call some of my favorites in the next area code. No doubt, though, you'll find ample stuff in your own backyard.

While you're online, I suggest you explore all of the resources of the BBS. The message board of a BBS is a great place to meet people, many of whom are anxious to lend a helping hand. You can post a message to "ALL" to introduce yourself, telling the members of the BBS that you're looking for educational shareware (or, later, maybe music and sound files) and would welcome advice. Check back for messages in a day or two and don't be surprised when you find helpful messages full of tips. Who knows, you just might find some kindred spirits out there online. More than one valuable friendship has been initiated online.

## Using Compressed Files

Although you're primarily hunting for library or educational shareware, you'll have to put off your search for a while until you've downloaded some key utilities known as "compression" or "archiving" programs. These are necessities of the online world and you can't get to first base without them. So before you look in the educational area, you need to locate the area which holds these vital programs.

In order to shorten the time it takes to transfer files via modem, several compression or archiving programs were developed which can "squeeze" software files to the smallest size possible. How this is done beats the heck out of me, but the trick is to reduce file size by eliminating redundancy. Here's a good example: A computer graphic file which is 90 percent black in color must say "black, black, black,..." over and over again for each dot of black in the graphic. A compression program squeezes this graphic file by storing it in a form which says "this whole area here is black." One would think all files should be stored this way but they aren't, again for the sake of speed, this time for the opposite reason: Compressed files take longer to open, so we usually store files uncompressed for rapid use on our computer.

For Macintosh users, the StuffIt Expander is the principal extraction utility. Files compressed using StuffIt have the file extension .sit. Most BBSs that cater to Mac users will have the StuffIt Expander (a freeware program from Aladdin) in an easily accessible folder, with a name like "Important Files," "Utilities," or "Free Downloads." StuffIt will also extract the BinHex files common on the Internet that have the extension .hqx. There is also a common self-extracting file with the extension .sea; double-clicking on the icon of this file will make it do its thing without needing any help from a utility. Of course, StuffIt, in self-extracting form, is available from different sites on the Internet.

In the PC world, there are three crucial compression utilities, known by their file extensions: .zip, .arj, and .lha. ZIP files are the most common ones on BBSs, commercial online services, and the Internet. You'll find many ARJ files on BBSs and a few floating around the online services. LHA is very popular in certain areas of the Internet, so you'll want a utility for it before you venture far from familiar territory. There's another one, ARC, which you might run into, but I wouldn't worry about it until you happen across an ARC file you must have. They're just not very common anymore. All PC BBSs have these programs readily available because they are vital to the online world. You'll usually find them in the "Utilities," "DOS Utilities," or "Windows Utilities" area. Many BBSs have a separate area for compression utilities. Find the right area and download these first. You can also download them from the major online services as well as several sites on the Internet. All three programs will be in the form of self-extracting .exe programs. When you execute the program, they extract themselves automatically. The easiest way to do this is to create a directory, put the self-extracting program in that directory, and execute the program. Later, you'll want to store the original on a floppy disk as a backup.

Here are the files you'll be looking for:

For Mac users:
    unstuffit3.07.sea—from Aladdin Systems

For PC users:
    pkz204g.exe—PKWARE's great PKZIP program
    lha213.exe—archive program by Yoshi (Japan)
    arj241.exe—popular archiving program
Optional:
    winzip60.exe—Great Windows ZIP program (also available for Windows 95)

*Note*: All these extraction utilities are listed in the shareware and freeware listing later in this book.

You may find these files with different names (the person who uploaded each file to the BBS might have given it another name), or there might be a new version with a new name, but chances are you'll know the files when you see them, by their names or their descriptions.

Using these compression/extraction utilities can be a little confusing, but if you read the accompanying documentation you should be able to figure them out. With PKZIP, for example, the command line for extracting is pkunzip [filename] [destination], where "filename" is the name of the .zip file you wish to unzip and "destination" is the directory where you want the files to go. Don't forget to state where the .zip file is, and don't forget to create the destination directory. (Example: pkunzip a:\ mdesk301.zip c:\ mdesk.) WinZip for Windows makes file extraction very simple, so I highly recommend it. In fact, WinZip will auto-install many shareware programs for you.

Mac users will find StuffIt to be extremely easy to use. Just drag and drop a .sit file on the StuffIt Expander icon and you're off and running.

*Note*: If you wish to use Windows shareware and freeware programs, you might need one or more of the following three special files: vbrun100.dll, vbrun200.dll, and vbrun300.dll. "vbrun" stands for "visual basic run time" and .dll stands for "dynamic link library." These special files allow different shareware programs to be properly run in the Windows environment. Sometimes they come included with the shareware program .zip file, sometimes not. If you find that you need them (and you will), they are available everywhere online: on BBSs and the commercial online services, as well as on the Internet. Search for them and download them as needed. Place them in your Windows\System directory.

# Chapter Four

# Tagging Programs
to the Curriculum

Whether you're a library media specialist helping others in your school or district, a computer or technology mentor trying to help your school get the most out of its computer resources, or a teacher who has decided to put his or her classroom computer more fully to work, the task of tagging a shareware program to the curriculum remains essentially the same. You want a program to be suited to the needs of the users. You do not want to waste either valuable hard disk space or the students' equally valuable time.

It's a simple fact, though, that unless you buy the often prohibitively expensive software created by your state-approved textbook publishers and tagged unit by unit to the curriculum, the software you do ultimately choose will in many cases have broad applications beyond your specific curricular requirements. This is true whether you acquire off-the-rack commercial software or shareware and freeware. It's not necessarily a bad thing and it's fairly easy to deal with.

In the shareware I've listed in this book, I've already tagged the various programs in the most reasonably narrow sense that I could. In each entry in the list, you'll find the grade range where the program will be of principal value. Outside of that range, its use is generally inappropriate, except in remedial situations or learning-impaired curricula. Very often, though, programs are broad in their application and defy exact tagging.

Math programs, those well-suited to drill and practice as well as those that teach, are often the broadest in their scope, in that a program may be so configurable as to be easily appropriate in classrooms from kindergarten to sixth grade and even in middle school remedial programs. That sounds as though it could be a problem but really it can be a funding godsend. If you negotiate an inexpensive district site license with a shareware author (or have luckily found a versatile freeware program), the value of being able to use a program broadly can be significant. Also, if a child can use the same program as he or she advances from grade to grade, the learning curve for utilizing that program flattens considerably over time. One such program I've listed, for example, called Show Me Math, can easily be used from kindergarten through eighth grade and above. As a child progresses year by year, he or she will have a declining need to be instructed on how to use Show Me Math, allowing more direct focus on actual learning.

On the other hand, there are a great number of math programs that are quite targeted and thus very easy to tag. Number recognition and counting games, for example, would rarely apply beyond preschool and kindergarten. Programs with only single-digit addition and subtraction would not be of value beyond first grade. This specific focus is usually the case with reading and phonics programs. Their value is limited to preschool through perhaps second grade, making them very easy to evaluate and tag. Spelling and vocabulary-building programs, however, especially those which allow entry or recording of new words, can be used at all elementary levels.

A general rule of thumb, then, for tagging is: Don't be afraid to distribute or use programs of broad applicability, but neither should you misdirect programs of narrow scope to inappropriate grades. In this sense, my listings will be a great timesaver for you. Once you feel, however, that you've exhausted the resources of these listings and wish to go online in search of your own finds, it would be good to put together a shopping list before you head out into cyberspace.

## Creating Your Shopping List

First, choose your platform. Then, choose your subject and target grade(s). You may be frustrated at first that there aren't always good file descriptions available at Web and FTP sites, and that you need to download files before you can truly know their efficaciousness and applicability, but remember that this is true as well for software off the shelf or out of a catalog. This is the beauty of shareware! If it doesn't apply, delete it, and you haven't spent a penny.

There are other ways of shaping your shopping lists. Public librarians may work together to improve their computer center offerings. Technology committee members at schools or in districts can offer their suggestions at meetings. Library media specialists may build up a list of requests from teachers in their schools or districts. District curriculum directors will have been listening to the broad needs articulated throughout their districts. Department heads at high schools might receive input from teachers in their departments. Individual teachers may ask others on their grade level what they'd like to see be made available. Advice can be sought in e-mail discussion groups. If you are one of those to whom the responsibility of shopping falls, organize the information you gather, make a coherent shopping list, and head to the online sites with an intelligent set of key words to facilitate your searches.

Many of the online sites will help with the tagging. A lot of the Web sites listed in this book will already be targeted to specific age groups, so the programs you come back with will likely already have a grade level indicated. If you go the "Tigger's Home" Web site at <http:/ /remarque.berkeley.edu/~tigger/>, for example, you'll find great shareware programs that are obviously appropriate for preschool through third grade. Thus, in a sense, you'll be downloading pretagged programs.

Depending on your situation and needs, there may be other factors that shape your tagging decisions. If you're a public librarian wishing to offer more programs in your media center or create a learning center atmosphere in your children's center, you may have more freedom in your shareware choices. Being free from state guidelines and school curricula can grant you some stretching room. Of course, if you're organizing a circulation library of freeware and shareware (you most certainly may distribute shareware as long as you don't circulate registered versions or fail to include all files), you'll want to let the borrowing parents or children know they're choosing appropriate programs. If you're choosing shareware for the classroom or computer lab, you may have guidelines or frameworks which will narrow the scope of your choices. Let's say that the mathematics framework that your district has adopted stresses the use of manipulatives to demonstrate basic math concepts. Two factors might shape your choices: one, you'll want to find a closer fit with the conceptual nature of the framework or, two, you'll want to flesh out the framework with shareware programs that teach and reinforce the algorithms that the framework addresses only conceptually. You'll want to be careful, however, not to abandon the framework and incur the ire of the district curriculum director or, worse, negatively impact the effectiveness of the original framework. Therefore, tagging a math program to both grade level and adopted framework may require you to evaluate its effectiveness as a bridge between framework requirements and extra-framework reinforcements. Working closely with technology committees and curriculum directors may facilitate the distribution of well-chosen and more widely accepted shareware programs.

In the end, though, I would advise savvy librarians and teachers to go with their instincts. If you've given a program a good look, you'll know whether it will be effective in teaching or reinforcing targeted skills in your particular situation. Do not shy away from employing resources you feel are a good fit. Surely you'll know if a program is merely a "filler" or if it's of considerable value and appropriate for your students or patrons.

## Test Before You Buy

Okay, you've listened to all this advice and you've downloaded many programs you think will be of value to whomever your target group might be. The beauty of shareware and freeware is that you may try it before you buy it, so by all means give it a good test drive before shelling out any bucks.

Some programs are very restrictive, providing you with a scant fifteen or thirty days before rendering themselves inoperative; fortunately these are relatively few. The majority of shareware authors place fully functional programs online for us to try. After giving them as careful an evaluation as time allows, load them onto your computers where students or patrons can try them out. Spend time watching the students using the program; ask them questions as to the program's effectiveness; find out what they like and don't like; find out if they have difficulty using the program. Track their progress with the program. See if they're catching on to its operation and whether they're gleaning any knowledge or skill from it.

With some programs, I've known the minute I've opened them up that they're winners. With others, I've discovered their value only after watching them for a while. With still others, I've failed to see their inadequacies until I've observed them in use for considerable time. Of course, I've deleted some programs minutes after extracting them from their compressed files, wondering why on earth anyone bothered to create them in the first place. Yet I've always been grateful for the free time to find these things out.

If the licensing guidelines included with the program allow for a good deal of evaluation time, take full advantage of it to make intelligent and thoughtful decisions. You'll know within a reasonable amount of time, through observation and interaction, whether to register the program and adopt it for full use.

There are a few significant failings of software programs to be on the lookout for. Often, programs are well-designed but have one fundamental flaw: The instructions and prompts of software for younger children require higher language skills than the target audience usually possesses. I don't know why this common mistake is made by programmers who are bright and creative in every other way. Another common weakness is the inability of these programmers to write a decent manual or "readme" file. Grammatical and spelling mistakes abound. The independent shareware author most likely has good programming skills but doesn't cut the mustard as self-editors go. Often this inability to write a manual or spell correctly doesn't detract from the program's effectiveness as a learning tool. Occasionally, however, I've had to toss a good-looking program because I haven't been able to figure the darned thing out. If you can't make it work, well, chances are good your younger charges can't either.

Taking the time to try the programs out will help you to both tag the program to the proper level and discover its strengths and weaknesses.

During the testing period, or even after you've decided to register a program and put it into use, you will want to check to see if your first impressions have proven correct. You may find after some time that the program, though of value, is inappropriately tagged. If you believe this, move it to another computer in another classroom and see if it's a better fit.

## Hard-to-Tag Programs

Librarians and the teachers they often supply with media should not be afraid to provide materials that are broad and difficult to tag to a curriculum. As long as the material generally contributes to a basic education, some aspects of a given program will fill a niche in the overall scheme. If we only accept material that is ideally suited for each purpose, we negate the value of materials that educate with a wider sweep. If we are inflexible in our set of choices, following only the rigid guidelines of a framework, we narrow not only our own choices but our students' ability to learn and grow as well. For example, a U.S.A. "learn the states" game can be educational and fun to sixth graders whose proper curriculum focuses on ancient history. Teachers merely need to distinguish between what is extra credit or recreational activity and what is curriculum-driven. Many of the shareware programs listed in this book, especially suites (groups of related programs) which offer multi-subject games, can fit in nicely with interdisciplinary approaches; certain programs can be grouped in such a way as to enhance or emulate interdisciplinary activities.

In this day and age, we're at the end of yet another cycle of ossification and are starting yet another reexamination of our beliefs and systems. This is no time to retreat; it is a time to experiment and find what works. If we need to break out of the mold, to abandon overly rigid guidelines and look for new ways to teach and new ways to provide for the growth and development of our children, then by all means let's do it. The computer and its resources are a continually emerging set of opportunities for us to explore. We'll need to feel free to take chances, to participate in some trial-and-error derring-do if we're to take full advantage of these resources.

As a final note of caution, however, I suggest we reach out to those around us who would stand in the way or drag us down in our efforts. It doesn't do to be so reckless as to alienate a principal or aggravate a district curriculum director. Take the time to keep them informed. Try to instill your own enthusiasm for the resources you've found and seek to build a consensus. In the end, we'll all be the more effective for having taken the time and expended the effort to improve the way we conduct the business of education, and we'll live up to the trust we've been granted.

# Chapter Five

# Strategies for
the CD-ROM

A couple of decades ago, library collections remained much the same in form as they had for hundreds of years. Notwithstanding the advances in printing and binding, the development of more organized print catalogs and reference works, and the later use of microform, the library has until very recently been a repository of mechanically processed print media. Librarians, viewing the process from the inside, no doubt saw improvements that had strong impacts on the way they did business, but patrons had witnessed little change from the basic library as it had existed for much of the twentieth century. In the last decade, and especially in the last five years, the library has undergone the greatest transformation since Johannes Gutenberg first began to pump out bibles back in the mid-fifteenth century. This transformation has been almost entirely a function of the personal computer and networking.

Apart from the automation of circulation and catalog functions enabled by computers, the most remarkable change patrons have witnessed is the vast increase in reference materials made available by CD-ROM technology. Hundreds of megabytes of text, graphics, and video can be stored and very quickly accessed from these disks, enabling users to locate mind-numbing amounts of information in a fraction of the time it took them using the old methods of browsing card catalogs, walking between stacks, and thumbing through dozens of volumes before settling on a few to take home for future study. Periodical searches were especially tedious, as were searches with the weighty volumes of encyclopedias. One thumbed through them searching for one article at a time, and copied relevant material by hand or clumsily copied them on the photocopier at a quarter a page.

## Multiply Your Library's Resources at Bargain Prices

There's no question that the old methods still hold precedence when tackling some of the more arcane topics of academic research, and patrons and students should never be encouraged to do slipshod work or incomplete research; but for the vast majority of users, the CD-ROM has allowed us to get our hands on more information in less time than anyone could have imagined five years ago. Many may surmise that this is another example of a society of people with shortened attention spans and a predilection for instant gratification, and I'd have a hard time arguing the point. The reverse of the implication may be true as well, that more information available more quickly enables more study and learning, not less.

Those of you managing a large public library in a large city may decline to accept many of the ideas I'll be promulgating here. You would hopefully have the resources to maintain a good collection of print encyclopedias. You would make sure to have a wide and diverse collection of the latest and best reference CD-ROMs, and you would know to attend to the regular updating and upgrading required of a first-rate collection. Though larger libraries have budget problems like those of the smaller ones, the size of your budgets will allow many of you to be able to take advantage of the proliferation of computer-delivered reference works and the many multimedia CD-ROMs coming onto the market weekly.

It's those of you struggling to acquire media for smaller public and school libraries that I most definitely address in this section. If you have severely limited funds or have made a slow start in acquiring the hardware to operate and access the new resources, you will have to be crafty and selective in the way you try to bring your enterprises up to current technological standards.

For purposes of discussion, it might be handy to devise some categories so we might take a look at the different needs and resultant strategies to cover those needs. Of course many libraries defy easy categorization, but let's hope you can find approximately where your institution would fit into a somewhat oversimplified scheme.

## Large Municipal and County Libraries

You may be freer of budgetary constraints and not as apt to have your technology money harshly limited, though you might appreciate some ideas for low-cost expansion of your CD-ROM collection and you may still be in need of strategies for lowering the cost of hardware acquisition. You may also have decided that you can expand your services by utilizing shareware and freeware in your media center or the computers in your children's library. You are beginning to experiment with the loan of software to students, parents, and teachers in much the same way that you now lend videos. You have discovered that CD-ROM indexes now replace your print indexes and that there are specialized CD-ROM resources that greatly expand access to materials in your subject departments. Because you have good Internet connectivity, you may be able to harvest the shareware and freeware that will be of value in many of your enterprises.

## Small-City Public Libraries and Neighborhood Branch Libraries

Many of you will have been experiencing budget squeezes that have held you back in your quest to use computer technology. Taking advantage of buying strategies may help you expand your offerings to your patrons. Remember that you provide the equity in your community! Patrons without hardware and/or software in their homes will depend on you to provide it to them. You may discover it is actually more economical to purchase your journals full-text on CD-ROM or your expensive reference materials in electronic format. You are faced with the many latchkey visitors who could make excellent use of their after-school hours experimenting in an electronic environment. You also want to experiment with software loan as a service to your community.

## High School Libraries

High school libraries play a critical role in assisting middle schools and elementary schools in their districts. Librarians and teachers from the lower-grade schools may look to you as a mentor and may rely on you for guidance in obtaining electronic media. You may have already made major headway in moving away from print to CD-ROM indexes and reference works. You will have found that students rely on the speed and flexibility of subject and key-word searches in the CD-ROM encyclopedias and you're not afraid to move away from upgrading your print reference materials. You could benefit by expanding your CD-ROM reference collection by shopping for bargains. Also, teachers may look to you to point the way to shareware programs that can assist their curriculum in the computer labs, whether they are located in the library or elsewhere. You are probably working on a software loan program and may find shareware to provide a wonderful set of resources for that.

## Middle School Libraries

You may truly find yourself in the middle. Your districts may not be ready to allow you to catch up to the level of technology in use at the high school level, but your students may actually be as much in need of quality reference works as their older brothers and sisters. You may be on your own when it comes to upgrading your computer media. You'll need to make your purchases carefully. You should possibly rethink your budget allotment—spending a bit less on print and a bit more on electronic resources. Encyclopedias, for instance, are a lot cheaper to replace on CD-ROM. Again, you may be able to help increase the depth of your school's computer labs through the acquisition of shareware and freeware programs. Your teachers and students may look to you for guidance and will appreciate any new software that furthers their goals.

## Elementary School Libraries

The consumer-oriented reference products and encyclopedias on CD-ROM may be just the thing for your kids, but limited or nonexistent budgets may require you to find inexpensive ways of getting both hardware and software. Your teachers will ask that you provide them with relevant subject-related software in much the same way you once provided them with print support. Kids are begging to borrow the resources you now have and shareware may be a very effective means. The K–6 schools with computers in the classroom may need help in effectively utilizing their hardware resources and would greatly appreciate the flexibility that shareware offers, especially in the area of multimedia document creation. They may benefit by low-cost acquisition of reference CD-ROMs for use in the classroom.

I have polled a number of librarians and have compiled a "must-have" list of children's electronic titles a library should first acquire from the major retail reference publishers in order to provide a core electronic reference collection before extending it with the consumer-oriented reference works that can be obtained by crafty, bargain-shopping methods.

■ **"Must-have" CD-ROMs for Small Public and Secondary School Libraries and Labs:**

ENCYCLOPEDIAS

*Note*: Many of you may not be able to afford all of these fine CD-ROM encyclopedias. The prices reflect the size of their databases, so use them as a guide for the breadth of material. If you have print versions of *World Book, Americana* or *Britannica*, you may want to spend your money on several of the lower-priced multimedia encyclopedias. However, all of these titles are in the "must-have" list because they are necessary if your goal is to provide the most material with the state-of-the-art search capabilities that today's patrons are coming to expect.

*Encarta 96*, Microsoft Corp., 800-426-9400, $54.95
*or*
*Grolier Multimedia Encyclopedia*, Grolier, 800-243-7256, $49.95
*or*
*World Book Multimedia*, World Book, 800-621-8202, $105

*Encyclopedia Americana*, Grolier, 800-243-7256, $595
*or*
*Encyclopaedia Britannica*, Britannica, 800-432-0756, $995

ATLASES

*Encarta 96 World Atlas*, Microsoft Corp., 800-426-9400, $54.95
*or*
*Picture Atlas of the World*, National Geographic, 800-368-2728, $79.95

MAGAZINE INDICES AND FULL-TEXT DATABASES (ONE OR MORE)

**SIRS Researcher**, SIRS Inc., 800-232-7477, $1,320 annually

**Infotrac**, IAC, 800-227-8431, TOM $2,048, SuperTOM $2,848, TOM Academic, $2,000

*ResourceOne*, UMI , 800-521-0600, from $930 to $1,270, depending upon amount of full-text

**MAS**, EBSCO, 800-653-2726, Elite, $2,390-3,190; Select, $1,799-2,199

*Readers' Guide,* Wilson, 800-367-6770, variety of prices depending on level of full-text ranging from $995 to $2,795 (for mega edition full-text)

*Newsfile,* NewsBank, 800-762-8182, $2,895

NEWSPAPERS

> *Note*: These products are excellent though expensive. It is, however, important to have good, searchable databases of newspaper articles available to your patrons. A lower-priced alternative may be at hand as newspapers across the country are establishing World Wide Web online daily newspapers and many of them are including searchable archives. Some of these services require subscription but will be substantially less than present CD-ROM versions.

*New York Times Fulltext,* UMI, 800-521-0600, $1,550 annually
*or*
*Washington Post,* UMI, 800-521-0600, $1,565 annually

**Knight-Ridder Information** (offers many dailies across the U.S.), Knight-Ridder, 800-334-2564, call for prices

**Your own daily metropolitan newspaper,** prices vary

BROADCAST DATABASES

**Broadcast News,** Primary Source Media, 800-444-0799, ranges from $495 to $1,285, depending on frequency

MISCELLANEOUS DATABASES

*Exegy,* ABC-CLIO, 800-368-6868, $650 per year; networked $975 per year

**Landmark Documents of American History,** Facts On File, 800-322-8755, $295

70

*Famous American Speeches*, Oryx, 602-265-2651, $129.95

*DISCovering Authors*, Gale, 800-877-GALE, $600

*Current Biography*, Wilson, 800-367-6770, $189

*Facts On File Fulltext News Digest*, Facts On File, 800-322-8755, $695

*American Medical Association Family Medical Guide*, Dorling Kindersley, 800-225-3362, $45.95

*McGraw Hill Encyclopedia of Science and Technology*, McGraw Hill, 800-722-4726, $1,300

■ **"Nice-to-have" CD-ROMs for Small Public and Secondary School Libraries and Labs:**

*Street Atlas USA*, DeLorme Mapping, 207-865-1234, $79

*Discovering Careers and Jobs Plus*, Gale, 800-877-GALE, $1,495

**American Journey series:** (Women, African-Americans, Hispanic Americans, Westward Expansion, Civil War, Primary Source) 800-444-0799, $149 each

■ **"Must-have" CD-ROMs for Elementary and Middle School Libraries and Labs, Grades 4 through 8:**

ENCYCLOPEDIAS

*Encarta 96*, Microsoft Corp., 800-426-9400, $54.95
*or*
*Grolier Multimedia Encyclopedia*, Grolier, 800-243-7256, $49.95
*or*
*World Book Multimedia*, World Book, 800-621-8202, $105

71

*Cartopedia*, Dorling Kindersley, 800-225-3362, $36
*or*
*World Vista Atlas*, Applied Optical Media Corporation, 215-429-3701, $59.95

MAGAZINE INDICES

**TOM Jr.**, IAC, 800-227-8431, $795; **Super TOM Jr.** $1,195 (more full-text)
*or*
**Middle Search**, EBSCO, 800-653-2726, $899 per year
*or*
**SIRS Discoverer** (article database), SIRS Inc., 800-232-7477, $750 (half-price with SIRS Researcher)

MISCELLANEOUS REFERENCE

*Macmillan Dictionary for Children*, Simon & Schuster Interactive, 800-983-5333, $19.95

*Junior DISCovering Authors*, Gale, 800-877-GALE, $325

*UXL Biographies*, Gale, 800-877-GALE, $325

*National Geo Mammals*, National Geographic, 800-368-2728, $69.95

*National Geo Presidents*, National Geographic, 800-368-2728, $69.95

*The Way Things Work*, Dorling Kindersley, 800-225-3362, $29

*San Diego Zoo Presents: The Animals!*, Mindscape Software Toolworks, 415-897-9900, $59.95

**Print Shop Deluxe**, Brøderbund, 415-382-4400, $99.95 (school edition)

**Kid Pix Studio**, Brøderbund, 415-382-4400, $46.95

**HyperStudio**, Roger Wagner, 800-497-3778, $112.95 (price varies)

**Multimedia Workshop**, Davidson, 800-545-7677, $51.95

**Student Writing and Research Center**, The Learning Company, 800-526-9247, $89.95

**Digital Chisel**, Pierian Spring Software, 800-472-8578, $119.95

■ **"Nice-to-have" CD-ROMs for Elementary and Middle School Libraries and Labs, Grades 4 through 8:**

*Dinosaur Adventure, Body Adventure* and others, Knowledge Adventure, 800-573-5223, $39.95

*BodyWorks 5.0*, Softkey, 800-227-5609, $29.95

*Ultimate Human Body*, Dorling Kindersley, 800-225-3362, $29

*Microsoft Dinosaurs*, Microsoft, 800-555-4512, $34.95 (also *Oceans, Dogs, Dangerous Creatures*)

*Microsoft Art Gallery*, Microsoft, 800-555-4512, $54.95

*Macmillan Dictionary for Children*, Simon & Schuster Interactive, 800-983-5333, $19.95

*New Macmillan Visual Dictionary*, Simon & Schuster Interactive, 800-983-5333, $38.95

*American Heritage Talking Dictionary*, SoftKey, 800-227-5609, $29.95

*Prehistoria*, Grolier, 800-356-5590, $69.95

■ "Must-have" CD-ROMs for Elementary School Libraries and Labs, Grades K through 3:

*First Connections: Golden Book Encyclopedia*, Hartley, 800-247-1380, $79.95

*My First Incredible, Amazing Dictionary*, Dorling Kindersley, 800-356-6575, $59.95

**Magic School Bus Series** (Human Body, Solar System) Microsoft, 800-555-4512, $44.95 each

**Knowledge Adventure Series** (Body, Dinosaur, 3-D Body, America, Bug, Discoverers, Undersea, Kid's Zoo,), Knowledge Adventure, 800-542-4240, prices range from $34.95 to 59.95 each

**Living Books Series** (*Dr. Seuss's ABC's, Arthur's Birthday, Arthur's Teacher Trouble, Just Grandma and Me, Little Monster at School, The Tortoise and the Hare*), Brøderbund-Random House, 415-382-3214, $34.95 to $39.95 each

PRODUCTIVITY PROGRAMS

**HyperStudio**, Roger Wagner, 800-497-3778, $112.95 (price varies)

**Multimedia Workshop**, Davidson, 800-545-7677, $51.95

**Student Writing and Research Center**, The Learning Company, 800-526-9247, $89.95

**Storybook Weaver Deluxe**, MECC, 800-215-0638, $79

**Kid Pix Studio**, Brøderbund, 415-382-4400, $39.95

■ **"Nice-to-have" CD-ROMs for Elementary School Libraries and Labs, Grades K through 3:**

**Millie's Math House**, Edmark, 800-426-0856, $31.95

**Bailey's Book House**, Edmark, 800-426-0856, $34.95

**Sammy's Science House**, Edmark, 800-426-0856, $31.95

**Microsoft Explorapedia Series** (World of Nature, World of People), Microsoft, 800-555-4512, $34.95 each

*My First Encyclopedia*, Knowledge Adventure, 800-542-4240, $32.95

*Macmillan Dictionary for Children*, Simon & Schuster Interactive, 800-983-5333, $19.95

*New Macmillan Visual Dictionary*, Simon & Schuster Interactive, 800-983-5333, $38.95

## Low-Cost Sources for CD-ROMs

There are a few ways that savvy shoppers in the computer world have learned to keep the cost of their software purchases down. Since bureaucratic institutions tend to get trapped by procurement procedures, it's common for individuals within these realms to be locked into buying only through standard catalogs or sales representatives. If you've got some discretionary money for purchasing products on your own, or if you're a teacher who is tired of waiting for the district to get its act together, there are ways to stretch your CD-ROM purchases. You can save hundreds of dollars, so if you're strapped for cash it's well worth using these methods. I found it to be great fun, too, but then I believe wholeheartedly in what Woody Allen's character said in the movie, *The Front*: "The greatest sin in our family was to pay retail!"

The single best way to obtain consumer-oriented CD-ROM programs is from the independent (non-chain) computer stores. They are everywhere throughout this country in major metropolitan areas. They are highly competitive and many of them specialize in heavily discounted CD-ROMs, often 70 to 80 percent off retail. Naturally they cannot offer the titles put out by the major scholastic and library-oriented producers such as SIRS and World Book, but when it comes to the consumer products like *Microsoft Encarta, Grolier Multimedia Encyclopedia, Compton's Interactive Encyclopedia,* or the *Living Books* series, they offer prices that make these products highly affordable to the cash-poor library or school.

This solution may not be convenient for libraries or schools in rural areas, but it could come in handy to know about it; maybe you can put together a shopping list for the next time you hit the big city. If you already live in a major metropolitan area, the best way to find these bargains is to get your hands on one of the free computer shopping guides. The most popular ones in my neck of the woods are *Computer Currents* and *MicroTimes*. These are widely available at computer stores. Each issue has advertisements for dozens of independent computer stores and acts as catalogs for these outlets. Many stores include lists of their hot CD-ROM titles in their ads. I've found fabulous savings on dozens of CD-ROMs and I didn't mind the extra bit of driving it took to go get them.

The independent stores are not the only ones offering discount CD-ROMs, to be sure. Many famous computer chains do offer excellent prices, so don't hesitate to check them out. They'll no doubt beat the retail prices in educational catalogs. Also, the large warehouse stores such as Price Costco are well worth keeping an eye on. They've often had excellent prices for software of all kinds.

Though I've made an effort to avoid promoting commercial ventures in this book, I can't avoid touting one large commercial enterprise when it comes to CD-ROMs. SoftKey International, which may rightly claim to be the largest provider of consumer CD-ROM titles, has an excellent variety of products of great value in the area of reference works and educational material. SoftKey produces many of its products in-house; others it licenses; still others it obtains from companies suffering hard times. Whatever the strategy, the result has been top-flight products at amazingly low prices. Rarely is a product higher than $29.95 (which seems to be the benchmark price) and when you order by mail from SoftKey's special offers, a worthy secondary title is usually thrown in as a free bonus. Thus, after tax and shipping, I've rarely paid more than $18 a title. Some of their better-known titles are:

*BodyWorks 5.0*
This is perhaps the best CD-ROM on the market today on the subject of human anatomy. It is highly interactive, with many great videos, including a set of tutorials on each area of anatomy.

*The American Heritage Talking Dictionary*
This combination dictionary-thesaurus is ideal for English-as-a-second-language classes because of its speech function—it pronounces every entry. Also, its search function helps users find words they can't quite remember. It allows for conceptual searches with multiple clues. It is loaded with pictures, animations, and videos. One powerful feature is the included macro that installs it as a menu item within Microsoft Word, thus allowing access within Word at the click of a mouse.

*InfoPedia 2.0*
This is a combination reference work, including the 29-volume *Funk & Wagnalls New Encyclopedia, Roget's Thesaurus, World Almanac, Merriam-Webster Dictionary, Merriam-Webster Dictionary of English Usage, Merriam-Webster Dictionary of Quotations, Webster's New Biographical Dictionary*, and *Hammond World Atlas*. Also included are more than one hundred fifty videos and animations, four hundred fifty sound clips, and over five thousand photographs.

Of course, SoftKey does not limit itself to reference or educational titles. There are many kinds of products in its catalog, from computer utilities to word-processing programs. But I know you'll find products of value from SoftKey and the prices will in most cases be helpful in staying within a budget.

SoftKey's customer service number is 800-227-5609. You may order products directly or ask to be put on SoftKey's mailing list. This will ensure that you are alerted to new releases and special offers.


## Classroom Resources

Many, if not most, schools have adequate libraries or computer labs for their students and most teachers will be glad to send their students there to find the information they need for papers and projects. The last thing I would want to see is librarians and teachers wasting valuable resources while working at cross-purposes.

But those teachers who find themselves adrift in schools with inadequate funding (my son's school not only does not have any computers in the library, it doesn't even have a librarian!) will find that a single computer stocked with a decent collection of CD-ROM reference works can instantly turn a classroom into a library.

A computer in each classroom is becoming more and more common, and if each of those computers is properly equipped with multimedia gear, the possibilities are great for expanding what can be accomplished within a classroom's four walls. If a topic comes up for discussion in any subject from history to science, it only takes a second or two for a quick key-word search to locate valuable information that can solve an arising mystery right on the spot. Productivity can be increased manifold when group or individual projects are assigned. Groups of students can take turns around the computer, researching their topics; more projects can be handled per term and more information shared among the class. Overall learning can rise dramatically.

Even in schools that have top-rate libraries I suspect librarians would be pleased if a lot of research were handled in individual classrooms. It could reduce the pressure on libraries that suffer from overcrowding, especially those libraries with limited computer labs. Though instruction in searching strategies will enable students to sift through vast amounts of information with greater confidence and skill, not all practice of these skills need occur in the school library. A classroom library might contain starting points for research.

I have met more than one teacher who has taken it upon himself or herself to develop a classroom computer lab. There are a number of good reasons for doing this: The students' general computer skills can increase dramatically; shareware and freeware learning programs can be used right in the classroom on a rotating basis, supplementing the textbook curricula; the multimedia CD-ROM programs often make learning more exciting for students, drawing them to enjoy exploring new areas of study; and the presentation creation programs can inspire creative efforts in a way that paper-based projects failed to do in the past. The end result will be well-rounded students ready for the world beyond the classroom where their technological skills will make the difference between success or failure.

The kinds of CD-ROMs best suited for the classroom are those listed earlier in this chapter, the consumer-oriented reference works and such. But I encourage teachers to look wide to find CD-ROM titles their students might enjoy. Naturally, I encourage everyone to use my bargain-shopping methods in the previous section whenever acquiring new CD-ROMs. It bears repeating, too, that shareware and freeware programs be utilized to their fullest!

# PART TWO

# Shareware, Freeware, and Internet Listings

# Introduction to Shareware and Freeware Listings

I have made every effort to locate and evaluate as many programs in as many categories of interest to librarians, teachers, and administrators as was practical. This list is by no means exhaustive, but it is representative of some of the finest shareware and freeware available online. If nothing else, these programs will serve as a full introduction to the value of shareware and the amazing ways you can use it to extend library services or classroom curricula. Some of the programs are specifically for use by librarians, teachers, and administrators to help them in their daily tasks, while others are useful in operating and maintaining computers and labs, on- and offline.

I hope, more than anything, to give you such a head start that you'll feel confident to look for new programs and tools in the future with your own searches of FTP and the World Wide Web.

There are some important things to know about this list, and shareware in general, in order to find programs easily and profit by them once you have them:

1. In the listings I have given the program name, a rating of one to five stars, downloaded file name, the download site I used, a description and evaluation of the program, system requirements, space requirements, price, and producer's name.

2. The star rating system runs from one to five. There are no entries in the list with a single star rating, as this would indicate a program of marginal value and thus would not warrant its inclusion. Two stars mean that the program is of general value; three stars indicate strong general worth; four stars mean that the program is of excellent quality; five stars put the program at the top of its category, even when compared to so-called retail or commercial programs.

3. The listed site is not the only site where a file can be found, not by any means. Using the World Wide Web shareware search engines such as c l net's shareware.com, Jumbo!, and others in the Web site listings, you can plug in various key words including file name, program name, or subject area to locate the programs you want. Sometimes you'll find a file by one means and not another, so try different types of search entries until you're successful. Where I give a complete World Wide Web or FTP address, it's to facilitate locating the file; where I've only given a home page, it's because a search engine is available to locate a program's file, or the site has an easy set of categories through which to search and easily find the file. AOL stands for America Online.

4. System requirements are based on documentation where available. This information was more often included in Mac

documentation than in that of PC programs. The Macintosh system information was based, additionally, on my testing the programs on a Mac LC with four megabytes of memory with a twelve-inch color monitor; thus most programs will run on most of the Macs in use today. Many of the low-end programs with no major memory requirements or need for color can run on a Mac Plus. Also, I took programs needing larger monitors to higher-end machines for testing. Occasionally, low-end programs will not work on Power Macs or Power PCs. As for IBM-PC programs, documentation of system requirements was almost wholly lacking. Here, though, is a fairly reliable set of guidelines: DOS programs will work on machines as low as 286s and definitely on 386s; Windows 3.x programs require at least a 386 and do well on a 486; Windows 95 programs require 486s or better and usually do best with at least eight megabytes of RAM (random access memory). Pentium machines are nice but not required for any program in this book. I tested all PC shareware on a 486-DX-120 with sixteen megabytes of RAM.

5. The space requirements are the amount of disk space needed for original installation. That will suffice for most educational programs with the exception that some additional space will be taken up by user records, saving of scores or games, and hall-of-fame entries. In many programs, though, resultant databases will grow according to the amount of data that is entered or the number of resultant files generated and saved. In some cases, this disk space can be extensive. Small programs which do not generate files that need to be saved can easily be placed on and run from floppy disks, thus saving space on machines with small hard drives.

6. Naturally, registration guidelines for shareware programs should be followed. Each author has his or her guidelines.

It is important to realize, though, that some shareware programmers may "go out of business," making registration of a program impossible. In that event, it may be ethical to continue to use the demo version as long as it is useful and functional. If a user has reason to believe that a useful program may be old enough that the registration process is obsolete, it may be wise to send a self-addressed, stamped envelope to the address of the programmer or company which is requesting a fee, instead of simply mailing a check. This would be a wise course to follow, whether you are a teacher, librarian, or administrator.

7. Each program listed has been downloaded and evaluated personally. Beyond the valuable information this process has provided you, there is one additional advantage. None of these programs contained any detectable virus. The antiviral programs installed on each machine detected no viruses at any time, and there remains no indication of infection or damage to any part of my machines. You can therefore download these programs without fear. In further explorations, use whatever precautions you deem necessary.

8. New Mac and IBM-PC shareware and freeware are coming online every day. Once you've checked out the programs in these lists, don't hesitate to keep your eyes out for new programs. Still, understand that, with shareware, old does not mean bad. I have some programs four or five years old that have not been surpassed in their delightfulness and effectiveness. There are many fine older DOS programs, both administrative and educational, that will run perfectly well on old 286 and 386 machines. Don't throw these machines out! Create a "dinosaur" computer lab and run the fine old DOS programs on them. The same can be done with Mac Pluses and old LCs. This may be an important use of shareware and freeware—the preservation of the value of older machines.

9.  The programs in these lists have been selected for their value to libraries and educational institutions. However, I encourage all of you to think about the value of shareware and freeware in the adjacent areas of computer enhancement. A good librarian, media specialist, or technology mentor should become well acquainted with what's available out there in the online world. There are programs of use in all areas of interest and application, from accounting to nutrition. Find stuff just for yourselves! Also, it isn't just shareware and freeware that's important, or just educational shareware you should be looking for. There's so much of value out there. You should learn how to locate and retrieve the latest drivers for various peripherals such as printers, video cards, and monitors. You can find exciting enhancement utilities for your operating systems. There are thousands of music and sound files, QuickTime movies, and other animations. For every conceivable aspect of computing and networking there is something available online to improve or extend its use. Take the ideas in this book, forge your own trail, and discover your own treasures.

10. Here are some important guidelines for downloading files. For most of you, the easiest way of locating and downloading files will be the World Wide Web and its many clearinghouses loaded with shareware and freeware. A good example of this is shareware.com. After you have located a program of interest using its search engine, you can click on a file name and be taken to a page of sites from which the file can be downloaded. These are invariably FTP sites around the world. When you choose which FTP site to use, think about what time it is in each time zone before you choose a site from which to download. For example, if it's 2:00 p.m. where you are, choose a site where it's the middle of the night, perhaps <ftp.archie.au> in Australia. The server there will be experiencing less demand at that time. You'll not only have an easier time connecting, but the file will be

sent to you much faster. If, on the other hand, you chose an American FTP site, chances are you won't even be able to log on, for many of the most popular ones such as <ftp:// wuarchive.wustl.edu> or <ftp://oak.oakland.edu> are too busy to allow anonymous users to connect. I like to go directly to FTP sites, for I've spent many a fine hour there browsing for files and finding many gems. Also, you can download the text files of complete program lists from different directories and later peruse them at your leisure to locate files. You can then log back on at a later time to bring the goodies back. Again, log on to these FTP sites at times when they're least likely to be crowded. I get a kick out of connecting to sites around the world in countries like Finland, Israel, Hong Kong, Japan, and Germany, knowing that it's the middle of their night. For more information and a list of valuable FTP sites, look to the FTP listings at the end of the World Wide Web sites chapter.

11. In the online world, shareware and freeware programs have been compressed to allow for rapid download. For Mac platforms the compressed documents have various extensions. The most common is .sit, which requires UnStuffIt (also available as StuffIt Expander) to uncompress. Drag and drop the .sit document on the UnStuffIt icon for automatic extraction. The Internet, especially at FTP and WWW sites, has many programs compressed in BinHex format with the extension .hqx. Drag and drop these documents on UnStuffIt and they will also be extracted. There are also the auto-extracting installation documents with the .Ins extension. Double-click on this kind of document and it auto-extracts and starts the installation program automatically. Lastly, for Macs, there is the self-extracting archive document with the extension .sea. Double-clicking automatically extracts the program and its related document. UnStuffIt is freeware and it is listed first in the Mac chapter.

12. There are also various compression schemes for the IBM-PC world. Number one by a long shot is the ZIP file. Unzipping (extracting) requires the use of the famous PKZIP program or WinZip, both of which are available everywhere on the Internet or online services. Also popular on the Internet are files compressed by LHA by Yoshi with the file extension .lha or .lzh. There is another less popular format, ARJ, which has the extension .arj. These programs are listed at the beginning of the IBM-PC chapter. Documentation for how to use them is included with each program. They are easy to use once you get the hang of it and the documentation is very clear. These programs are all available in the self-extracting format with the extension .exe. Double-clicking on a self-extracting file's icon will cause it to autoextract, so, naturally, you don't need an extraction program to extract it! Also, these programs allow you to build compressed files for uploading or attaching to your e-mail, or for archiving to save disk space (that can really come in handy). Thus, I suggest you learn how to use them. The last word: if you have Windows, definitely get WinZip. It's a miracle worker and really streamlines the extraction process.

Well, happy harvesting. I hope these lists prove to be a great boon to you. I know you will find many useful programs and tools to make your institutions more effective and your daily lives happier and more productive.

# Chapter Six

# Macintosh Shareware and Freeware

## File Extraction Tools

### UnStuffIt ★★★★★

unstuffit3.07.sea.hqx

http://www.shareware.com

This self-extracting archive contains UnStuffIt 3.0.7. UnStuffIt joins segments and expands archives from StuffIt versions 1.5.1 to 3.0.7. It can also expand StuffIt SpaceSaver files without SpaceSaver being present. Can be used to extract most BinHex files such as .hqx files popular on the Internet. Requires any Mac. Requires 90k hard disk space. Freeware. Aladdin Systems.

# Antiviral Programs

## Disinfectant ★★★★★

Disinfectant.sea

CompuServe

This top-rated antiviral program is already in use on thousands of Macs throughout the world. With it, the user can scan and disinfect both floppy disks and hard disks. If a virus is discovered, the suspect disk can be repaired in most cases. The Disinfectant protection INIT file installed in the system or extensions folder will stay on the alert for viruses. As with any antiviral program, watch for and download the latest release or update in order to keep up with emerging viruses. Works on any Mac with System 6 or higher. Requires 345k hard disk space. Freeware. Northwestern University.

## VirusScan ★★★★★

msc100e1.hqx

http://www.mcafee.com

This program supports all Macintosh computers with an extensive array of features to keep your system immune from viruses. It offers easy initiation of background protection and automated scanning during system startup and automatically captures viruses as programs are executed for immediate virus elimination. VirusScan scans all system areas to provide extensive security including local and network drives, CD-ROMs, floppies, and any mounted storage device, as well as files and folders. In the vast majority of cases, it accurately cleans virus infections and restores systems to their virus-free states. It can discover viruses within driver-level compressed files such as StuffIt, Compact Pro, and DiskDoubler. As with any antiviral program, watch for and download the latest release or update in order to keep up with emerging viruses. Requires any Mac with System 6.0.5 or higher. Requires two megabytes hard disk space. $65. McAfee.

## Computer Security

### Abracadabra ★★★★

abracadabra-15.hqx

ftp://mirrors.apple.com/mirrors/Info-Mac.Archives/gui

This small program may save system administrators, lab coordinators, library media specialists, and teachers a lot of grief! Its simple task is to show/hide the system folder. With a single click, it's hidden; with another, it's back. A perfect remedy for clever students with prying eyes or mischievous intent. Requires any Mac. Requires 29k hard disk space. $7. Nightfall Software.

### AutoLock ★★

auto-lock-15.hqx

ftp://mirrors.apple.com/mirrors/Info-Mac.Archives/gui

AutoLock is a small application intended to alleviate some problems associated with running children's applications (games, etc.) under the System 7 Finder. It can help to prevent small children from accidentally sending a game to the background. AutoLock's Shell Mode provides a limited launching functionality that can be used in place of the Finder, somewhat like At Ease. Requires any Mac with System 7.0 or higher. Requires 72k hard disk space. Freeware. Singular Systems.

### The Cloak ★★★

cloak-10.hqx

ftp://mirrors.apple.com/mirrors/Info-Mac.Archives/gui

This clever little program allows you to make files visible or invisible. You can prevent the launching of off-limits programs as well as protect data or system files. Requires any Mac with System 7.0 or better. Requires 34k hard disk space. $10. Little Dog Software.

### Filelock ★★

filelock-131.hqx

ftp://mirrors.apple.com/mirrors/Info-Mac.Archives/gui

Filelock is a simple drag-and-drop security program. Its sole purpose is to lock files which are unlocked and, conversely, to unlock those that are locked, and it prevents any number of files from being opened. Requires 68K or Power Mac. Requires 109k hard disk space. $10. Rocco Moliterno.

## Internet Tools

### CyberFinder ★★★★

cyber-finder-20.hqx

ftp://wuarchive.wustl.edu/system/mac/mac-info/app

CyberFinder makes it easy to go from one type of Internet site (such as a Web page) to another (such as a newsgroup). Double-click a CyberFinder bookmark and CyberFinder automatically launches the appropriate application (you must, naturally, have your own Internet browser and connection) and takes you to the chosen site. You can use a special "hot key" to jump to Net sites from within any application—even a word processor. This bookmark tool would be handy for organizing and storing large numbers of bookmarks or for setting up your computer in a way that guides students or patrons to appropriate sites (others could be declared "off-limits"). Requires Mac SE or greater running System 7.1.1 or greater. Requires about one megabyte of hard disk space. $30. Aladdin Systems.

### GrabNet ★★★

gnmac2.sea.hqx

http://www.ffg.com/

GrabNet is a browser companion tool enabling users to intuitively collect and organize information gathered from the World Wide

Web. Users can casually grab snips of information, including images, text and URLs, for reuse, navigation, and organization within a customized collection of folders on the local desktop. $19.95. ForeFront Group Inc.

## Microsoft Internet Explorer ★★★★★

Various file names for different Macintosh computers

http://www.microsoft.com

Currently, Microsoft has joined battle with Netscape to determine who shall dominate the Web browser market. The fortunate result is Internet Explorer 3.0, as state-of-the-art as Netscape Navigator, and free to all. Various versions are available depending on which Mac you use. Follow the easy download instructions at the above site. Naturally, eight megabytes of memory is required. Required hard disk space differs according to your version, but expect to use up ten megabytes or more. Freeware. Microsoft.

## Netscape Navigator ★★★★★

2_01Nets.hqx or latest version

http://home.netscape.com

Netscape, the leading producer of tools for browsing and utilizing the World Wide Web, has made its premier Web browser, Netscape Navigator, available to students, educators, and librarians free of charge. Netscape Navigator brings Web exploration, e-mail, newsgroups, and FTP right to your fingertips with all the state-of-the-art refinements and capabilities together in one package. To take advantage of this generosity, visit the Netscape Web site and download the software directly. Web browsing requires a color Mac with eight megabytes (sixteen megabytes are much better) of memory. Requires 2.25 megabytes hard disk space. Freeware. Netscape.

### WebWhacker ★★★★

_wwmac1_.hqx

http://www.ffg.com

> WebWacker allows you to "whack" single pages, groups of pages, or entire sites from the World Wide Web and save them for later viewing. Patrons and students can then browse these sites without maintaining an open Internet connection. This program will allow you to share the resources of the Internet while saving valuable online time and controlling Internet use. Requires 1.74 megabytes hard disk space. $49.95. ForeFront Group Inc.

## Library Cataloging Programs

### Bibliography Manager II ★★★

bibliography-manager-ii-20.hqx

ftp://wuarchive.wustl.edu/system/mac/info-mac/text

> This is a HyperCard stack template for creating a bibliography database. It could be used to catalog and manage circulation for small libraries, or it could be used in large research projects. The template allows data entry of most typical bibliographic information, plus a large scrolling note section. You can search by keywords, mark and unmark cards, print cards, and create a journal list. Requires any Mac with HyperCard 2.1 or later. Requires 789k hard disk space. $20. David Tremmel.

### Bibliophile ★★★

Bibliophile 2.0.sea

AOL

> A HyperCard stack library cataloging system. There is a well-designed form for data entry, as well as a variety of sort functions. Records can be exported as text files in bibliography or catalog form.

New records are easily added. Records have room for large descriptive text entries. Requires Mac Plus or higher and HyperCard 2.x or Player. Requires 120k hard disk space. Freeware. Unknown.

## CS Library ★★★★★

Library CS (v1.07).sea

AOL

A program for the control of small libraries. It is a full-featured program, set up to print and use bar-coded patron ID cards and book bar-code labels for check-in/check-out of materials. There are listings for both patrons and books, and the book catalog entries have the ability to contain and display PICT files for each book. There are search functions, as well as a number of report functions. This seems to have a substantial number of the bells and whistles that a fully functioning library would need, including password requirements to control access to librarians' operations. Requires any Mac System 7.0 or better. Requires 1.28 megabytes hard disk space. $49. CopperHead Software.

## Generic Library Stack ★★★

GenLib.sit

AOL

A HyperCard library catalog program. The program features scrollable entry fields and thorough, easy search functions. Records the borrower and date out. This program could do very well for the small library or classroom library. Requires any Mac with HyperCard 2.x or Player. Requires 158k hard disk space. Freeware. The Library Stack.

## On Your MARC ★★★★★

on-your-marc-demo.hqx

ftp://wuarchive.wustl.edu/system/mac/info-mac/app

On Your MARC is a stand-alone, online card catalog. It features online help; Boolean, subject/author/title, and key-word searches; printable scrolling list of matches that includes local call number;

bibliographic "zoom" on list item, with found words highlighted; and much more. The program works at blazing speeds on even small Macs. Requires Mac with at least four megabytes of memory running System 7.0 or better. Requires 350k hard disk space for every thousand bibliographic records. $499.95 for up to thirty-two thousand bibliographic records (send MicroLIF files from your circulation program and the company will send you On Your MARC preloaded); included is the right to have the program installed on any and all computers on-site, from libraries to classrooms to offices. Requirements uncertain (inquire with company). InSite Software.

## Teaching Aids

### BasicFacts Maker II ★★

BasicFac.sea.hqx

http://wuarchive.wustl.edu/

BasicFacts Maker generates math worksheets with twenty-five addition, subtraction, multiplication, or division problems for practicing basic math skills. An unlimited number of different worksheets can be made for students along with a teacher answer sheet. This is a very fast, helpful program, with the limitation that specific levels cannot be set. The range for subtraction and addition is good for K–3 (sums to 18 and minuends to 18) and the range for multiplication and division is appropriate for 4–6 (products to 81 and dividends to 81). Requires any Mac, though it may need two megabytes of available memory. Requires 979k hard disk space. $10; $30 site license. Jim White.

### Crossword 1.0 ★★

Crossword 1.0.hqx

ftp://wuarchive.wustl.edu/system/mac/info-mac/font

This is not a program but a set of fonts that enables you to create crossword puzzles in any word processor. By a simple case change, you can hide the answers. Teachers may wish to encourage their students to try their hand at making crossword puzzles. Requires any Mac. Requires 121k hard disk space. $10 or less, depending on use and financial situation. Benn Coifman.

## Desk Planner ★★★

Desk Planner™ 4.1.3.sit

AOL

A lesson plan program with advantages over paper planners. It looks and feels like a standard lesson plan book, but it is reformattable for special needs and has scrollable data fields with unlimited text entry. With the click of the tab button, an expanded field window pops up for easy reading. The program comes with a template to allow the user to get started easily. This program can run in either ClarisWorks or SimpleText (when you start it, it looks for what's available to run it). Requires Mac Plus or higher with System 7.0. Requires 644k hard disk space. $11.50 ($4 per teacher for site licenses). John Barber.

## Eagle GradeBook ★★★

eaglegradebook3.1a folder.sit

CompuServe

This program was written to help teachers track a class of students. It can record attendance, record assignments and grades, compute student grades, and produce reports. A spreadsheet is used as the primary method of entering and maintaining data. Grades may be entered using a letter grade, points, percents, pass/fail, or plus, check, and minus. You may also define your own letter grades. Calculation of grades may use a straight average, even average, or weighted average. The spreadsheet looks very much like a standard print-form teachers' gradebook, making it an easier and more intuitive operation to enter the data. This program has been used by teachers around the world from kindergarten to college level. It can very successfully streamline the grading and class-tracking process. Requires any Mac with one megabyte of memory. Requires

575k hard disk space. Freeware, but the author would like a post-card sent to him. Rex Evans.

## Flash ★★

Flash.sit

AOL

A HyperCard stack speed-reading tutorial and driller. It presents the basics of speed-reading in a clear, direct fashion; then it provides user-configurable, multilevel drills to increase reading speed and comprehension. This stack can be useful for students who wish to increase their reading speed or for teachers whose students complain that they cannot finish reading assignments. Perhaps a session with this program will alert students that there are different, more effective ways to read. Not for everyone, but may be helpful from fifth grade through college. Requires any Mac and HyperCard or Player. Requires 49k hard disk space. $15. Tim Constantine.

## Gradebook Manager ★★★

gradebook-manager-35.hqx

ftp://wuarchive.wustl.edu/system/mac/info-mac/text

Gradebook Manager can record scores for forty students on forty assignments is each quarter of the school year. You can group assignments into seven categories, compute grades using category weights or total points earned, excuse any assignment for any student, or drop the worst score in any category. You can choose to have your final exams contribute to the quarter, semester, or final grade. Requires any Mac. Requires 132k hard disk space. $20. Daniel Ethier.

## Instant Fractions ★★★

Instant Fractions © 1.1.sea

CompuServe

A HyperCard stack for producing fractions worksheets and tests. Menus feature catchy, entertaining sound clips. Choose between addition, subtraction, multiplication, or division; select the value limitation for numerator and denominator; specify whether or not to allow negative numbers for answers; then click and print. Worksheets and tests can be printed with or without answers. The automatic problem generator allows for unlimited random problem creation (within the set parameters, of course). This stack should be a very helpful tool for all teachers of grades 3 through 9. Requires any Mac with HyperCard. Requires 638k hard disk space. $10. France & Associates.

## Instant PerCents ★★★

InstantP.sea.hqx

http://wuarchive.wustl.edu/

A HyperCard stack, Instant PerCents will prepare tests or worksheets, as well as answer keys, for conversion between percents, integers, decimals, and fractions. You can then print the worksheets and answer keys on 8½-x-11" paper. The program is capable of creating an unlimited number of random problems. Requires any Mac with HyperCard. Requires 419k hard disk space. $10. France & Associates.

## K-8 Pioneer Activities ★★★★

K-8_Pioneer_Activities.sit

AOL

A program of well-conceived pioneer activities (expansion of the old west and Canada). The activities are ingeniously tagged to art, environmental study, math, music, drama, physical education, reading, spelling, and writing. Each category provides two activities. K–8. Requires color Mac with four megabytes of memory. Requires 700k hard disk space. $12 individual; $20 lab; $30 site license (registration brings many extra activities). E3 Inc.

## Math Worksheet Creators ★★★★

math-worksheet-creators-hc.hqx
ftp://wuarchive.wustl.edu/system/mac/info-mac/app

This HyperCard stack creates randomly generated math worksheets in practically any format for the drilling of elementary school math concepts, including addition, subtraction, multiplication, and division. The sheets can be individualized, with control over constants and range. Each worksheet can be named and dated. Problems can be individually edited before the final worksheet is printed. This is a very versatile program of great value to all elementary teachers from K through 6. Requires any Mac with HyperCard. Requires 255k hard disk space. Freeware. Nathan M. Smith, Jr.

## MathHomework 3.1 ★★★★★

MathHomework 3.1.sit
AOL

This is one fabulous program. It allows students to enter and do their math homework with a program which takes them step-by-step through each operation, whether it be multidigit multiplication, division, addition, or subtraction of whole numbers, fractions, or mixed numerals. When a mistake is entered, the program takes the student back until the correct number is entered. The final product can be a neat, finished, printable assignment to hand in. Though it may be impractical for all students in a class or school to have this program at home, it can be made available in labs or right in the classroom for practice. The program is not a calculator; the student must perform the computations; but, by taking students step-by-step through each operation, it thoroughly teaches them how to do each kind of problem. Not only can students complete assignments or drills, but teachers can also use the program to create worksheets that can be printed and completed in longhand or solved with the program itself. This is one very complete program for assisting the teaching of almost all K–8 math skills. Valuable as a standard or remedial teaching tool. Requires any Mac. Requires 485k hard disk space. Operates for a two-week evaluation period. $24; site license $79. Steve Smith.

### Proverbs ★★★

Proverbs.sit

AOL

A HyperCard stack of one thousand proverbs. An excellent program for essay and journal topics or, naturally, the study of proverbs and the wisdom contained in them. Proverbs can be displayed at random or can be located by built-in search tool. Can be useful for grades 5–12. Requires any Mac and HyperCard 2.x or Player. Requires 153k hard disk space. $5. Poor Richard's Publishing.

### Wonderful Word Search ★★★

Wonderful WordSearch 1/2/1B.sit

AOL

A simple, straightforward, very easy-to-use HyperCard program for generating and printing word-search puzzles. Enter your word list and the program does the rest. Size and style are easily configurable. Ideal for reinforcing spelling. K–8. Requires any Mac with HyperCard 2.x. Shareware: pay whatever you think it's worth. Running Dog Enterprises.

### Word Find ★★★

Word Find 1.3 *f*.sit

AOL

A program which easily generates and prints word-search game sheets. Grid size, word direction, and fonts are easily selected and configured. Hot tip: Set keyboard to caps lock in order to enter word list. This is a useful tool for generating custom word-search sheets for rainy day activities or spelling reinforcement. Effective for grades 1–6. Requires any Mac with System 7.0 and at least a twelve-inch monitor. Requires 149k hard disk space. Freeware. Brett C. Helbig.

## Wordsearch Creator ★★★

WORDSE.sit

CompuServe

> An easy-to-use word-search puzzle generator. There's no mystery to using this one: enter words in the list screen and select "make puzzle" from the menu bar. The puzzle is automatically generated and is ready to print. The ability to use foreign-language alphabets and select your favorite font makes this a very versatile little program. Another nice feature is the ability to copy and paste puzzles into word-processing or graphics programs. Requires any Mac. Requires 67k hard disk space. $15. Kevin D. Lee.

# Suites

## KKGames ★★

KKGames1.0 *f*.sit

CompuServe

> A suite of learning games for preschool to third grade. Wordspell is a spelling game. Mosaic Patterns allows the creation and printing of block color patterns on a grid. Color shapes is a paint program using only basic geometric shapes. Five-In-A-Row is a competitive addition program similar to bingo but played on-screen with dice. PlayNotes introduces children to the piano keyboard and musical notes. Requires a large-screen color Mac (thirteen-inch or greater) with four megabytes of memory. Requires 1.23 megabytes hard disk space. Freeware. Kurt Kaufman.

## Laser Learning ★★★

Laser Learning 1.1.sit

CompuServe

> An entertaining arcade-style program which can use various learning modules. This version comes with the math and state capitals modules. The player is the pilot of a spaceship surrounded by other

103

spaceships. Answering math problems or identifying state capitals lets the player know which ships are friendly and which are the enemy. Blast the enemies and win points. The graphical interface of the cockpit and the accompanying sounds make this an appealing program for kids. The math module is configurable for difficulty level and type of problem. Negative numbers are allowed. K–8. Requires a color Mac with System 7.x or higher. Requires 877k hard disk space. $15. MultiMedia Designs.

## Mathematics

### Algebra II Made Easy ★★★

Algebra II Made Easy.sea

AOL

A program which allows the user to plug in numbers to solve quadratic equations, distance problems, and linear equations, and to find the vertex of quadratic equations. Also included is a list of the more common formulas needed when taking Algebra II. The program is well designed, with balloon help throughout. It could be a helpful educational diversion for high school math classes. Requires a color Mac, System 7.0 or above and HyperCard 2.1. Requires 409k hard disk space. $15. Steve Toub.

### Baseball Math ★★★

Baseball Math.sit

AOL

This is a math baseball game that quizzes using multiple-choice word problems. Fun interface, with ball players running the bases accompanied by humorous sounds (which aren't necessary for the operation of the game). Fourth grade through middle school (or basic math classes in high school). Requires a Mac with a large-screen monitor and four megabytes of memory. Requires 1.46 megabytes hard disk space. Freeware. James Hall and Jeff Allnutt.

### CirculusMaximus ★★

Circulus.sea.hqx

http://wuarchive.wustl.edu/

A HyperCard stack which automatically calculates many dimensions of a circle, including area of a circle, segment of a circle, segment of a circle with a base, area contained between two concentric circles, and part of an area contained between two concentric circles. The stack can be used to demonstrate many principles of geometry involving the circle. Requires any Mac with HyperCard. Requires 80k hard disk space. Author requests discretionary amount under $10. Donovan O. Hendrick.

### Creepin' Critter Math ★★★

CC Math 3.1.sit

AOL

A suite of arcade-style math games in which the student squashes a critter on the wall (or, as a peaceful alternative, pops a bubble) to recognize numbers or to solve equations. Multileveled from counting to all four arithmetic operations, including borrowing and carrying. Appealing to kids. K–4. Requires any Mac with HyperCard 2.x or Player. Requires 907k hard disk space. $10; site license $50. BAP Software.

### Descriptive Geometry ★★★

DESCGEOM.sit

AOL

A stand-alone stack program which comprises a unit on basic geometry. It teaches basic geometrical definitions, types of angles, the measurement of complementary and supplementary angles, how to find the missing angle in triangles, etc. A self-paced tutorial, it allows students to proceed to the next topic only if they score 80 percent on each quiz. Easy to operate without many frills, it is nonetheless a very effective program for introducing the basics of geometry. Can be useful especially in middle school or basic math in high school, and for bright fifth and sixth graders as well. Topics and problems are printable as flashcards. Requires any Mac. Requires 550k hard disk space. No fee is mentioned for this program, but it's $10 for future programs covering chemistry, physics, and math. B & C Educational Resources.

### Dinosaur Rock Math ★★★★

D.R. Math 1.3.sit

AOL

A well-designed suite of math games which teach number order and the four arithmetic operations. Of special interest is a game called "Eliminator," in which the child must construct equations that will eliminate numbers from the screen. Great for developing math reasoning skills. This program is very intuitive and has excellent graphics. K–4. Requires 2.34 megabytes hard disk space. Requires color Mac with System 7.0 or better. $15; site license $25. Saratoga Software.

### Early Fractions ★★★

Early Fractions V1.0.sit

AOL

A HyperCard tutorial on fractions. The program does not show how to perform any computations, but is nonetheless a very clear presentation of the concept of fractions, and teaches how to recognize the values of basic fractions. It would be a fantastic introductory course or an excellent remedial tool. K–3. Requires any Mac with HyperCard 2.x or Player. Requires 111k hard disk space. Freeware. Elation Software Development.

### Graf ★★

Graf.sea.hqx

http://wuarchive.wustl.edu/

A program for plotting graphs. Suitable for late high school and college. Requires any color Mac with at least four megabytes of memory. Requires 788k hard disk space. Freeware. Ralph S. Sutherland.

## GraphPlot II ★★★

GraphPlo.sea.hqx

http://wuarchive.wustl.edu/

GraphPlot II is a program for creating graphs for mathematical, scientific, or engineering documentation, or for exploring mathematical functions. It can be used in late high school and college mathematics courses. Graphs may be printed or saved as PICT files. They can be imported into word-processing or presentation programs via the clipboard. Requires a Mac with four megabytes of memory and works best on a large screen. Requires 405k hard disk space. $20. Graham Cox.

## Guessing Game ★★

Guessing Game.sit

AOL

A little number-guessing game. Students type in numbers between 1 and 100, are told whether they're too high or too low, and guess again until they discover the number. No frills, but good for teaching elementary values. K–4. No documentation comes with it, though it's easy to understand and seems to be freeware. Requires any Mac. Requires 39k hard disk space. Unknown author.

## HyperGeometry ★★★

HyperGeo.sea.hqx

http://wuarchive.wustl.edu/

A HyperCard stack that solves a great number of geometric equations, including slope. It is blazing fast and can be a helpful teaching tool in that the vital formula for solving each type of shape is given on each calculation page. Grades 5–12. Requires any Mac with HyperCard. Requires 77k hard disk space. $10. RMK Software.

## HypoGraph ★★

HypoGrap.sea.hqx

http://wuarchive.wustl.edu/

> A HyperCard stack for plotting graphs. Lets you plot functions, parametric equations, and polar equations. Useful in late algebra, pre-calculus, and calculus classes in high school and college. Requires any Mac with HyperCard. Requires 60k hard disk space. Freeware. Dominic Yu.

## MacEmatics ★★

MacEmati.sea.hqx

http://wuarchive.wustl.edu/

> A HyperCard stack math drilling game. All four arithmetic operations are tested. Games can be selected by type and the level of difficulty can be set. There are some sounds and graphics for reinforcement, but the emphasis is on the math, not the entertainment. This program works very well and cleanly. K–6. Requires any Mac with HyperCard or Player. Requires 340k hard disk space. $8.95. APPS.

## Math Bee ★★★★

MathBee.sea.hqx

http://wuarchive.wustl.edu/

> An interactive math game for one or two players. Students are quizzed on the four basic arithmetic operations. The program uses Speech Manager, Plain Talk, or Macintalk 1.5 to provide speech; though the speech is entertaining and reinforcing, it is not necessary for the operation of the game. The games are fully configurable as to the kind and difficulty of the problem sets, up to the number 120,000. The problems can be set up for manual answer entry or different difficulty levels of multiple choice. The colorful graphical user interface makes this a pleasant experience for the students. The demo version allows only the use of addition. K–6. Requires color Mac with four megabytes of memory. Requires 550k hard disk space. $15. David Bagno.

## Math Factory ★★★★

MathFact.sea.hqx

http://wuarchive.wustl.edu/

> This game is quite similar to Math Bee, except for the incredibly flexible way it allows the teacher to pick exactly which set of problems to work on. For example: adding by ones, twos, etc.; multiplication tables by fours, fives, nines, etc.; division by three, eight, eighteen, etc. This would be a very creative way to teach groups of specific algorithms. The demo version is limited to addition. K–4. Requires color Mac with four megabytes of memory. Requires 527k hard disk space. $15. David Bagno.

## Math Flash Card! ★★

Math Flash Card!™ folder.sit

AOL

> A HyperCard stack for teaching the four basic arithmetic operations. It has a nice Egyptian theme, with a pharaoh smiling or shedding a tear depending upon the answer, while a pyramid is built by correct answers. Difficulty levels are easily set, so this program can be useful from kindergarten through sixth grade. Requires any Mac with HyperCard 2.x or Player. Requires 406k hard disk space. Shareware, but the price was omitted. A. Britt Anderson.

## Math School ★★★★

MathScho.sea.hqx

http://wuarchive.wustl.edu/

> This game is quite similar to Math Bee, except that it allows problems with up to four factors. The demo version is limited to addition. K–4. Requires color Mac with four megabytes of memory. Requires 527k hard disk space. $15. David Bagno.

## Math Stars ★★★

Math Stars3.0.1.sit

AOL

A nice, color math quizzing program with a very friendly interface. The answers are easy to enter and students are rewarded with sound and gold stars for successful runs at ten problems. The options menu allows full configuration of game according to problem type (all four basic arithmetic operations are included), timer settings, difficulty level, and the inclusion or exclusion of negative numbers. Allows up to ten players' names entered. K–5. Requires color Mac with System 7.0. Requires 163k hard disk space. $7; site license $50. Roger M. Clary.

## MathHomework 3.1 ★★★★★

MathHomework 3.1.sit

AOL

This is one fabulous program. It allows students to enter and do their math homework with a program which takes them step-by-step through each operation, whether it be multidigit multiplication, division, addition, or subtraction of whole numbers, fractions, or mixed numerals. When a mistake is entered, the program takes the student back until the correct number is entered. The final product can be a neat, finished, printable assignment to hand in. Though it may be impractical for all students in a class or school to have this program at home, it can be made available in labs or right in the classroom for practice. The program is not a calculator; the student must perform the computations. But, by taking students step-by-step through each operation, it thoroughly teaches them how to do each kind of problem. Not only can students complete assignments or drills, but teachers can also use the program to create worksheets that can be printed and completed in longhand or solved with the program itself. This is one very complete program for assisting the teaching of almost all K-8 math skills. Valuable as a standard or remedial teaching tool. Requires any Mac. Requires 485k hard disk space. Operates for a two-week evaluation period. $24; site license $79. Steve Smith.

## Reckon ★★★

Reckon2.sea

CompuServe

A color HyperCard math game. This is a challenging, imaginative game involving all four arithmetic operations. From four numbers, using any operation or series of operations, shoot for a target answer from nine numbers on a grid. Students can choose to win by hitting any three targets, three in a row (as in tic-tac-toe), or by hitting all nine target numbers. Students could well get very absorbed in this game while learning and practicing multiple operations. K–6. Requires any color Mac with HyperCard or Player. Requires 121k hard disk space. Freeware. Thomas C. Bretl.

## xFunctions ★★★

xFunctio.sea.hqx

http://wuarchive.wustl.edu/

A graphing program designed to aid in teaching calculus and pre-calculus courses. New functions can be input as single formulas, split functions, graphs, or tables. A knife tool can be used to cut out a rectangle on a graph for enlargement. Seven special "utility" operations include: plotting several graphs on one axis; animation of a family of functions of the form $f(x,k)$; graphing of derivatives and tangent lines; Riemann sums, with graphical display; graphs of parametrically defined curves; integral curves of vector fields; and three-dimensional plots of functions $z = f(x,y)$. A limited printing facility is provided. High school and college. Requires any Mac. Requires 295k hard disk space. Freeware. David Eck.

# Alphabet, Phonics, Spelling, and Reading

### Alphabet Pro 2.0 ★★★★
Alphabet Pro 2.0.sit
AOL

> A very useful tool for teaching the alphabet, phonics, and spelling. The user can record words and letters in his or her own voice, then the program quizzes the student on location of letters in words and spells them aloud. The user interface is well designed, intuitive, and encouraging as it uses animation to drive the point home. Due to its user-input format, the program can be suited to a teacher's exact needs and lesson plans. Because sounds are instructor-created, this program can be used with foreign languages. Ideal for K–2, but useful for remedial and learning disability programs. The demo program allows only four-word lists. Requires Sound Manager, Mac System 6.7 to 7.5, two to three megabytes of memory, and recording capabilities. Requires 600k hard disk space to start, but this will grow fast as sound database files are created by the user. $20. David Bagno.

### Crystal's FlashCards ★★★
Crystal's FlashCards.sit
AOL

> A HyperCard stack of over 150 words on the first-grade level. Its colorful background and use of synthesized sound to pronounce words enhance this flash card program for teaching early vocabulary. Individual students can view the cards or groups of students can be led in activities in rooms with computers with larger screens. K–2. Requires any color Mac (though it would probably display well on black-and-white) with regular sound manager and HyperCard 2.x or Player. Requires 673k hard disk space. $7. Custom stacks up to two hundred words (you send the word list) are available for additional $10. Katz Designs.

## Find the Missing Word ★★★

Find Missing Word folder.sit

AOL

This multiple-choice game asks the student to fill in the missing word to complete the sentence. It has a very colorful, intuitive interface and comes with a plentiful word list. A wonderful reading teacher, it can be used to reinforce writing skills as well. It needs Speech Manager or Macintalk Pro to utilize the speech functions, but the program works fine without sound. K–3. Requires any Mac (color is best). Requires 612k hard disk space. $15. David Bagno.

## Letter Land ★★★★★

Letter Land *f*.sit

AOL

A colorful and entertaining program to teach the alphabet and numbers to preschoolers and kindergartners. The program has wonderful graphics and sound, and is easy to use. It asks "What picture begins with the letter…" and successful answers are rewarded with a game in which children learn their numbers while trying to snare varying numbers of graphics of the last presented word in a butterfly net. It's loads of fun and very effective. Most any Mac should be able to run it. Requires 1.56 megabytes of hard disk space. $8. Keith Productions.

## Libby's Letters ★★

Libby.sit

CompuServe

A HyperCard stack that teaches the alphabet and word recognition while serving as a very basic typing teacher. There are two games. In "ABC," the child is shown a letter; when it is typed, the child is rewarded with sound and graphics. In "Words," the child is shown a highlighted word with five word boxes below it. The child is given sound and graphics rewards when the corresponding word is clicked. The child need not know how to read, only to be able to click on identical words. The games can be edited for more complex words as desired. Preschool to kindergarten. Requires any Mac with HyperCard. Requires 99k hard disk space. Freeware. Rick Montgomery.

## Phonic Building Blocks ★★★★

Phonic Building Blocks 1.1.sit

AOL

By the author of Alphabet Pro, this program uses the same user-recorded sound database files to teach phonics. A word is recorded, then a multiple-choice question is created by recording four sounds such as "sh," "ch," "th," and "t." Word and question lists are built up until a quiz can be given by the program. The user interface is attractive, intuitive, and friendly. This phonics program can be shaped by the instructor to suit any lesson plan. This could be an ideal program for K–2, but could also be used in both remedial and learning disability situations. Requires any color Mac. Requires 523k hard disk space. $20. David Bagno.

## The Reading Factory ★★★

The Reading Factory v1.1.sea

AOL

An effective program for teaching basic phonics, spelling, and sentence construction. Using synthesized speech, the program offers multiple-choice games which test oral word comprehension and rhyming word recognition. Another game asks the student to make sentences out of offered words. It's very kid-friendly and colorful, with learning and reinforcing animation. It comes fully functional. K–2 and remedial situations. Requires any color Mac. Requires 523k hard disk space. $20. David Bagno.

## Sentence Builder ★★★★

Sentence Builder 1.3.sit.

AOL

As its name implies, this program aids in teaching children how to construct simple sentences. An out-of-order word list (2–8 words) is presented and the child has to click on the words in the right order. The program's interface is colorful and intuitive, and, if your computer is equipped with Speech Manager or Macintalk (downloadable from several sources, including <ftp.dhmc.dartmouth.edu>), the computer prompts the child with sound. This is a helpful reading and writing reinforcement tool for K–3. Requires color Mac with two megabytes of memory. Requires 659k hard disk space. Speech Manager or Macintalk are enhancing but not required. $20. David Bagno.

## Spell Tutor ★★

Spell Tutor.sit

AOL

An uncomplicated spelling program which allows the user to record a word list to be tested via a simple user interface. Correct words fall in one column while incorrect entries fall in another. A retest of missed words is offered. This is a simple way for students to practice their spelling. It has applications for grades K–8 as well as remedial programs. Requires any Mac and a microphone. Requires 115k hard disk space, plus additional space for created word lists. $7. Roger Clary.

## Talking Spelling Bee ★★★

Talking Spelling Bee v2.sea

CompuServe/AOL

A competitive spelling bee program featuring digitized speech. The program requires Speech Manager or Macintalk to fully utilize the speech capabilities, but it can be configured to show the word briefly

115

if either of those programs are not installed. Older students can type in words or younger students can use a mouse to select letters from the colorful, well-designed graphical interface. Extensive word lists are provided. Registered owners can enter their own word lists. K–6. Requires any Mac (color is best) with 800k available memory. Requires 521k hard disk space. $20. David Bagno.

## Unscramble ★★★

Unscramble .sea

CompuServe

A colorful scrambled-word spelling game. It can be played by one or two players. An extensive word list is included with the program. This can be an effective spelling learning game for first through third grades. It works best with Speech Manager or Macintalk installed, but works fine without sound. Requires any color Mac with four megabytes of memory. Requires 536k hard disk space. $15. David Bagno.

## Word Mania ★★★

Word Mania.sea

AOL

This HyperCard stack is a suite of five word games: Scramble (solve the scrambled word), Hang'im (hangman game), Blankity Blank (a storymaker where the student chooses nouns, verbs, and adjectives which are then injected into stories with hilarious results), Shake-Up (a word-spotting game), and Letter Rip (a vocabulary game). Word Mania can be a useful vocabulary and spelling reinforcement tool while also functioning as a rainy day activity or reward for completed work. Recommended for grades 4–8, as a couple of the games are a little difficult. Requires any Mac with HyperCard or Player. Requires 186k hard disk space. $20. Dancing Rabbit Creations.

116

### Word Match ★★★

Word Match.sit

AOL

A concentration-style game in which students compete to match antonyms, synonyms, and homonyms. Users can create their own lists, so the level of difficulty can be set by the individual teacher or lab supervisor. The program comes with a number of well-designed lists. Curriculum level is flexible, but would be best for third to sixth grades, or in certain remedial programs. Should play on any Mac (color suggested). Requires 161k hard disk space. $7. Roger M. Clary.

### World Championship Bee with Clarence the Bee ★★

Clarence's Bee.sit

CompuServe

A HyperCard stack spelling bee game. This simple program is well designed, with a cute bee (Clarence, one would think) congratulating those who give the correct spelling of a misspelled word. It comes with a large database of prepared spelling bees in beginning, intermediate, and advanced levels, but the word selection is much too difficult for the supposed elementary-school target group (judging by the graphics and the honey bee theme). An excellent feature is the capability of creating your own spelling bees. Grades 1–6. Requires any Mac with HyperCard or Player. Requires 334k hard disk space. $5. Michael E. Abrams.

## Writing Tools and Resources

### Mac Language Arts Resources ★★★

Mac Language Arts Resources.sit

AOL

This is not a program but an online catalog of shareware and freeware resources compiled by an organization, SchoolHouse Mac, dedicated to making the best education tools available and easily accessible to educators. This catalog contains the best programs they've found in the language arts area of study. It can be used as both an introduction to the concept of online shareware and as a timesaving device for locating such. Dozens of programs are evaluated and rated. Articles on a number of related subjects are included. Requires any Mac. Requires 266k hard disk space. No charge. SchoolHouse Mac.

## Online English Handbook ★★★★

Online English Handbook1.2.sea

AOL

This is a marvelous resource tool. OEH is a concise, menu-driven grammar handbook. Click on the appropriate topic and concerns are answered in clear, concise language. Students could have this program open while they are writing compositions in computer labs; when a grammatical problem arises they could have instant access to a solution. Teachers could use the handbook as a resource for developing units on different areas of grammar and compositional skills. Librarians might find it a useful resource for answering questions concerning grammar. Foreign students will find it helpful in understanding English grammatical structure and rules. Recommended for fifth grade through college. Requires any Mac with at least a twelve-inch screen. Requires 185k hard disk space. $10. Tom Haglund.

## Story Starters ★★

Story Starters.sea

AOL

This HyperCard stack contains fifteen opening paragraphs for stories as well as an equal number of dramatic endings. Useful for creative writing projects in grades 5–9. Cards can be printed for distribution to students. Requires any Mac with HyperCard or player. Requires 45k hard disk space. $10. Dancing Rabbits Creations.

## Style and Grammar Tutorial ★★★

Tutor.sit

CompuServe

This HyperCard stack is a lesson (Quiz topics A-C) on correct usage in the form of a multiple-choice quiz. The questions are well constructed and deal with mainstream grammatical issues; wrong answers elicit an explanation of correct usage. The program could be used as a resource or as a framework for a lesson on style. To help chart a student's progress, reports on performance (showing weak areas) are generated and printable. Fifth grade through college. Requires Mac System 6.07or higher with HyperCard 2.x or Player. Requires 130k hard disk space. Freeware. Michael E. Abrams.

## Writing an Expository Paragraph: Structuring and Supporting ★★★

Exposition.sit

AOL

This HyperCard stack, written by an English teacher, can be of great value to any English class trying to teach students how to write effective essays. It has a step-by-step tutorial on constructing the expository paragraph, followed by cards that help the student write and print the paragraph, as well as creating and printing an outline for an essay. This stack is clear, well constructed, laced with humor students can relate to, and succeeds in getting straight to the core of what opening paragraphs are all about. Teachers can use this valuable resource to help students get over the very common roadblocks to getting an essay started. This stack can be used by teachers from grades 6–12 and can be especially helpful as an aid to students trying to pass their proficiency tests. Requires 92k hard disk space. Requires any Mac with HyperCard 2.x or Player. This is shareware with a twist: the author asks for a $10 donation to a specific wilderness cause. John M. Gorbacz.

## Foreign Languages

### FlashWorks ★★★★
FlashWorks 1.0.7 f.sea
AOL

A flashcard program designed to help students learn foreign language vocabularies. The student enters the meaning of the word and compares it with that of the word list. The program is equipped with a search function which allows the student to choose only those words in a word list he or she wishes to study. Teachers can create their own lists in any language. Extensive word lists in French, Spanish, German, Greek, and Hebrew accompany this program. Middle school through college. Requires any Mac. Requires 800k hard disk space. $3 (this modest shareware fee is waived if the user creates a word list and makes it available online). Dr. William D. Mounce.

### Landkartenspiel Europa ★★
Europe game 1.5German.sit
AOL

A simple HyperCard stack European geography game with a twist: It's in German! Teaches the countries and capitals in multilevel games. This would be a fun diversion for high school German classes. Requires any Mac with HyperCard 2.x or Player. Requires 171k hard disk space. Postcardware (send the author a postcard!). Ron LeMay.

# Geography

### Africa ★★
Africa.sit

AOL

This is a HyperCard stack for learning the countries and capitals of Africa. It is simple and effective. Grades 3–8. Requires any Mac with HyperCard or HyperCard Player. Requires 53k hard disk space. $5 donation. Calapooia Middle School.

### Asia Map Game ★★
Asia Map.Game.sit

AOL

A HyperCard stack for learning the countries and capitals of Asia. Allows competition among classmates and a Hall of Fame listing. Simple and direct. Grades 3–8. Requires any Mac with Hyper-Card 2.x or HyperCard Player. Requires 153k hard disk space. Postcardware. Ron LeMay.

### GeoGenius U.S.A. ★★★★★
GeoGenius U.S.A.sit

AOL

Like its worldly sister program, this one provides a colorful and friendly interface for learning about the United States. It has four modes: name the states, capitals, time zones, and regions. Each offers a quiz mode. In addition, "Fast Facts" allows the student to click on a state to learn its nickname, motto, flower, and song, and view a thumbnail sketch of its history. This program is an excellent resource for any purpose where the U.S.A. is concerned. Grades 3–12. Requires a Mac with at least a fourteen-inch monitor and three free megabytes of memory. Requires 978k hard disk space. $15. LittleFingers Software.

## GeoGenius World ★★★★★

GeoGenius World.sea

AOL

A very well-designed, colorful, and effective world geography program. It teaches the names of the countries of each continent, plus the states of the U.S.A. and provinces of Canada; then, in quiz mode, it tests students on their knowledge of each continent's countries. The interface is beautifully designed and very easy to operate. Sounds accompany and reinforce the quizzes nicely, but are not required. An excellent program all around. Grades 3–12. Requires a Mac with at least a fourteen-inch monitor and three free megabytes of memory. Requires 978k hard disk space. $16. LittleFingers Software.

## U.S. Map ★★

U.S. Map.sit

AOL

A simple HyperCard stack. Clicking on a state reveals its capital, flower, bird, nickname, and motto. The process will teach the location of the states; it's a good resource for students of any level who are learning about the states for the first time. Requires any Mac with HyperCard or Player. Requires 38k hard disk space. Freeware. Richard Wanderman.

## World Discovery ★★★★

World Discovery Demo 1.02b.sit

AOL

An interactive tool for learning the geography of the world. Players must identify countries from fourteen different world regions plus work with detailed maps of countries such as Canada, Mexico, and the United States. Players discover major cities (including capitals), rivers, lakes, seas, oceans, mountain ranges, and deserts. World Discovery tracks students' progress as they learn. The colorful puzzle format of the games turns the learning lessons into a great deal of fun. A very wide-ranging educational package, the program will be helpful to all in the K–8 range, and may be of use to high-schoolers too. The demo version contains only the maps of world regions and South America, but has plenty to allow a good evaluation and student road testing. Requires 368k hard disk space. Shareware with unspecified price. Great Wave Software.

## Social Studies

### Freedom Stack ★★★★
Freedom Stack 1.3.sit
AOL

This is a wonderful resource HyperCard stack full of myriad documents relating to freedom and democracy, centering around the Colonial period, Revolutionary period, and the early years of the United States. In categories named Pre-Constitution Docs, The Constitution, Post-Constitution Docs, and Quotations are some of the most famous documents of all time relating to the pursuit of freedom. Included are the Magna Carta, the Mayflower Compact, the Constitution of the Iroquois Nation, Patrick Henry's famous "Liberty or Death" speech, the Declaration of Independence, the U.S. Constitution, and more. Ideal for a lengthy unit on the birth of our nation. Not only is this a great teaching tool, but instructions are included for using the stack as a template for creating similar text stacks to produce your own units. Included with the program is the address for obtaining more than twenty-five other social studies stacks. A valuable classroom or library resource. Appropriate for fifth through twelfth graders. Requires any Mac and HyperCard 2.x. Requires 817k hard disk space. Freeware. SchoolHouse Mac.

# Science

### Prefix Game ★★★
PrefixGame1.0.sit
AOL

This creative HyperCard stack teaches common prefixes used in the world of science. Some examples are: photo-, di-, tri-, hydro-, tele-, hypo-, and some suffixes. This program represents a good way to introduce students to the concept of prefixes and word roots while incorporating the learning into a fun game. Middle school and high school. Requires any Mac with HyperCard 2.1. Requires 165k hard disk space. Freeware. Ken Dunham.

## Astronomy

### MPjAstro ★★★★
mpj-astro-13.hqx

ftp://mirrors.apple.com/mirrors/Info-Mac.Archives/sci

MPjAstro is a very handy planetarium program which can show you the day or night sky at any hour at any location from 2000 B.C. to 6000 A.D. It is very easily configurable and allows star and planet location, as well as labeling of many important celestial objects without obscuring the view. It includes various charts to help you locate objects and even lists the major meteor showers with peak dates and rates per hour. This program can be a very good introduction to the science of astronomy. It comes with very good documentation. K–12. Requires any Mac (color better). Requires 2.1 megabytes hard disk space. $25. Microprojects.

### StarAtlas ★★★
staratlas 0.8.cpt.hqx

ftp://mac.archive.umich.edu/misc/astronomy

StarAtlas is a good, simple planetarium program. It is easily configurable and displays a full set of stars. It can be set to atlas, planetarium, or solar system view (which shows the current relative location of the planets in their orbits). It relies on the control panel "Map" setting for viewing location. This is a good stargazing and teaching tool. K–12. Requires any Mac (color better). Requires 346k hard disk space. Postcardware (send the producer a postcard). Youhei Morita.

# American Sign Language

## Sign Finder ★★
Sign Finder 2.0 Demo .sit
AOL

This program is an interactive dictionary for words in sign language. Click on a word from the list and, in an adjacent box, you'll see an animated demonstration of how to sign the word. In another box is a text description of the sign. There are many options including printing and cutting and pasting to other documents. The demo version is limited to thirty-eight words, while the registered version comes with over nine hundred. Requires 584k hard disk space. Requires any Mac. $27.50. SoftScience.

# Typing

## Al Bunny's Typing Class ★★★
Al Bunny's Typing Class.sit
CompuServe

A colorful, graphics-based, game-style typing tutor. It may have special value in that children not ordinarily drawn to enhancing their keyboard skills would find this game friendly and inviting. Multileveled and fully configurable. Grades 4–8 (older kids might be turned off by the bunny theme). Requires any Mac with a large color monitor. Requires 790k hard disk space. $10. SUNMOON USA.

### TypingTutor ★★

TypingTutorJr3.3.sit

CompuServe

An effective typing tutorial with four different modules: free typing, letter drill, word drill, and paragraph drill. This is a fairly straightforward program without any bells or whistles but it would be effective for teaching anyone to type. Best suited to fifth grade through college. The program should work on any Mac. Requires 200k hard disk space. $12.50. W. Rogers.

## Classroom Publishing

### Book ★★★

Book ƒ.sea

AOL

A color HyperCard template created to help students write and illustrate their own books with text, drawings, animations, draggable buttons, and icons. Easy to use with clear instructions, it comes with a couple of sample books to suggest how it works. K–6. Requires System 7.0 and HyperCard 2.x or Player. Requires 253k hard disk space. Freeware. Diane Bundy.

### DOCMaker ★★★★★

DOCMaker4.6.sit

CompuServe

This application creates stand-alone, self-running documents. It features scrollable and resizable windows, graphics, varied text styles and fonts, and full printing capability. You may create up to sixty separate 32k chapters within each document, with a table of contents and a "find" feature. Full-color graphics can be added. Pages and fonts can be in various colors. "Hot pictures" act like buttons within the documents for playing sounds, showing Quick Time movies, sending Apple Events, and jumping to other applications.

These stand-alone documents are self-executing and can be distributed to other computers which do not have DOCMaker loaded. This is a full-featured electronic book creator, presentation creator, or highly versatile word processor plus. It can be used by students (fifth grade and up), teachers, librarians, and administrators. The program is available in many languages, including Japanese. Requires any color Mac with System 7.0 and four megabytes of memory. Requires 1.15 megabytes of hard disk space. $25. Green Mountain Software.

## Electronic Textbook ★★★

Electronic Textbook .sit

AOL

This is no KidWorks II, but considering what you get for free, it could be a handy addition to any learning environment. The program is a HyperCard writing tool that allows students to enter text which can be read back with synthesized voice by clicking the sound icon at the top of each page. Using the painting tools, students can draw art to accompany text. Combining all of the available tools in one page, one can enter text, then hide it and draw over it: clicking the sound icon, the hidden text becomes a narration to tell the story contained in the artwork! Quite cool in a stack requiring only 144k hard disk space. The program also allows the creation of navigational buttons. Good for all levels from grades K through 8. Requires any Mac with System 7.0 and HyperCard 2.1 or later. Freeware. Ken Dunham.

## SoftAD Pro ★★★★

SoftAD Pro 1.5.ins

CompuServe

SoftAD is a predefined interactive presentation program. Though designed to create marketing and promotional tools, it has all the bells and whistles of a high-quality presentation or interactive-document creator, thus making it valuable for librarians, teachers, administrators, and students from grade 5 through college. Requires a large-screen Mac (at least thirteen inches) with four megabytes of memory. Requires 1.92 megabytes hard disk space. $149. Techno-Marketing Inc.

## Painting and Coloring

### IconBOSS ★★★

IconBOSS.sit

CompuServe

A full-featured icon editor which allows editing in eight-bit, four-bit, and one-bit formats. It's very simple to use. You can choose to edit or design icons in Apple icon color or 256 system color. Use is not limited to any group, as both teachers and students may have need to edit icons for use in a number of ways. The program is so simple that even kindergartners could conceivably make use of it. Full documentation provided. Requires any color Mac. Requires 132k hard disk space. $25. Scott A. Johnson.

### Kid Pix ★★

KidPix.sit

CompuServe

A black-and-white paint program. While it seems there would be no need for such a program when color versions are available, it's included here because of the many teachers who might want children to draw simple pictures to include in an electronic book or HyperCard stack. Kid Pix has all the standard paint tools and a good variety of controls, plus a very nice collection of shapes and pictures in the form of stamps for children to add spice easily to their art work. Simple icon menus make this a good choice for the youngest grades. Requires any Mac. Requires 102k hard disk space. Freeware, though you may order the commercial version for $25 to get color capabilities and more tools and stamps. Craig Hickman.

## Let's Color ★★★★

Let's Color...™ Sampler 1.3.sit

CompuServe

A coloring program equipped with ten templates for children to color. The user interface requires no language skills, so any age can use it with ease. The program uses 256 colors and comes equipped with a number of pleasing patterns. The templates are very well done, with pictures of dinosaurs, fish, snakes, and butterflies. Children of all ages (including adults!) should have great fun with this coloring book. K–6. Requires any color Mac with four megabytes of memory. Requires 1.2 megabytes initial hard disk space. Freeware, but an additional $19.95 brings dozens of new templates. TOTO Multimedia.

## Mandala ★★★

Mandal.sit

CompuServe

This is a paint program with a twist: It creates mandalas, or kaleidoscopes, either with your help or automatically. There are a number of controls available to manipulate the shapes and direct the fills. The results are astounding, very creative, and highly entertaining. Children of all ages will be fascinated and the resulting pictures can be used in a variety of ways, from pure art to inclusion in multimedia works or presentations. The concepts necessary for operating the program may limit this to older children and adults, but with supervision, all ages can enjoy Mandala. Requires any color Mac. Requires 315k hard disk space. $25. Gordon M. Green.

## MattPaint ★★★★

MattPaint1.9.4.sit

CompuServe

A full-functioned color paint program. You'll find all the bells and whistles of a standard paint program with easily accessible tools and palette. It has a built-in icon editor. Can read and produce PICT documents. Requires a color Mac with Color Quick Draw. Requires 211k hard disk space. $20. Matt Battey.

## Desktop Publishing and Graphics Management

### Color SnapShot ★★★

Color SnapShot.sea

CompuServe

> A screen capture for the Macintosh. This utility enables the user to graphically capture the whole screen or any window on the desktop. It supports MacPaint and allows online capture of GIFs. It should work on any Mac, but the online manual could not be read on a small-screen Mac LC. Requires 295k hard disk space. $12 donation to UNICEF. Josh Blume.

### Designer Draw ★★★★

DesignerDraw 4.4.2.sea

CompuServe

> A program for drawing diagrams. It is useful for such things as structure charts, flow charts, organization charts, dataflow diagrams, and other diagrams which have boxes containing text connected by lines. This could be helpful for science teachers wishing to create diagrams or administrators who need to build organization charts. It could come in handy for developing presentations. Requires Mac II or higher. Requires 102k hard disk space. Freeware. Paul Hyman.

### DOCMaker ★★★★★

DOCMaker4.6.sit

CompuServe

> This application creates stand-alone, self-running documents. It features scrollable and resizable windows, graphics, varied text styles and fonts, and full printing capability. You may create up to sixty

130

separate 32k chapters within each document, with a table of contents and a "find" feature. Full-color graphics can be added. Pages and fonts can be in various colors. "Hot pictures" act like buttons within the documents for playing sounds, showing Quick Time movies, sending Apple Events, and jumping to other applications. These stand-alone documents are self-executing and can be distributed to other computers which do not have DOCMaker loaded. This is a full-featured electronic book creator, presentation creator, or highly versatile word processor plus. It can be used by students (fifth grade and up), teachers, librarians, and administrators. The program is available in many languages, including Japanese. Requires any color Mac with System 7.0 and four megabytes of memory. Requires 1.15 megabytes hard disk space. $25. Green Mountain Software.

## GraphicConverter ★★★★★

graphicconverter-222-fat.hqx

ftp://utexas.edu/pub/mac/graphics

If it's a computer graphic or animation (even Atari, Amiga, or IBM-PC), you can convert it to any Mac format with GraphicConverter. This is one powerful program. The types of files it imports or exports are so extensive that they defy listing. It handles every kind of graphic or animation that I've ever heard of. You can also edit, alter, or dither files with a number of filters/transformers. It can convert whole folders or sets of pictures from one format to another with one command (batch conversion). Requires a Mac with Color Quickdraw, System 7.0 or later, with two megabytes of free memory (though I'd recommend more memory). Requires 2.7 megabytes hard disk space. $35. Lemke Software.

## JPEGView ★★★

JPEGView 3.2.1 (680x0 only).sit

CompuServe

A fast, flexible image viewer for 68000-based Macs (common Mac processor). It can open and display images in JPEG, JFIF, PICT, GIF,

TIFF, BMP, MacPaint, or Startup Screen formats. It can run slide shows. It has special features that reduce JPEG graphics to 256 colors (when necessary) while preserving the best quality possible. Quick Time is required for the decompression of JPEG images. Requires 68000-based Mac (JPEGView is also available for Power PCs). Requires 800k hard disk space. Postcardware (send a postcard to the author). Aaron Giles.

## PickTureDemo ★★★★

PickTureDemo.sea

CompuServe

PickTure expands the "Open" dialog box of any application to show a scrolling list of miniature pictures (thumbnails) of your files. These thumbnails are created automatically as you work with your files. From the "Open" dialog box, you can open a file by double-clicking on its thumbnail. PickTure's ability to create thumbnails is not limited to any specific file format; if an application can open a document, PickTure can create a thumbnail for it. PickTure is installed in the Control Panels folder and works seamlessly with your computer. This program can be a great streamliner for working with graphics and it can allow students unfamiliar with the graphics library on a given computer to make more rapid searches for desirable graphics. PickTure works on any black-and-white or color Mac, and it runs under both System 6 and System 7. Requires 108k hard disk space. $65. Right Answers.

## Super Dither! ★★★

SuperDither v1.0.sit

CompuServe

A simple, easy-to-use PICT viewer. Drag the icon on to the desktop, then drag and drop any number of PICT files onto the icon. Super Dither will display the files in a continuous slide show. Configure the program for the length of display, auto-display or self-activation, or to display PICTs in original size or largest size allowed by monitor. Super Dither is a convenient way for students,

teachers, and librarians to scan PICT collections. Requires any Mac.
Requires 51k hard disk space. Freeware. Ken.

## Resumés

### Resumaker ★★★

Resumakr.sea

CompuServe

A quick, easy resumé creation program. This could be a useful teaching tool for resumé design or helpful in the career guidance center in high school or college. It makes electronic resumés. Requires color Mac with thirteen-inch or larger screen. Requires 1.1 megabytes hard disk space. $49. Techno-Marketing Inc.

### Resumé Template ★★★

Resumé Template (word).sea

CompuServe

A set of Microsoft Word for Mac templates for resumé creation. It comes with a cover letter template and a mail merge document for merging addresses. This set of templates would be ideal for teaching about resumés or for career counseling. Requires a Mac with enough memory to run Microsoft Word. Requires 161k hard disk space. $20. Stephen Dacarie.

## Music

### Keyboard ★★

keybd.sit

CompuServe

A HyperCard Stack that introduces young students to the piano keyboard and musical notes. The keyboard can be played with the

133

mouse and the notes can be recorded for playback, thus demonstrating the rudiments of musical computation. Songs can be played
back in synth, harpsichord, "boing," mouth harp, organ, or horns.
K–3. Requires any Mac with HyperCard. Requires 47k hard disk
space. Freeware. (No name included).

## Word Processing

### Excalibur ★★★

excalibur-221.hqx

ftp://wuarchive.wustl.edu/system/mac/info-mac/text

This is a spell-checker for LaTex documents, though it can be op-
tionally switched to check plain text documents as well. It can spell-
check the clipboard, making it a good spelling checker for any text-
based application such as Alpha, BBEdit, or Eudora. Requires any
Mac with System 6.0.5 or higher. Requires 836k hard disk space.
Freeware. Rick Zaccone.

### Scorpio ★★★★

scorpio-101p.hqx

ftp://wuarchive.wustl.edu/system/mac/info-mac/text

Scorpio is a full-featured word-processing program with an easy-
to-use, powerful tool bar. It features background paper color, color
text, color pictures, and color printing. Registered version comes
with full spell-checker. All formatting tools are very intuitive. This
is one of the easiest and best shareware word processors. Requires
any Mac (color needed for color work). Requires 353k hard disk
space. Promotional version is free; full-featured version is $19.95.
Abbot Systems.

## UpWord ★★

up-wor-12.hqx

ftp://wuarchive.wustl.edu/system/mac/info-mac/text

This is a straightforward word-processing program. You can select fonts, formats, and page and text layout, and print in color. It has find-and-replace functions. It's very simple to use and its small space requirements may be handy. Requires any Mac with System 6.0 or greater. Requires 180k hard disk space. $35. Jeffrey P. Turnbull.


## Spreadsheet Applications

## Mariner ★★★

mariner f.sit

CompuServe

A spreadsheet program with the following features: split-window interface, variable row and column size, individual cell formatting (size, font, style), command bar menu shortcuts, tear-off tool and pattern menus, multiple undo, values calculated using extended precision, data hot-linked to charts, importable/exportable worksheets (ASCII text), basic chart types able to be combined in layers, and MultiFinder support (large worksheets can be recalculated in the background). This is a fully functional spreadsheet program that may be used by teachers, librarians, or administrators who require spreadsheet capabilities, or it may be used by students from grades 5 to 12. Requires any Mac. Requires 298k hard disk space. $40. William Paar.

# Chapter Seven

# IBM-PC Shareware and Freeware

*Note*: Program applicability is noted as DOS, Windows (meaning Windows 3.x), or Windows 95. All Windows 3.x programs work well in Windows 95, but do not attempt to run Windows 95 programs in Windows 3.x. Most DOS programs work well in Windows 95, but those using Windows 3.x should run DOS programs in DOS mode, unless you know how to edit and use PIF files.

## File Extraction Utilities

### ARJ archiver ★★★

arj241a.exe

http://www.shareware.com

DOS

ARJ archiver, version 2.41, is easy to use. It is, however, not a very common format; you may find .arj compressed files occasionally on the Internet and more often on BBSs. You can wait to obtain it until after you encounter a file needing this program. Requires 360k hard disk space. Price unavailable. Robert K. Jung.

## LHA by Yoshi ★★★★★

lha213.exe

http://www.shareware.com

DOS

This is the LHA compression-extraction program for .lzh and .lha files with documentation in English. This is handy for many files you'll encounter on the Internet, though you may want to wait until you run into one before you download it. Requires 80k hard disk space. Freeware. Yoshi.

## PKZIP ★★★★★

pkz204g.exe

http://www.shareware.com

DOS

PKWARE's PKZIP, PKUNZIP, PKZIPFIX, ZIP2EXE for .zip files. This suite of programs has been the state of the art for DOS since they were first introduced. Requires 355k hard disk space. $47. PKWARE, Inc.

## WinZip ★★★★★

winzip95.exe (thirty-two-bit Windows 95 version)

wz60wn16.exe (sixteen-bit Windows 3.1x version)

http://www.winzip.com/winzip/download.htm

Windows 95 and Windows

This absolute best of the best in ZIP programs brings the convenience of Windows to the use of ZIP files without requiring PKZIP and PKUNZIP. It features built-in support for popular Internet file formats, including ARJ, LHA, LZH, TAR, GZIP, and Unix compress. It can read and expand most Microsoft-compressed files. WinZip interfaces to most virus scanners. Requires 843k hard disk space. $29. Nico Mak Computing, Inc.

## Antiviral Programs

### F-PROT Professional Antivirus System ★★★★
fp-221.zip

http://www.infoscandic.se/f-prot/

Windows and DOS

> F-PROT Gatekeeper is a native device driver for Windows (.vxd), which uses the award-winning Secure Scan technology to scan all executed or copied files. F-PROT Gatekeeper works for both Windows applications and DOS applications. One special feature is the quick ability to choose just what to scan. For example, you can set it to scan only compressed files; in other words, recently downloaded files where viruses could enter your system. This is a highly recommended antivirus program. Requires 1.12 megabytes hard disk space. Freeware with inconsequential charges for educational and institutional (noncommercial) use. Frisk Software International.

### VirusScan ★★★★★
vs95i20e.zip (Windows 95)

wsci229e.zip (Windows)

scni229e.zip (DOS)

http://www.mcafee.com

Windows 95, Windows, DOS

> This top-rated program supports Windows 95 with an extensive array of features to keep your system immune from viruses. It has an enhanced thirty-two-bit scanning engine assuring fast and protected virus scanning; New Virtual Device Driver (VxD) technology to automatically detect viruses in memory; and on-access scanning technology to capture viruses on program execution for constant, transparent virus isolation. It scans all system areas to

138

provide extensive security including local and network drives, CD-ROMs, floppies, boot sectors, file allocation and partition tables, folders, files, and compressed files. It accurately cleans most virus infections from files, master boot sectors, partition tables, and memory. It has New Recursive scanning to identify and repair complicated, multiple reinfections. VirusScan easily adapts to your computing environment and productivity needs. New Migration installation allows VirusScan to intelligently install on either Windows 3.1 or Windows 95 computers (disk version only)—protecting present and future Windows 95 users. The emergency scan disk can eliminate viral damage even if Windows 95 becomes corrupted. It provides multiple on-demand scanning options such as file, file type, detection action, and reporting to meet all user requirements. The user can configure predefined actions on detection including logging, moving, deletion, and isolation for unattended operation. It displays a virus response prompt with customized messaging to respond swiftly to identified viruses. All versions require one to two megabytes hard disk space. $69. McAfee.

## Computer Security

### LOCKtite ★★★

locktt24.zip
http://www.shareware.com
Windows

LOCKtite is a utility designed to help manage Windows security. It works with the Program Manager to allow you to easily restrict the available options on the menu, to add or remove program groups from display, and to password protect the running of any application. It is particularly useful in educational settings where more than one user has access to a computer. LOCKtite can also make network security easier. This version of LOCKtite works only with the standard Windows Program Manager shell. It will not work with other desktops, such as the Norton Desktop. In addition to

LOCKtite, two small utility programs to help manage security on a network, CTRLBRK and REBOOT, are also included. Requires 287k hard disk space. $30 for individual or site license. Digipac Microcomputer Software Ltd.

## ProGuard ★★★

prgrd-22.zip

http://www.shareware.com

Windows

ProGuard is a Windows utility that prevents guest users from running selected programs with a double click on icons in Program Manager. Once a particular program's icon has been protected by ProGuard, the guest user will find that a password will be needed before the actual program will start. Logical icons to protect might include those for Windows Setup, Control Panel, PIF Editor, System Editor, File Manager, and the MS-DOS Prompt, and it's a simple matter to add ProGuard's protection to any other application's icon as well. ProGuard can also prevent the guest user from starting any program that is not present as an icon in Program Manager, and can prevent the guest user from creating, copying, moving, or deleting icons, or changing any of their properties. Requires 475k hard disk space. $20; site license $75. Cetus Software.

## Sentry ★★★

sentry45.zip

http://dragon.acadiau.ca/~910318b/readme.txt

Windows and Windows 95

Sentry will allow you to set up accounts on your computer, one account for each person allowed access. Those who don't have an account, don't get in. Each user has a separate account and password, making it easy to track who logs in and when. Since Sentry doesn't use a "master access" password, you can close a single user's account without affecting any other users. Sentry records each log-in attempt in a log file which can be viewed by the "SuperUser" at any time. You can set accounts to expire on a certain date, effectively barring access to the specified user after that date. Requires 246k hard disk space. $40 (educational discounts available). NightShade Computing.

## Toybox ★★★★★

toybox202.zip

AOL

DOS

Toybox is an excellent graphical interface shell program. Organize your DOS programs for kids with multiple pages of one-click icon buttons for easy launch. The program is easy to configure and includes a built-in icon painter for custom-made icons. Use Toybox for a convenient and secure shell to prevent access to other programs and data on your computer. Requires 250k hard disk space. $29. Virtual Magic Software.

## WinU Menu System for Windows 95 ★★★

winu202.zip

http://www.shareware.com

Windows 95

WinU is a menu system with timeout and security access features. It features three distinct levels of security control, and many flexible configuration options. The program allows you to use any Windows bitmap as its background image. Use the bitmap to display maps or educational material, or a favorite graphic. You can display the image full-screen behind the buttons, or put the image in the top half and the menu buttons on the bottom to give an unobstructed view of the image. Requires 401k hard disk space. $29.95. Data Outlet.

# Internet Tools

## Grabnet ★★★
gnwin2.zip (Windows 3.1)
gnwin95.2.zip (Windows 95)
http://www.ffg.com/
Windows 3.1 and Windows 95

>GrabNet is a browser companion tool enabling users to intuitively collect and organize information gathered from the World Wide Web. Users can casually grab snips of information, including images, text, and URLs, for reuse, navigation, and organization within a customized collection of folders on the local desktop. Two to five megabytes hard disk space, depending on version. $19.95. ForeFront Group Inc.

## Microsoft Internet Explorer ★★★★★
dlfull31.exe (Windows 3.1)
msie30m.exe (Windows 95)
http://www.microsoft.com
Windows 3.1 and Windows 95

>Microsoft gets up to speed with its Internet Explorer 3.0, and reaches the state-of-the-art level of Netscape. Currently, IE is free to all. This all-in-one Internet package includes access to the World Wide Web, FTP, gopher, newsgroups, as well as built-in Internet Mailer, ActiveMovie, and HTML Control. Requires ten to twenty megabytes hard disk space, depending on options. Freeware. Microsoft.

## Netscape Navigator ★★★★★
Various file names depending on operating system
http://home.netscape.com
Windows 3.1, Windows 95, DOS

>Netscape, the leading producer of tools for browsing and utilizing the World Wide Web, has made its premier Web browser, Netscape Navigator, available to students, educators, and librarians free of

charge. Netscape Navigator brings Web exploration, e-mail, newsgroups, and FTP right to your fingertips with all the state-of-the-art refinements and capabilities together in one package. To take advantage of this generosity, visit their Web site and download the software directly from them. Web browsing requires at least a 386 computer with eight megabytes of RAM. Requires about eight megabytes hard disk space, depending on your operating system. Freeware. Netscape.


## WebWhacker ★★★★

wwwin.zip (Windows 3.1)

_wwwin95.zip (Windows 95)

http://www.ffg.com

Windows 3.1 and Windows 95

WebWhacker allows you to "whack" single pages, groups of pages, or entire sites from the World Wide Web and save them for later viewing. Patrons and students can then browse these sites without maintaining an open Internet connection. This program will allow you to share the resources of the Internet while saving valuable online time and controlling Internet use. Requires 1.74 megabyte hard disk space. $49.95. ForeFront Group Inc.


## Library Cataloging Programs and Aids


## Bibliotek ★★★

bib28a.zip (1 of 3); bib28b.zip (2 of 3), bib28c.zip (3 of 3)

http://www.shareware.com

Windows

Recordkeeping system for individual, professional, or institutional book-collection records. Various sort command options in Form or Table Views. Reports, on-line docs. Requires 2.08 megabytes hard disk space. $29.95. RCCO Research.

## BookBank II ★★★

bookb2.zip

AOL

DOS

Personal Library Management System for book collectors, libraries, businesses, and churches. Tracks books you have, want, or have
loaned. Menu-driven for easy use. Configurable reports as well as
mail-merge-style data files can be created. Simple and very straightforward. Requires 400k hard disk space. $35. Data by Design.

## Book Catalog ★★★★

ambc41.zip

http://www.shareware.com

Windows

This is an impressive book/magazine cataloging program. It features unlimited number of entries, easy search functions, summa-
ries with bar or pie graphs in color, plenty of room for notes for
each entry, multiple database files, display filters, and more. A really sharp package with an attractive, intuitive graphic user interface. Requires 600k hard disk space. $17. PrimaSoft PC, Inc.

## BookStore ★★★★

bookst12.zip

AOL

Windows

A very user-friendly, well-integrated program for cataloging books.
Good search functions, sorts by categories, well-designed database.
Requires 1.64 megabytes hard disk space. $25. John Lullie.

## ScrollZ ★★

scrlz210.zip

http://www.shareware.com

DOS

A simple, menu-driven library cataloging system. Though not as slick an interface as others, this program has the special advantage of being preset to receive entries of books, periodicals, newspapers, and graphic novels (the program's name for comics?). Valuable features include the numerous data-entry fields for costs, condition of materials, a notes entry field with a five-thousand-line capacity for each catalog entry, and a "Facts & Figures" report function. It has a number of search and list functions, with many print options including automated Rolodex® card printing in two sizes. Requires 342k initial hard disk space. $25. Unicorn Software Limited.

## Square Notes ★★★

sqn35.zip

http://www.sqn.com/

DOS

A cross-referencing text utility that can be of use to writers, researchers, librarians, and anyone needing to collect and organize information into searchable databases. It is organized along the line of stacks of index cards, each card being able to hold ten pages of notes. The notes are organized by subject, allowing related ideas to be called up into a stack by a subject search. Very good organizational tool for personal information, research, or any information in need of organization. Requires 525k hard disk space. Shareware limited version requires no registration, but if you want the full version, the cost is $67. SQN, Inc.

## Windows Barcode ★★★★

wbar19.zip

ftp://oak.oakland.edu/simtel/win3/barcode/

Windows

This is a program which generates bar codes (i.e., 3 of 9, UPC, Postnet, library, bookland, etc.) that can be copied to the Windows Clipboard. Once in the Clipboard, you can then paste the bar code into other programs such as Windows Write, Microsoft Word for Windows, or Paintbrush, as well as other Windows programs that can accept bitmaps or metafiles from the Windows Clipboard. This program would allow librarians to produce bar codes for books, media, and patrons' cards. It is very simple to use. Requires 154k hard disk space. $25. Stellar Technologies.

## Administrative Aids

### Schedule Master ★★★

sched.zip

http://wuarchive.wustl.edu/edu/administrative/

DOS

A course and instructor scheduling utility. The program allows the user to enter information for each course and instructor. A warning is issued if any time conflicts arise. This program was designed to assemble course schedules for colleges and universities, but could be used to do the same on the middle and high school levels. It could also be used by librarians or computer lab monitors to schedule library and lab usage to avoid conflicts. The user can print a number of reports. Requires 400k hard disk space. Freeware. Wes Reynolds, Vincennes University.

### SchoolWrite ★★★★★

swkids22.zip

ftp://oak.oakland.edu/SimTel/msdos/teaching/

DOS

This program is for K–12 classroom administration and could conceivably be used to maintain student records for an entire school without risk. With additional available modules, it appears to be able to handle the complete administration, accounting, and billing for private schools. It keeps full details about students throughout their school life, including academic records, discipline details, absenteeism, positions held, accidents and illnesses, immunization status, emergency phone numbers, and more (including band and instrument management!). It prints end-of-semester reports with

146

marks, assessments, grades, and teachers' comments. The many different student printouts and lists it produces are amazing. Among the many special features of this program are a pop-up calculator, note pad, and mini-spreadsheet. Included is an automatic records backup program to prevent loss of data. It is also password-configurable. SchoolWrite for MS-DOS is compatible with Windows, and with all major networks. It has full online documentation. Requires 1.27 megabytes hard disk space. Shareware version includes the full Student module. $120, plus additional fees for additional modules (Timetable Printing, Parent Billing, Future Enrollments, Past Students, Ledger, and Payroll). Brennan Bates & Associates.

## Teachers' Aids

### BizXword ★★★★

bxword11.zip

http://www.jumbo.com/

Windows

This seems to be the Cadillac of shareware crossword generators. It is very powerful but may be too complex and time-consuming for most librarians or teachers. Those ambitious enough to master it may find it a fabulous teaching tool. The demo version is fully operational but limited to 9 x 9 grids. It comes with a sixty-thousand-word dictionary, with the ability to create more dictionaries and word lists. Requires three megabytes hard disk space. $25. Belding Computing Devices Ltd.

### Computer Word Search ★★★★★

cws50.exe

ftp.hea.ie/part9/cica/games/

Windows

A comprehensive word-search game, with nice touches like background graphics and simple sound. It can be played onscreen or printed for copying. It comes with nineteen puzzles, including presidents, state capitals, fruits and vegetables, inventors, animals, and countries. Personalized word lists can also be created. A really nice little program. K–6. Requires 414k hard disk space. Sound is nice but not necessary. $9.95 for a single user or a whole site. CanalRun, Inc.

## Crossword Compiler ★★★★

ccwin3.zip

http://www.jumbo.com/

Windows

A very quick and intuitive crossword creator. You can do just about anything you would need for the classroom with this program. It has autofind and autofill capabilities, though it's a little limited in the demo version. In general, though, puzzles are created and printed with minimal difficulty with a good deal of help from the program. It's great for making anagram puzzles with anagram clues. The registered version allows the creation of word lists for the autofind and autofill features. No onscreen solving of puzzles. A bit costly at $45, but the features may be worth it. Also, puzzles can be saved in RTF format for transferring to Mac platforms for printing without needing the program. Requires 836k hard disk space. Anthony Lewis.

## Crossword Construction Kit ★★★★

cwkit120.zip

ftp.monash.edu.au/pub/win3/games/

Windows

This program features the unique ability to make puzzles in fun shapes with over twenty-five predefined puzzle shapes (diamonds, doughnuts, trains, etc.), with the added ability to create unlimited

148

new shapes, up to a 30 x 30 grid. Print options include skeleton or filled box, answer key, font selection, metafiles and more. Requires 750k hard disk space. $18. Insight Software Solutions.

## Crossword Mania! ★★★★

cwm102-1.zip (1 of 2), cwm102-2.zip (2 of 2)

http://www.jumbo.com/

Windows

A full-featured crossword-puzzle generator. It comes with a number of crossword puzzles. It's great fun to solve the puzzles within the program itself, but the included puzzles and those you create can be printed. Lots of tools to streamline crossword-puzzle generation. The shareware version cannot save puzzles until registration. This is a very capable package. Has sound, which is helpful but not required. Requires 2.96 megabytes hard disk space. $24.99. Saturn Software.

## Exam Bank ★★★★

examba20.zip

ftp://oak.oakland.edu/SimTel/msdos/teaching/

DOS

This program offers teachers not only a means to create tests of various kinds but a place to store them safely until later use. A test can be formatted as multiple-choice, true/false, cross-match, short answer, or short essay; printed tests can be all of one type or mixed as desired. Student instructions can be included as well as standard headings, such as student name, date, etc. The program automatically prints an answer sheet for the teacher's use (assuming the answers were entered in the appropriate places during test creation!). This is a very versatile, straight-to-the-point program and could be an invaluable time-saving tool. Requires 243k hard disk space. $30; site license $60. Education Software.

## Grader ★★

grader51.zip

ftp://oak.oakland.edu/SimTel/msdos/teaching/

DOS

An easy-to-use grading program. Spreadsheet layout allows intuitively easy entry and modification. Output controls are powerful, flexible, and simple. Requires 305k hard disk space. The shareware version is limited to thirty student entries until registered. $30. D. S. Hirshberg.

## Graph Crazy ★★★★

grcrazy11.zip

ftp://oak.oakland.edu/SimTel/win3/educate/

Windows

This program is designed to make quick, attractive graphs. There are eleven basic graph types (including 2-D and 3-D bar, 2-D and 3-D pie) with a variety of options for each, including fonts and colors. Graph Crazy will let you do quick data entry or you may import data either through the Windows Clipboard or through the Data Import menu. For graphs that must be independently saved, Graph Crazy lets you save your graph as either a BMP bitmap file or a WMF metafile. Librarians and administrators will find this program very helpful in creating graphs to use in presentations. Teachers can use the program to teach about graphs in general, or to teach how to use graphs to illustrate specific data; thus, it can be very useful in math classes. It has broad-ranging applications for curricula from third grade to college. Requires 804k hard disk space. $19.95. WordSmith Document Design Inc.

## LessonPlanZ ★★

lplnz260.zip

ftp://oak.oakland.edu/SimTel/msdos/teaching/

DOS

> This is a lesson-planning kit. Entries can be made in areas for methodology, goals, objectives, evaluation methods, and supplies. Each section can hold from one to five thousand lines using a full-featured text editor. It has supplemental entries for lesson number, title, subject, dates covered, teacher's name, and school. Requires 316k hard disk space. $29. Unicorn Software Limited.

## Math Problem Generator ★★

mathprob.zip

ftp://oak.oakland.edu/SimTel/msdos/teaching/

DOS

> A random problem-generation program for the four basic arithmetic operations. Teachers can save time by producing worksheets in seconds for immediate printing. Answer sheets accompany the worksheets. This program can be especially helpful in producing targeted worksheets for remedial, reinforcement, or testing situations. The printing is slightly unusual as it uses ASCII characters in certain places, but nonetheless is still highly workable. K–6. Requires 30k hard disk space. Freeware. John Pirog.

## On This Day ★★

otd201.zip

http://www.shareware.com

DOS

> A program showing the historical events, birthdays, and religious events on each day of the year. Also included are the dates according to the Gregorian, Julian, Hebrew, and Islamic calendars. Requires 264k hard disk space. $30. The Software Construction Co.

## On This Day for Windows ★★★

wotd201.zip

http://www.shareware.com

Windows

> The same as the DOS version, only better and easier to use. Requires 380k hard disk space. $30. The Software Construction Co.

## Pencil and Paper Activity Maker ★★★★

papam2.zip

AOL

DOS

> If you want a continuing source of fun learning activities for the classroom, PAPAM would be ideal for you. This highly versatile program can create such puzzles and activities as hidden messages, shadow messages, hidden pictures, color-by-numbers, dot-to-dot puzzles, silly pictures, crazy messages, missing letters, acrostic puzzles, word-crossover puzzles, word-search puzzles, decoding puzzles, scrambled-word puzzles, scrambled-verse puzzles, matching puzzles, math puzzles, mazes, and more. Make them yourself or, after a little training, turn the kids loose with the program. A nice feature is that PAPAM creates activities in a half-sheet format, saving considerable paper. K–6. Requires 347k hard disk space. $16. Impact D. Publishing.

## StarCharts ★★

starch10.zip

ftp://oak.oakland.edu/SimTel/win3/educate/

Windows

> This program was created to assist parents in getting their children to become self-reliant and cooperative in getting their chores done, but can be just as handy in creating classroom charts to assign tasks to students. Teachers could use this program to create a template which can be copied and reused throughout a school year, or

could be altered and printed weekly with assigned children's names. K–6. Requires 637k hard disk space. $19.95. StarBrite Software.

## Teacher Assistant ★★

ta100b.zip

ftp://oak.oakland.edu/SimTel/win3/educate/

Windows

A class list management system. Teachers can maintain student records of all types, including name, I.D. number, birthdate, parents' names, addresses, phone numbers, status, lunch category, bus schedule, test scores, miscellaneous information, plus an open-ended notes section. The data entry interface is simple and direct. Records can be printed. Requires 119k hard disk space. $15. Chiam Yih Wei.

## Test Writer ★★★

twrite2.zip

ftp://oak.oakland.edu/SimTel/msdos/teaching/

DOS

This is a word processor/database designed for test creation. Tests are divided into groups of similar question types called Sections. Teachers may have up to ninety-eight sections per test, with up to one hundred fifty questions in each section. One may create individual tests or test databases, grouping questions for an entire class or subject together under one test name. The user can then easily create customized, individual tests as needed using the "Get" capability. With Get, the user can copy a series of questions or an entire section from an existing test. The "borrowed" questions can be edited or deleted without affecting the original test. Test Writer supports five different question types: multiple choice, matching, identification (short essay), essay, and true/false. Grades 5–12. Requires 310k hard disk space. Freeware. R. R. Merritt.

## Test Writer for Windows ★★★★

ttwin15.zip

ftp://oak.oakland.edu/SimTel/win3/educate/

Windows

This is a program designed to create, edit, and output printed tests. It is most beneficial as a "test bank" to accumulate questions for a particular class over several successions of the class. With a large "bank" of questions already inputted, the need for new questions will be greatly reduced. Creating a new test will be a simple case of picking the appropriate questions based on the subjects covered in the current term. The program supports six question types: essay, multiple choice, true/false, identification, matching, and group answer. Good for any grade where tests and quizzes are given. Requires 1.23 megabytes hard disk space. $20. R. R. Merritt.

## VAR Grade for Windows ★★★★★

vgw102.zip

ftp://oak.oakland.edu/SimTel/win3/educate/

Windows

VGW allows you to grade, record attendance, and do seating charts for your classes. This is a complete grading system, and will do just about anything that you need or want to do regarding class records. In particular, it will allow you to record, analyze, and print grades and attendance, do seating charts, and maintain a database. In general, the program allows an almost unlimited number of students, grades, attendance, database items, reports, and analyses. You can do the following: sum, average, weight, and scale assignments, discard the lowest, convert scores to percentages, assign extra credit, assign final grades, and much more. There are numerous tutorials and hints that show you how to get started with the program. VGW also has help and context-sensitive help available. Although some elementary-level teachers may wish this kind of powerful grading assistance, the program is probably best suited to middle school through college. Requires 2.86 megabytes hard disk space. $50. VARed Software.

## WinFlash ★★★

flash_31.zip

http://www.jumbo.com/

Windows

A flash-card creator. This program has the ability to include BMP Windows graphics and/or sound files in the questions and answers, as well as use regular text. For that reason alone this is a valuable program. Requires 490k hard disk space. Sound card is not required unless you wish to use sound capabilities. $19.95. Open Windows.

## Word Search Construction Kit ★★★★

wskit200.zip

http://www.winsite.com/pc/win3/games/

Windows

Another word-search generator, but this one features the unique ability to make puzzles in fun shapes with over twenty-five predefined puzzle shapes (circles, apples, hearts, etc.). It has the ability to create unlimited new shapes. Create your own word lists. Grids can be up to 30 x 30 size. Print options include upper/lowercase, grid, answer key, font selection, metafiles, and more. K–6. Requires 853k hard disk space. $15. Insight Software Solutions.

## Wordsearch Mania! ★★★

wsrch113.zip

http://www.winsite.com/pc/win3/games/

Windows

A word-search puzzle game which can be played onscreen or printed for classroom use or homework. It comes with a number of very creative puzzle files, though you can also build your own. You can work on up to ten puzzles simultaneously. K–8. Requires 405k hard disk space. $19.99. Michael J. Baker.

## WordSearch Puzzle Maker ★★★

wdschgen.exe

http://www.winsite.com/pc/win3/games/

Windows

A program that generates word-search puzzles. Words to be searched for are listed below the puzzle. The program is unique, because it accepts foreign language accents, which are printed in the puzzle. This is unusual, partly because the standard IBM printed character set does not include accented capitals, and partly because accented capitals are not usually used in print. The ability to display accented capitals makes the program especially useful for teachers of languages such as French, German, Spanish, Italian, Portuguese, and Scandinavian languages, particularly in elementary schools. K–8. Requires 91k hard disk space. $15. Lane C. Showalter.

## WordWiz ★★★★

wordwiz3.zip

http://www.jumbo.com/

Windows

This is a design and construction tool for crossword puzzles, word and number fill-ins, and word searches. It comes with a thirty-thousand-word pool for automatic puzzle construction, but you can also create individual word pools. The program is very intuitive and easy to use, with great control over words, clues, design, and printing. The shareware version allows grids up to 9 x 9, with different prices for grids up to 25 x 25. The recommended education package goes up to 17 x 17 with a price of $49, but smaller packages are less expensive (as low as $19) and may be fine for younger students. This may be an ideal word-game tool for the classroom teacher. K–12. Requires 594k hard disk space. Jim Buccigrossi.

# Suites

## Big Math Attack! ★★★

bigma221.zip

http://www.shareware.com

DOS

A suite of games that test math, spelling, typing, and metric conversion skills in a fun, graphical, arcade environment. Multiple skill levels are available, making this program suitable for grades K–8. Top scores are maintained to track progress. Users can create their own spelling lists for use within the program. Requires 189k hard disk space. $11.95. For an additional $4, a math problem editor will be provided by the producer. Philip P. Kapusta.

## Crayon Box ★★★★★

crayon41.zip

CompuServe

DOS

This wonderful suite of programs will delight and edify any young student. It's one of the greatest and best first programs for children. The suite includes counting, addition, states and capitals games, coloring book, piano and music, concentration-style memory challenge, spiral-pattern create-and-color, and entertaining music without need of a sound card. K–2. It will run on low-end PCs. Requires 341k hard disk space. $12. Philip P. Kapusta.

## Farnsworth Ferret's Fun Pack for Kids ★★★

farn12.zip

AOL

Windows

Suite of very good programs, including math, spelling, memory, painting, and concentration-style games. Needs sound. Bad point: starts Windows Write or Windows 95 WordPad with registration order form every time one exits a game, making road-testing with kids difficult. K–3. Requires 3.59 megabytes hard disk space. $19. Elpin Systems.

## Flix Productions Animated Learning Series ★★★★★
Various file names
http://www.eden.com/~flixprod/
DOS

Flix is famous for its "animated" series including: Animated Word, Animated Clock, Animated Math, Animated Multiplication and Division, Animated Addition and Subtraction, Animated Money, Animated Shapes, and Animated Alphabet. All the files for these programs may be downloaded from Flix's above Web site. With these programs, you can turn a bunch of obsolete PCs into a computer lab for K–4. Shareware. As low as $10. Flix Productions.

## Pirate School ★★★
pirate1.zip
AOL
Windows

A well-designed suite of games that teach letters, spelling, reading, elementary grammar, same/different, counting, addition, and telling time. Preschool to second grade. Fully functional. Requires 577k hard disk space. Send whatever dollar amount you like. Gerald Myers.

## Preschool Pack ★★★
pspak.zip
AOL
DOS

Using five effective and entertaining activities, preschoolers and kindergartners will learn about counting, number recognition, the alphabet, colors, matching, and classifying. Activities include "Animal Homes," where animals must be placed in their appropriate homes—either farm, forest, or circus; "Balloons," where the user must click on a color block matching the color of a rising balloon before it pops; "Matching," a memory game with an animated bee rewarding the user who locates all matches; "Counting," where the user counts along with the computer as a variety of colorful images, from dinosaurs to dolls, is displayed; and "ABCs," where the user must find all letters which match a displayed letter. "ABCs" uses speech to pronounce each letter as it is selected. All activities are reinforced with animation sequences. Requires 1.12 megabytes hard disk space. $10 registration brings fifty more animations. PractiComp.

## School Crazy ★★★

scrazy30.zip

http://www.shareware.com

Windows

This suite is an excellent set of challenges for a wide age group of children. It has games called Math Squares, Math Wizard, TypeWriter, Charts, Numero, and Moving Words. Though the games are targeted for nine- to fourteen-year-olds, it can be fun for younger children as well. A very nice suite. Grades 1–8. Requires 193k hard disk space. $19.95. WordSmith Document Design Inc.

## School Mom Plus ★★★★★

schlmom6.zip

CompuServe

DOS

School Mom Plus has multiple levels of instruction for math, English, art, music, the alphabet, spelling, and telling time. It also has a multiple-choice exam generator with some exams already provided. The art option has a very nice coloring-book option that allows you to create your own pictures, store them for later use, and color them with a large selection of colors. Use the other options to generate beautiful screen art. The English section will teach your child all about sentence structure and subject-verb agreement. The math section has multiple-level instruction for addition, subtraction, multiplication, division, fractions, and basic algebra. It also has arcade-style games. This large math section provides most of the tools you need for a child from kindergarten to sixth grade level in math. Use the Music option to write and edit music, then store tunes for later use. Some tunes are already provided. Use the spelling option to practice spelling. Enter your own words or use the large files of existing words. Maximum word size is sixteen characters. The spelling program features large graphical characters. Also, if you have a sound card, the words are spelled for you with a real human voice. Young children can use the Telling Time option to learn how to read a clock, starting with on-the-hour times and progressing to more difficult times. The digital time is also shown. Want to teach geography, history, science, or social studies? Use the multiple-choice exam generator. This version of School Mom comes with fifty exams already written but you can write your own. K–6. It'll work on low-end machines if you have a VGA video adapter. Requires 1.12 megabytes hard disk space. $25 and a generous site license schedule. Motes Educational Software.

## Teach Your Children ★★★

tyc2_0.zip

http://www.shareware.com

Windows

A program which teaches addition, subtraction, multiplication, spelling, and word recognition. A fine program with little flair, yet it is exceptional because it inputs numbers in the correct fashion from right to left (so many math programs force children to do all the computation before entering multidigit answers!); thus it reinforces multidigit operations well. K–6. Requires 2.16 megabytes hard disk space. $19.95. Q&D Software Development.

# Math

### Algebra, A Skill-Oriented Approach ★★★
soav10.zip
CompuServe
DOS

A course in basic algebra, formatted as a series of exercises and tests which can be printed with answer keys. The program may be able to help supplement an algebra class, regardless of chosen textbook. Middle school and high school. Requires 1.11 megabytes hard disk space. Included in the ZIP file is Gmath, a program that produces exercises and tests for basic arithmetic operations for integers, decimals, fractions, and percents. First grade through middle school. Requires 220k hard disk space. Also included in the ZIP file is an address database program called Dbase. Requires 170k hard disk space. All programs are freeware. Alfred D'Attore.

### Algebrax ★★★
algbr212.zip
ftp://oak.oakland.edu/simtel/dos/math
DOS

This is Professor Weissman's Algebra Tutorials 2.12: random problems with step-by-step solutions. The program maintains a record of the student's progress and has five levels of difficulty. Additional sets of problems are available from the author. This tutorial is very clearly presented and can be of great use either as an introductory or remedial tool for slow starters. Middle school to high school. Six different disks are available. $30. Professor Weissman's Software.

161

## Amy's Fun-2-3 Adventure ★★★★★

fun23_21.zip

http://www.portal.com/~devasoft/

DOS

> An adorable puppy named Amy guides young children through four entertaining activities which help teach number recognition and counting skills. Outstanding animated graphics and real speech and sound effects add to the counting fun. One portion of the program allows children to play a xylophone, choosing a song and playing by the numbers. A sound card enhances the program, but the PC speaker will suffice. Requires 1.93 megabytes hard disk space. Registration gives you three more programs: Amy teaches the alphabet and shapes, plus a colorful memory game. $24.95. Devasoft.

## Arithmetic Trainer ★★★★★

arith.zip

AOL

Windows

> This creative program can teach, not merely reinforce, difficult concepts such as borrowing and carrying, using a charming combination of graphics, music, and animation. Concepts are well-illustrated and children as young as four or five will quickly be adding three-digit numbers and fully understanding what they are doing. K–4. The demo version comes with addition; registration brings the other three arithmetic operations. Sound card required to enhance the experience. Requires 337k hard disk space. $25. Opal Productions Software.

## As Easy As 123 ★★★★★

math090.zip

ftp://plaza.aarnet.edu.au/micros/pc/garbo/windows/educgames/

Windows

> This is a very special little program. There are no bells and whistles, just perfect demonstrations of all four basic arithmetic operations,

at levels from the simple to the more complex. Every stage of computation is illustrated, with numbers entered right to left, in the proper way. Carrying is automatically shown, while the student is alerted to wrong moves and congratulated for correct answers. This program has no super graphics, music, or other positive reinforcement tools. But what it does provide—crystal-clear demonstration of mathematical computation—is worth its weight in gold, teaching-wise. K–6. Requires 400k hard disk space. $5. CrossTech.

## BasketMath ★★

bm.zip

AOL

DOS

Math quizzing game using basketball animation. Tests most areas up to pre-algebra. Printable test results show areas needing remediation. Its principal usefulness is in testing for a student's weak points. Does not teach. Drawback: can only be used once to evaluate, then expires, thus disallowing road-testing with kids. Grades 7–9. Requires one megabyte or more hard disk space. $29. Science Academy Software.

## CalcuMemory ★★

calmem12.zip

http://winsite.com/

Windows

A cute, concentration-style memory game for teaching the four basic arithmetic operations. Behind the tiles are problems and answers for students to match. Successful answers reveal a cute graphic. Configurable for type(s) of operation, difficulty level, and bitmap graphic. Sound is fun but not required. K–4. Requires 535k hard disk space. $17.95. Hummelen Educatief.

## Chalkboard Math ★★★★★

cbmath15.zip

http://www.shareware.com

Windows

> Chalkboard Math is easily the cutest and most effective basic math program available for Windows. A cute mouse scampers about the chalkboard whenever the student solves a problem. The interface is brilliant and intuitive. It quizzes on addition, subtraction, multiplication, and division. When Auto-Advance is on (indicated by a checkmark next to the pull-down menu selection), the program automatically increases the difficulty level when five correct answers are recorded at the current level. The program can also be set for one of eight levels of difficulty. There's an honor roll for high scores. Another great lab program. K–4. Requires 229k hard disk space. $16. Pegasus Development.

## Dino Match ★★

dmatch32.zip

http://www.shareware.com/

Windows

> This matching game teaches pattern and number recognition. Preschool–K. Sound card not required but enhances the program. Requires 1.83 megabytes hard disk space. $20; three-game bundle $30. DynoTech Software.

## Dino Numbers ★★★★

dnumbr33.zip

http://www.shareware.com/

Windows

> This game is highly effective at teaching math reasoning skills in basic operations. Grades 2–5. Sound card not required but enhances the program. Requires 2.68 megabytes hard disk space. $20; three-game bundle $30. DynoTech Software.

## Graph Crazy ★★★★

grcrazy11.zip

ftp://oak.oakland.edu/SimTel/win3/educate/

Windows

This program is designed to make quick, attractive graphs. There are eleven basic graph types (including 2-D and 3-D bar, 2-D and 3-D pie) with a variety of options for each, including fonts and colors. Graph Crazy will let you do quick data entry or you may import data either through the Windows Clipboard or through the Data Import menu. For graphs that must be independently saved, Graph Crazy lets you save your graph as either a BMP bitmap file or a WMF metafile. Librarians and administrators will find this program very helpful in creating graphs to use in presentations. Teachers can use the program to teach about graphs in general, or to teach how to use graphs to illustrate specific data; thus, it can be very useful in math classes. It has broad-ranging applications for curricula from third grade to college. Requires 804k hard disk space. $19.95. WordSmith Document Design Inc.

## Introduction to Basic Math ★★★

math.zip

AOL

DOS

A menu-driven comprehensive set of quizzes that reinforces knowledge of all basic math operations and functions taught from fourth grade through middle school. Includes elementary algebra and geometry. The shareware package is limited but warrants a look. Requires 1.54 megabytes hard drive space. Sound enhances the program but is not required. $20. Algebra 1 for Windows (algebra2.zip) is also available on AOL. LF Software.

## Kitty123 ★★★

kitty123.zip

CompuServe

DOS

> A well-designed program for teaching number recognition from one to twenty. It features a talking kitty. Language skills not required. Preschool–K. Sound required. Requires 325k hard disk space. Freeware. Bozo Bob.

## Lugnut City ★★★★★

lugnut.zip

ftp://info.forthnet.gr/pub2/teacher-2000/msdos/kids/math/

DOS

> This benevolent, arcade-style game is one of the most effective I've seen in teaching basic math skills. There are twelve skill levels for teaching number recognition, addition, subtraction, multiplication, and division. A cute, laser-toting robot gallops around a wonderful set of mazes while confronting and conquering a variety of problems in different, fun formats. Children will thrill with enjoyment as the math concepts are reinforced effortlessly. K–3. Lugnut City is an excellent choice for labs using older PCs. Requires 171k hard disk space. $10 buys both single-user or school-wide registration, while $35 brings a package of seven programs by the author. Paul T. Dawson.

## Math Fun-Damentals ★★

1mathfun.zip

AOL

DOS

> Good set of math games, teaching all operations with whole numbers, fractions, decimals and percents, and pre-algebra. Bad point: numbers input backwards. Some functions not supported in the demo, but enough there to road-test with the kids. K–6. Requires 1.09 megabytes hard disk space. $25. Scholastic Software.

166

## Math Invaders ★★

mathinv.exe

AOL

Windows

An arcade-style game that teaches all four basic arithmetic operations. Sound not required but enhances the fun and positive reinforcement. Grades 4–6 (or bright third graders). Requires 1.51 megabytes hard disk space. $15. Allen Creveling.

## Math Rescue ★★★★★

1math.zip

CompuServe

DOS

This is one entertaining and educational arcade-style game. A boy or girl, fighting the "Gruzzles," scampers through different enchanting landscapes and labyrinths, solving number and word problems, while collecting objects for extra points. Children will have so much fun playing the game that they'll acquire lasting math and logic skills without a moment's pain. The downloadable version contains addition problems but with registration come other operations. Sound card is required to enjoy the music but is not required to operate the game. K–2. Requires 850k hard disk space. $15 each for different modules; special deals on packages. Apogee.

## MathCounts 1+2 ★★★★★

mc12v1.zip

CompuServe

DOS

This brilliant suite of math learning games, quizzes, and tutorials can teach elementary math as well as many others with more flash. This program automatically remembers mastered skills and takes children on to more difficult levels, thus speeding up the learning curve. It stresses counting; pattern and shape recognition; addition; subtraction; multiplication; early concepts in fractions; telling time; and word problems. This would be an excellent program for computer labs. K–2. Requires any basic PC. Requires 212k hard disk space. $29.95, with good discounts for site licenses. Able Art Software.

## MathCounts 3+4 ★★★★★
mc34v1.zip
CompuServe
DOS

This is a more advanced suite of math learning tools designed along the same lines as MathCounts 1+2, and just as brilliant. The program creates a progress graph for each student and lets them know what areas of study they have or have not worked with enough. It tutors, in a very encouraging way, the following areas: counting, place value, addition, subtraction, multiplication, division, estimating, big numbers, word problems, fractions, decimals, and shapes. This would be an excellent program for computer labs. Grades 3–4. Requires any basic PC. Requires 310k hard disk space. $29.95, with good discounts for site licenses. Able Art Software.

## Mathtest ★★★★
mathts30.zip
CompuServe
DOS

An educational mathematics problem-solving game. It lets players practice addition, subtraction, multiplication, and division problems, with varying skill levels and difficulties. Selectable options allow players to practice advanced problem types, such as multidigit problems, negative numbers, decimals, carrying, borrowing, and long division. This math program is ideal for students who are learning basic math problems, and also for students who are familiar with basic math problems but need to either practice advanced problems or improve speed and accuracy with basic problems. The program is completely configurable for speed and difficulty level. Students are rewarded by arcade-style games for each successful answer. Like many DOS educational games, this one is simply yet very effectively designed. Answers are entered in the correct order especially for the more complex levels, thus properly teaching children the various algorithms. K–8. Requires 272k hard disk space. $20; site license $50. Kenneth Perrine.

## Monster Math ★★★★

mmath.zip (Windows)

mmath32.zip (Windows 95)

AOL

Windows and Windows 95

> Shoot-'em-up game for grades 1–4 for all four arithmetic operations. Very good and very friendly, no drawbacks. Sounds are fun but not necessary. Fully functional. Requires 830k hard disk space. $10. Dart Consulting.

## Mouse Math ★★★

mousma.zip

AOL

Windows

> Three games in one which teach counting, digits and digit placement. Preschool–3. Fully functional. Cute animation using mice. Requires 262k hard disk space. $2. Robert Allen Low.

## Multiplication Drill ★★★

md.zip

CompuServe

Windows

> A perfectly fine multiplication drill program with encouraging sound and graphics. Quizzes through 9 x 9. There is no instruction, but through fourth grade or so, this could be a positive reinforcement or testing tool. Sound card required. Requires 1.13 megabytes hard disk space. $15. Richard F. Retter.

### PC Kid Math ★★★

km_fw10.zip

ftp://oak.oakland.edu/SimTel/win3/educate/

Windows

> This program is a timed test-giver for the four basic arithmetic operations. The interface is very friendly and should be relaxing to children. The special value of this program is that it is highly configurable, handles the results of up to one hundred tests, and can issue reports based on a student's overall performance; and it can save hours of grading timed tests. This time-saving, automatic tracking of student progress can be very helpful. K–6. Requires 65k hard disk space. $8.95. Uniproducts Co.

### Roxie's Math Fish ★★★★

Various file names (use "roxie's" in a key-word file search)

CompuServe

Windows

> A variety of versions including Roxie's ABC Fish, Roxie's Reading Fish, and the aforementioned. Absolutely entertaining and educational, Roxie the Cat teaches while playing the classic card game Fish. Preschool–2. Sound required. Requires 1.09 megabytes hard disk space. $9.95. LatticeWork Software.

### Sea School ★★★

1sea13.zip

CompuServe

DOS

> This has a suite of six math games in the shareware demo version. The sea themes are cute and effective, with penguins, fish, seahorses, and Eskimos. The accent is on number recognition, counting, addition, and subtraction. Preschool–K. Sound card is nice to have but not required for the program. Requires 1.15 megabytes hard disk space. $29.95 (registered version comes with two more suites on the alphabet and reading). MVP Software.

## Senari Programs Long Division ★★★★

long_div.zip

AOL

DOS

This program does for long division what its multiplication counterpart does for multiplication (see below). It is excellent. Grades 1–5. Requires 187k hard disk space. $15. Micki Fitzpatrick.

## Senari Programs Multiplication ★★★★

mb_mult.zip

AOL

DOS

This versatile program teaches basic multiplication skills. It has a wonderfully simple tutorial demonstration and configurable problems for drilling. It will produce printed worksheets for teachers and progress reports for each student. The program is very impressive in the way it graphically explains multiple-digit multiplication, including decimals. Grades 1–5. Requires 270k hard disk space. $15. Micki Fitzpatrick.

## Show Me Math ★★★★★

sm_math.zip

AOL

DOS

I've not seen a math teaching and drilling program as broad as this one. It makes an amazing selection of math concepts available on its extensive menu, taking students to literally hundreds of demonstrations and drills. It can grade and track the progress of each student, and illustrate student performance through graphs. Show Me Math is not a game or flash-card program; it literally shows children what they are doing step-by-step in math operations from number recognition to basic algebra and geometry. If used properly, this program is capable of significantly accelerating math learning at every level. I would call this the must-have math program of this list. Preschool through college. Requires 1.52 megabytes hard disk space. The documentation makes no mention of cost; this program may be freeware, and if so the author, R. Webster Kehr, is a hero. Show Me Math Software.

## Sir Addalot ★★★★

adalot.zip

CompuServe

DOS

A wonderfully peaceful knight-versus-dragon math game. Sir Addalot goes off to dodge the dragon's fireballs while solving basic math problems. Successful completion allows the child to add fish and plants to the castle moat. Addition and subtraction come free with the demo; registration brings more levels as well as multiplication and division. K–4. Sound card enhances the game but is not required. Requires 894k hard disk space. $19.95. Landmark Solutions.

## Treasure Hunt Math ★★★★

thmath.zip

AOL

DOS

This suite of math games teaches the four basic arithmetic operations plus fractions and decimals. The graphics follow a treasure-hunt-island-and-sea theme. There are solve and study modes. Children enjoy this simple and kind program and seem to learn concepts well with it. K–6. Requires 384k hard disk space. $19.95; lab price is $79.95. Adventure LearningWare.

## XYSee ★★★★

xysee40.zip

ftp://oak.oakland.edu/simtel/dos/math/

DOS

This is a highly interactive, visually oriented program for the study of high school and college algebra, geometry, and trigonometry. A powerful resource for investigating the functions and forms within the X-Y coordinate system, it covers SAT, ACT, and math placement test material. It has an excellent 3-D interface with colorful icons, button bars, in-cell editing, and HP-Laser support. Also included are a comprehensive tutorial, and "how to" and context-sensitive help modules. VGA graphics required. Requires 347k hard disk space. $30. Insight Advantage.

# Alphabet, Phonics, Spelling, and Reading

## Bago ★★
bago320.zip
http://www.shareware.com
Windows

A challenging word game in which the object is to make as many words as possible by following paths through adjacent letters. There are multiple levels as one plays against the computer in timed competition. Good for developing cognitive, analytical, and word recognition skills. Grades 4–12. Requires 178k hard disk space. Freeware. H. G. Wrekshun.

## Color My World ★★
color12.zip
http://www.jumbo.com/
Windows

Simple little color recognition game. Click on the color and a geometric shape changes to that color with the word both shown and spoken. Preschool–K. Sound card required. Requires 92k hard disk space. $5. Mei-Hsin Jenny Chang & Ling Siow Chang.

## Cross Pix ★★

cpix11.zip

http://www.jumbo.com/

Windows

A graphical crossword simulation that uses bitmap pictures for clues. The program is designed as a spelling aid for young children. Colorful graphics, speech and sound effects enhance the game to keep children's attention. A built-in scoring system allows players to compete for high scores. Preschool–6. Requires 1.97 megabytes hard disk space. A sound card is not required but highly recommended. The shareware version has eight puzzles but registration brings one hundred more. $15. Patchworks.

## Danny's First Program ★★★★★

danfirst.zip

ftp.orst.edu/pub/mirrors/simtel/msdos/educatin

DOS

A truly wonderful, simple little program. It offers a colorful screenful of the letters of the alphabet. A child presses one of the letter keys and wonderful things happen: For W it's colorful windmills, for Y it plays the "Yellow Rose of Texas" with the words displayed, P and it's a prelude by Bach, E and it's ellipses, I and it's a sonnet from Shakespeare, and so on and on. Through its simplicity, a child learns the alphabet and so much more. Unless a child can press X for exit followed by Y for yes, the entire keyboard is locked and secure while the youngster is at work. A learning tool for both preschool and kindergarten, it is a tribute to the shareware world. All sounds are played by the PC speaker, requiring no sound card. Requires 148k hard disk space. $15. All-American Kidware Co.

### Dino Spell ★★★

dspell32.zip

http://www.shareware.com/

Windows

An enjoyable game that teaches spelling skills. Allows the creation of custom word lists. Grades 1–4. Sound card not required, but enhances the effectiveness of the program. Requires 3.32 megabytes hard disk space. $20; three-game bundle $30. DynoTech Software.

### Dollars and Dinosaurs ★★★

dino01.zip (1 of 2), dino02.zip (2 of 2)

AOL

DOS

Dollars and Dinosaurs offers four language and spelling activities for young computer users, divided into eleven levels. The activities are: flash cards, spelling, matching written words to a picture, and recognition of moving letters. Each of these activities helps develop skills which are necessary for reading and writing. K–4. Requires 764k hard disk space. $29. Right to Left Software.

### Fun with Letters and Words ★★★★

flw25.zip

CompuServe

DOS

An old but very nice program for learning the alphabet, building vocabulary, and developing a sight word vocabulary. Vocabulary and graphics can be personalized so that children's names and personal information are intermixed with the original vocabulary built into the program. Also, the program is multilingual, and personal information can be entered in both primary and secondary languages. American sign language is also included! Preschool–3. Requires 336k hard disk space. $19. Wescott Software.

### Living Letters ★★★★★

llabc20.zip

AOL

Windows

> Alphabet and reading program for preschool to first grade. This program has excellent graphics, animation, and sound. This is a top-of-the-line, effective introduction to language. Limited to A to C in demo version. Sound needed. Requires 915k hard disk space. $19. LarKen Software.

### Multimedia Spelling Bee ★★★

bee10a.zip (1 of 2), bee10b.zip (2 of 2)

http://www.shareware.com

Windows

> This program lives up to its name, using sound, graphics, and special effects to tantalizingly test children on spelling. It's a wonderful program but…it may be a bit much. However, it's a well-designed program, and you may feel it meets your school's needs. Its main drawback is that there is no user input of words and, thus, the user is dependent on the provider for word modules. K–6. Requires 1.55 megabytes hard disk space. Sound required. $34.95 for the program with two hundred words, and $9.95 each for fifty-word add-on modules. Indigo Software.

### My Spelling Bee ★★★

msbsetup.exe

AOL

Windows

> A very interesting, competitive spelling bee program which allows the recording of spelling words and phrases of encouragement. Allows multiple players. K–6. Demo is functional up to thirty words. Requires 1.6 megabytes hard disk space. $19.95. Cutlass Associates Inc.

## Phonics ★★★

phow156a.zip (1 of 2), phow156b.zip (2 of 2)

CompuServe

Windows

This looks to be a full-featured phonics and reading program, at least in the registered version. It has quite a few limitations in the shareware version. Although well done, it has some annoying flaws, including nonstandard accents in the voice files as well as a certain amount of distortion. It is, however, one of the best shareware phonics packages around and thus deserves a good look to see if it meets your needs. Preschool to first grade (and up, for remedial purposes). Sound card required. Requires 4.32 megabytes hard disk space. $39; CD-ROM version, with many more sound and graphics files, available for $99. DareWare, Inc.

## Phonics Reading & Spelling System ★★

phonic.zip

CompuServe

DOS

This program will teach children and adults the phonetic reading and spelling methods. Interactive teaching method with graphic, music, and voice. This is a complete hearing, seeing, and saying package with real speech. K–6. Requires 3.31 megabytes hard disk space. Sound required. $39.95. DareWare Inc.

## Spellbound! ★★★

spell210.zip

http://www.shareware.com

DOS

Spelling tutor with a good selection of spelling lists. The graphics are a bit primitive, but the words in the lists are well grouped. The program includes a mini-editor for creating your own word lists. One hundred word lists included in the shareware version. K–6.

Requires 473k hard disk space. $15, or more if you want additional word lists and word search puzzle generator included. Spellbound Software.

## The Spelling Voice ★★

spvoic12.zip

http://www.shareware.com

Windows

A spelling tutor and quizzer which allows you (if you have a microphone) to create word lists and record the words in your own voice (or your students'). The voice files that come with the program are a little rough, but registration allows the customization of all voice files. A good point is that the program tracks performance and initiates automatic reviews. K–8. Sound card required. Requires 952k hard disk space. Extended Version (allows customization of all voices in the program) $15; Professional Version (supports and tracks the progress of an entire classroom) $35; more for school or district site licenses. Bob Dolan.

## Talking Teacher for Sound Boards ★★

teach25.zip (DOS)

teachwin.zip (Windows)

AOL

DOS and Windows

An educational package with real human speech that teaches children the alphabet, reading, spelling, and how to use a computer. You can record your own voice and use it in this package. Spelling words can be changed to match children's weekly spelling words. K–6. Sound required. Requires 1.54 megabytes hard disk space. $25. DareWare Inc.

## Voice Match ★★

vocmch20.zip

ftp://oak.oakland.edu/SimTel/win3/educate/

Windows

This compact, direct program allows the user to record spelling words and test them two different ways: multiple-choice selection or direct quiz. Its simplicity is its best aspect. Requires 392k hard disk space. $15. NianQing Huang.


## Wonder Word ★★★★

wonder.zip

http://www.shareware.com

DOS

This wonderful program has a little monkey climbing around a crossword-style game board helping children spell the words correctly. This program is very good for both spelling and vocabulary building. Preschool–3. A sound card is useful but not necessary. Requires 1.22 megabytes hard disk space. $9.95. Software Avenue, Inc.


## Word Rescue ★★★★★

1rescue.zip

http://www.shareware.com/

DOS

This delightful arcade-style vocabulary-building game is one of the most entertaining and educational around. A boy or girl scampers around landscapes and castles, matching words with pictures and scoring points. The trick is to avoid the "Gruzzles" or slime them into submission. If you've got a sound card, music plays in the background, but it's not needed to play the game. K–3. It will work on low-end machines. Requires 800k hard disk space. $15, with special deals on bundles of modules. Apogee.

### Words Alive ★★★

wrdalive.zip (DOS)

winwa.zip (Windows)

AOL

DOS and Windows

> Three games in one: spelling, word recognition, and time-telling multiple choice to spell a secret word. The DOS game is basic, but simple and effective. Uses PC speaker to play music and say letters and words. Animation rewards correct answers. Preschool–1. Requires 700k hard disk space. $19. Lana Chakoff.

### Wordy ★★

wordy313.zip

http://www.shareware.com

DOS

> A text-based educational word construction game. The object is to make as many words as possible from the given letter set within the allotted three-minute time limit. A simple yet worthwhile game for developing cognitive skills. K–8. Requires 1.17 megabytes hard disk space. It comes with a variety of associated word utilities. A mere $2. M\Cooper.

### Zpeller ★★★

zplr410.zip

http://winsite.com/

DOS

> Spelling and vocabulary teacher. It can handle up to thirty-two students. You can enter correct spelling and definitions for up to thirty-two thousand words. There are seven different types of tests, and the program tracks wrong answers for immediate retest. A major plus is the automated test battery for problem words that are constantly missed. This program has no particular bells or whistles, but its greatest strength is its combination of spelling and definitions,

and the ease with which new words and definitions can be added. K–8. Requires 517k hard disk space. $19.95. Unicorn Software Ltd.

# Language, Writing, and Grammar

### Advanced English Computer Tutor ★★
aect20.zip
CompuServe
DOS

A tutorial for English speakers who have a good grasp of the language but are puzzled by certain subtleties of usage such as inversion; problem words such as affect and effect, anticipate and expect, and more are also explained. Generally well done, this program could be helpful to high school students who wish to hone their English skills and could also serve the foreign speaker as a way of preparing for TOEFL tests. Requires 303k hard disk space. $65.50. MaxTex International.

### Grammar Expert ★★★
gramxprt.zip
http://www.shareware.com
Windows

This Windows Help file is an online, HyperText reference book for the rules of English grammar, punctuation, and effective writing. Grammar Expert contains practical answers, guidelines, and advice on thousands of grammar-related points for businesses, writers, students, and people learning English as a second language. The online index and table of contents can be used to locate the information you need quickly. Grammar Expert explains the grammatical rules involved and provides plenty of examples. Appropriate for middle school and high school (or any adult writer). Requires 186k hard disk space. $30. Wintertree Software Inc.

181

## Grammar Slammer ★★★

gramslam.zip

http://www.shareware.com

Windows

An online grammar guide. When installed, a button bar sits on top of any word-processing program. When the writer is troubled by a point of grammar or style, he or she clicks on the appropriate button and a Windows Help file opens with a menu of topics. Grammar Slammer offers an exhaustive set of guidelines, including style and usage, capitalization, abbreviations, punctuation, letter writing, common mistakes, and choices. HyperText links jump to related menus, with ample explanations and HyperText pop-up definitions. This grammar utility could be an excellent aid to teaching English composition as well as for preparing students for writing proficiency tests. Appropriate for middle school and high school (or any adult writer). Requires 570k hard disk space. $25. James Blair.

## Grammar Slammer for Microsoft Word ★★★

gsw4w.zip

http://www.shareware.com

Windows

Microsoft Word for Windows version. It offers the same grammar and style guidance as the generic Grammar Slammer and is different only in the way it can be installed directly into Word, either as a macro, menu item, or task bar button. Appropriate for middle school and high school (or any adult writer). Requires 848k hard disk space. $25. James Blair.

## Grammar Slammer for WordPerfect ★★★

gswp4w.zip

http://www.shareware.com

Windows

WordPerfect for Windows version. It offers the same grammar and style guidance as the generic Grammar Slammer and is different only in the way it can be installed directly into WordPerfect, either as a macro, menu item, or task bar button. Appropriate for middle school and high school (or any adult writer). Requires 848k hard disk space. $25. James Blair.

## WinProof ★★★

winprof1.zip

http://www.shareware.com

Windows

This grammar checker can detect many subtle and complex errors such as dropped words, extra words, or words that have been misspelled into another word. It can also detect many other grammar errors including subject/verb agreement, missing articles, commonly confused words, double negatives, and passive voice. WinProof is compatible with WordPerfect, Word, Works, Word for Windows, ProWrite, PC-Write, WordStar, and other word processors. Network support is also provided. A nice feature is the ability to proofread text in the Windows Clipboard. Middle school and high school (and adults). Requires 834k hard disk space. $45. Intellect Systems.

# Foreign Languages

## Anna's Language Tutor ★★★

lngtut22.zip

AOL

DOS

This program needs individual language modules in order to operate (also available at AOL). The interface is the old DOS style, but the presentation is quite orderly and menu-driven. The learner proceeds step-by-step through topics on the target language. Drills, games, memory tests, translations, adventures, and history of the language are presented. Users can customize the program and even create their own language modules. Ready-made modules are available in Spanish, German, Italian, Swedish, Portuguese, Lithuanian, and Romanian. Seventh grade through adult. The program can run on low-end machines. Requires 250k hard disk space plus additional space for each module. Freeware, but donations from $5 to $20 are appreciated, and $10 registration brings added features and a manual. Abavagada Software.

### Earth Words ★★★

ewords10.zip

http://www.jumbo.com/

Windows

A multimedia vocabulary-building program, available in a myriad of languages, including English, French, Spanish, German, Italian, Dutch, Portuguese, Greek, Hebrew, Yiddish, Hungarian, Chinese, Japanese, Korean, Russian, Polish, Czech, and Turkish! This may be a pricey package for a hundred words of vocabulary per language module, but deserves to be checked out. K–8. Requires three megabytes hard disk space. Sound card required. $25 for English only; $35 for a three-language package. Right to Left Software.

### Ultimate Language Tutor ★★★★

4lang32a.zip

http://winsite.com/

Windows

A very straightforward vocabulary tutor in four languages: French, German, Italian, and Spanish. This has tests by parts-of-speech categories and reviews for missed words. You may edit and add to word libraries, allowing you to enter the current chapter's vocabulary. Students can be individually tracked in their progress and a Top Ten is maintained. This program is very well designed without any nonsense or wasted effects. Middle school and high school. Requires 310k hard disk space. $20. Ultimate Software.

## Social Studies

### The Constitution ★★★
const1_3.zip
http://www.jumbo.com/
Windows

> This a Windows Help file of the Declaration of Independence and the U.S. Constitution. Straightforward and easy to use. One of the benefits is being able to send the text home with students for projects. Middle school to high school. Requires 611k hard disk space. $10. LeftJustified Publiks.

### FactsUSA ★★
usa.zip
AOL
Windows

> A quiz program about the states. Simple, yet fun and educational, it quizzes state shape recognition, capital, and nickname. Grades 4–6. Requires 441k hard disk space. $10. Bruce Forbes.

### The Federalist ★★★★
fed30a.zip (1 of 2), fed30b.zip (2 of 2)
http://www.shareware.com
Windows

> The Federalist Papers are a collection of articles that were published by newspapers in New York from late 1787 to 1788. Published originally under the pseudonym PUBLIUS, these eighty-five essays were written by Alexander Hamilton, John Jay, and James Madison to explain the benefits of the proposed Constitution to the people and to defend it against its many critics. Presented in Windows Help

185

file format. Very easy to use and a wonderful resource for government and history students. Middle school through college. Requires 1.88 megabytes hard disk space. Freeware. LeftJustified Publiks.

## History Alive, The Northwest Passage ★★★★

nwpdemo.zip

http://www.shareware.com

Windows

A Lotus ScreenCam demo of an interactive in-depth presentation of the lengthy search for a northwest passage around North America. Full of text, maps, and graphics, this is a profoundly creative way to present a unit on this fascinating subject area. Remember, this shareware file is only a demo. You must then order from the company. There are others in the series, but they appear to be primarily of interest to Canadians. Middle or high school. Requires 2.21 megabytes hard disk space. $18.95. IDON East Corporation.

## We the People ★★★

wtp3_2.zip

CompuServe

Windows

An exploration of democracy throughout the centuries, We the People is a Windows Help file which contains the full text of the Magna Carta, the declarations and resolves of the First Continental Congress, the Declaration of Independence, the Articles of Confederation, the U.S. Constitution, the U.N. Declaration of Human Rights, the complete constitutions of Japan, Germany, China, and Iran plus excerpts from those of seven other countries. Sixth grade to high school. Well done, no nonsense. Fully functional. No sound. Requires 913k hard disk space. Unspecified registration fee. LeftJustified Publiks.

# Geography

## Europe! ★★★★★
eurwin22.zip (Windows)
eurv22.exe (DOS)
AOL
Windows and DOS

This is the shareware tryout version of Around the World!. The very best all-around geography package, with quizzes about Europe, its capitals, geographic features, and trade and manufacturing centers. Registered version gives you the whole world, its continents, plus the U.S. and Canadian states and provinces, even the solar system. Top-notch package. K–8. Requires 376k hard disk space. $15. Torpedo Software.

## States ★★
states10.zip
http://www.shareware.com
DOS

This program draws a map of the United States and quizzes students, at their option, on various aspects of each state, including name, capital, largest city (as of 1991), abbreviation, song, bird, flower, motto, nickname, date of entry, and order of entry into the Union. The user can choose exactly what to be quizzed on. The program keeps time and statistics as it requires the correct answer for every state. If the user misses, the program will come back to that state later. Graphics are decent, and simple sounds are included and may be turned off or on at any time. The user can request that spelling not be strictly enforced. Documentation is built-in. Grades 3–8. VGA graphics are required. Requires 180k hard disk space. Freeware. Will Menninger.

## Ultimate Geography ★★★

usgeo110.zip

http://www.shareware.com

DOS

This is a great resource and game program for the United States. It has quizzes for both the states and their capitals, cued to a well-designed map. Additionally, it functions as an interactive gazetteer of information on population, population distribution, state size, crime statistics, trivia, industries, marriage, and divorce. It can produce a number of graphic representations of population distribution by time and ethnic origin, using 1990 Census statistics. The program gives a wider view of life in the U.S. than most. Grades 4–12. Requires 331k hard disk space. $15. Ultimate Software.


## USAPuzzle! ★★★★★

uspuzl10.zip

AOL

Windows

This is the shareware tryout version of GeoPuzzle!. This entertaining and educational package includes a states puzzle and a state capitals Quiz. Register and get the whole package, GeoPuzzle!, that includes puzzles and quizzes for all the continents, the U.S., and Canada. Very user-friendly and educational. K–8. Requires 338k hard disk space. $15. Torpedo Software.


## World Empire II ★★★★

wemp15.zip

CompuServe

Windows

A well-designed computer version of the classic strategy game Risk. This may be an entertaining way to teach or reinforce world geography. It isn't for every class or grade, but if this kind of game-playing education appeals to you, it's worth checking out. Fairly functional in the try-out version. Grades 6–12. Requires 2.38 megabytes hard disk space. $25. Viable Software Alternatives.

## Science

### ChemLab 1.0 ★★

chemlab.zip

http://winsite.com/

Windows

ChemLab is an interactive simulation of a chemistry lab. Common lab equipment and procedures are used to simulate the steps involved in performing a chemistry lab experiment. Lab equipment is added to the workspace by either selecting from the toolbar or equipment menu. Additional lab equipment can be added by selecting from the chemicals menu and specifying a particular lab container. General lab or fractional crystallization can be simulated. High school. Requires 670K hard disk space. Free beta version. Model Science.

### Dictionary of Organic Chemistry ★★★★

organic.zip

http://www.shareware.com

Windows

A Windows Help file resource on the topic of organic chemistry. It is well organized with glossaries, graphics, and essays explaining all the basic tenets of organic chemistry. It is suited to high school and college biology and chemistry classes; it would be a welcome resource at high school and college libraries. Requires 421k hard disk space. Freeware. Ian McGuinness.

189

### Physicist ★★★

physicst.zip

http://winsite.com/

Windows

A HyperText physics tutorial in the form of a Windows Help file, written for a wide range of users, including students, technicians, engineers, chemists, and physicists. It features a unique property chart which graphically shows the relationships among the physical properties, and a particle chart which graphically shows the relationships among the subatomic particles. Good reference work. High school. Sound is not necessary but provides comic relief. Requires 1.30 megabytes hard disk space. $10. Tom Potter.

### The Rock Cycle ★★★

rockcy14.zip

http://www.shareware.com

Windows

This nifty little labeling program teaches children the elements of the rock cycle, the various stages rocks go through as they form. It's a nice addition to a geology unit. Grades 3–8. Requires 1.16 megabytes hard disk space. Freeware. Thomas W. William-Powlett.

### Stoichiometry ★★★★

stoic10.zip

ftp://oak.oakland.edu/SimTel/win3/educate/

Windows

Learning about stoichiometry can be very difficult for the introductory chemistry student. This program is designed to be a nonthreatening device which can provide the student with practice in both balancing chemical equations and solving stoichiometry problems. Students using the program in a computer lab will be presented with the reactions in a different order. When registered, the user will receive thirteen more reactions for the balancing portion of the lab and fourteen more reactions for the

190

stoichiometry section. High school and college. Requires 350k hard disk space. $10. (This fee entitles the user to a site license for the program and a copy of a lab which can be used with the program will be included.) Timothy J. Allen.

# Astronomy

## SkyGlobe ★★★★★

skyglb36.zip

http://www.shareware.com/

DOS

SkyGlobe is an award-winning planetarium program that is fast and easy to use. It has over twenty-nine thousand stars (it has support for up to two hundred fifty thousand stars), and its viewing modes, times, and locations are easily configurable. Its display is top-notch and can be quickly adapted to your preferences. Fifth grade through college. Requires 424k hard disk space. $20. KlassM Software.

## SkyMap ★★★★★

skymap30.zip

http://www.jasc.com/jmcdl.html

Windows

SkyMap is a "Planetarium" program for Microsoft Windows 3.1, 95 or NT. It will display a map of the sky as seen from any point on Earth for any date between 4000 B.C. and 8000 A.D. Two different types of map can be drawn—a horizon map showing the observer's local horizon, and a sky area map showing a detailed view of a small area of the sky. You can get information about any object displayed on the map by simply pointing at the object with the mouse and clicking the button. The display of additional information, such as constellation figures or star labels, can be switched on and off with a click of the mouse button, making it easy to see exactly what you want without being overwhelmed by unwanted information. When you have the map just as you want it, you can print it on any printer supported by Windows, in either black-and-white or color. This is the best astronomy program yet seen for Windows. K–12 (with teachers' help for the early grades). 2.37 megabytes hard disk space. $49. JASC Inc.

## Painting and Coloring

### Bert's Series ★★

Various file names

http://www.coast.net/cgi-bin/SimTel/msidx?bert%27s

DOS

These easy-to-do coloring programs can be a hit with younger children and be a good early mouse manipulation learning tool. The series includes Bert's Dinosaurs, Bert's African Animals, Bert's Christmas, Bert's Whales and Dolphins, and Bert's Prehistoric Animals. Preschool–2. Space requirements vary, but average about 300k hard disk space per program. $20. Theron Wierenga.

### The Color Wizard ★★★★★

clrwiz12.zip

ftp://uoknor.edu/pub/simtelnet/asp/programs/educaton/

DOS

A most amazingly wonderful paint and color program. It features pictures from different books such as *Aesop's Fables* and *Rapunzel*, as well as dinosaurs and more. Not only can you paint the various pictures but there is a tutorial mode in which the original artist paints the picture before your very eyes, teaching such techniques and concepts as perspective, shading, and color values. This is the only program I've seen that can actually impart artistic skills. K–8. Requires 1.36 megabytes hard disk space. $29.95 (Save $11 if ordered from their BBS by modem). ImagiSOFT, Inc.

192

## Coloring Book 2.0 ★★★

cbook20.zip

http://www.shareware.com

DOS

A very easy-to-use coloring book program. There are a number of entertaining pictures to color. The interface will be easy for young children to understand and reading skills are not necessary. Finished products can be printed. K–3. Sounds provided by PC speaker. Requires 243k hard disk space. $15 (the registered version provides an additional twenty-five pictures to color). Russell Holloway.

## Magic Color ★★★★

magic01.zip

http://www.shareware.com

Windows

This paint and coloring program is very innovative. From a menu at the bottom of the screen, you can: choose to enter text; select surface style; fill colors; paste ready-to-color black-and-white pictures from a library of clowns, teddy bears, animals, boats, greeting cards, etc.; draw lines or geometric shapes; or design and enter 3-D images. The whole interface has been designed to be easily understood by young and old alike. The workings are accompanied by amusing sounds, which are entertaining but not necessary to the functioning of the program. There are many creative possibilities to this program without being overly technical. K–8. Requires 1.42 megabytes hard disk space. $20. J. Minet.

## Tuppy ★★★

tuppy1.zip

CompuServe

Windows

A paint-by-the-numbers picture-generation program which prints numbered grid pictures for children to color. No onscreen activities.

The pictures are cute and the program easy to operate. Most valuable for preschool through third grade teachers to teach colors and numbers and associative skills. Requires 261k hard disk space. $10. PiGAS Inc.

## Classroom Publishing

### Storymaker+ ★★★
storyv24.zip
AOL
DOS

With this program, children will be able to produce their own stories, complete with graphics, animations, text, and music. You can compose your own music with the melody maker; write your story with the text editor; create or place PCX graphics using the scenery and shape editors; assemble the story and animate it using the story editor; and interactively play back the story or have Storymaker+ play it for you. K–6. It uses a speech synthesizer to play back text. Sound card is optional (the program will work with the PC speaker). Requires 1.2 megabytes hard disk space. $20. Elson Embry.

## Desktop Publishing and Graphics Management

### GrafCat for Windows ★★★★★
gctw.exe
http://www.north.net/alchemy/gctw.html
Windows

This handy program will allow you to print your image file collection in high-resolution thumbnails to any printer supported by Windows. It prints in color or black-and-white, and will allow you to select between six and forty-eight images per page. It works with most popular bitmapped image file formats, including PNG, GIF, TIFF, JPEG, PCX, Kodak Photo-CD, IFF/LBM, PC Paint Pictor PIC, Targa TGA, Windows/OS2 BMP/DIB, Windows 3 RLE, Microsoft Paint MSP, Halo CUT, PFS:First Publisher ART, Sun Raster RAS, HRZ SSTV, WordPerfect Graphics bitmapped WPG, MacPaint, and GEM/IMG. It will print in two-color dithered monochrome, 256-level grayscale, and twenty-four-bit true color. Requires 1.87 megabytes hard disk space. GrafCat for Windows is bookware. The registration fee is buying Steven William Rimmer's novel *Wyccad* and reading it. Alchemy Mindworks.

## GrafSaver ★★★★★

grafsv16.exe

http://www.north.net/alchemy/grafsave.html

Windows

This is a Windows screen saver that allows you to integrate your own graphics into the software. When GrafSaver for Windows blanks your screen, it will display the images you've selected. It will also allow you to select from a library an animated special-effects transition for each image, and add sound effects to your pictures. It includes optional password protection to guard your system when you're away from your desk. If used creatively, this screen-saver could be an innovative teaching tool. GrafSaver for Windows is bookware. The registration fee is buying Steven William Rimmer's novel *Wyccad* and reading it. Alchemy Mindworks.

## Graph Crazy ★★★★

grcrazy11.zip

ftp://oak.oakland.edu/SimTel/win3/educate/

Windows

This program is designed to make quick, attractive graphs. There are eleven basic graph types (including 2-D and 3-D bar, 2-D and 3-D pie) with a variety of options for each, including fonts and colors. Graph Crazy will let you do quick data entry or you may import data either through the Windows Clipboard or through the Data Import menu. For graphs that must be independently saved, Graph Crazy lets you save your graph as either a BMP bitmap file or a WMF metafile. Librarians and administrators will find this program very helpful in creating graphs to use in presentations. Teachers can use the program to teach about graphs in general, or to teach how to use graphs to illustrate specific data; thus, it can be very useful in math classes. It has broad-ranging applications for curricula from third grade to college. Requires 804k hard disk space. $19.95. WordSmith Document Design Inc.

## Graphic Workshop ★★★★★

gwswin11.exe (Windows)

grafwk70.exe (DOS)

http://www.north.net/alchemy/gww.html

Windows and DOS

This is a premier graphic image viewer and converter. You can create and view thumbnail catalogs of all your graphics in virtually any format (e.g., BMP, PCX, TIFF, GIF, etc.) as well as convert from image type to image type. There are a host of different ways to resize, dither, and alter your various graphic image types. You can view MPEG, AVI, FLI/FLC, QuickTime, and MPEG movies and animations. A very versatile screen capture camera is also included. You can choose to password-protect certain graphics! This is a must for all who work with graphics or wish to have a handy way to have students look for graphics to select for multimedia projects. Requires 2.67 megabytes hard disk space. $40. Alchemy Mindworks.

## Illuminatus ★★★★

ilm3eval.zip

http://www.jasc.com/jmcdl.html

Windows

Multimedia publishing and presentation for Windows made easy and inexpensive. Combine text, sound, graphics, slide shows, animation, and video into thrilling interactive multimedia publications, presentations, and promotions of all kinds. Publish them on floppy or CD. No programming, no royalties! Requires 3.59 megabytes hard disk space. The evaluation version is a restricted demo, with no save function. $169. JASC Inc.

## Media Center ★★★

jmc202.zip

http://www.jasc.com/jmcdl.html

Windows

This program allows you to organize your multimedia and graphics by creating albums of thumbnails. You can arrange image thumbnails in the album using drag-and-drop, and locate them using numerous sort options available such as by name, type, size, etc. You can catalog your multimedia and graphics files using keywords and comments for future searches. Clicking on a thumbnail displays the graphic in full-screen mode. This is a very fast, easy-to-use program. Requires 2.21 megabytes hard disk space. $39. JASC Inc.

## Paint Shop Pro ★★★★★

psp311.zip (Windows 3.1x)

psp32bit.zip (thirty-two-bit version for Windows 95)

http://www.jasc.com/pspdl.html

Windows and Windows 95

Paint Shop Pro is a complete Windows graphics program for image creation, viewing, and manipulation. Its features include painting, photo retouching, image enhancement and editing, color enhancement, image browsing, batch conversion, and TWAIN scanner support. Included are twenty standard image-processing filters and twelve deformations. The program supports Adobe-style image-processing plug-in filters. Over thirty file formats are supported, including JPEG, Kodak Photo-CD, PBM, GIF, PCX, BMP, TIFF, and more. Paint Shop Pro is not only very handy as a graphics viewer but also has graphics filters and paint tools not available in Windows Paintbrush or Windows 95 Paint. One of its very best features is a built-in applet, PSP Browser. PSP Browser is a visual file system for Paint Shop Pro, which uses an album-and-thumb-nail format to make accessing and handling image files easier and more intuitive. Just open any directory with graphic images, and the browser automatically creates and displays thumbnails which can be clicked on to open the paint program for editing. Winner of SIA and ZiffNet awards. Requires 3.8 megabytes hard disk space. $39. JASC Inc.

## Professional Capture Systems ★★★

pcs20.zip (includes both Windows and DOS programs)

http://www.jasc.com/jmcdl.html

Windows and DOS

This is actually two programs in one: JasCapture and DosCapture. JasCapture allows for the capturing of a defined area, full screen, window, client area, or object under Windows. Captures can be sent to disk, printer, or clipboard. Formats supported include BMP, PCX, and TIFF. DosCapture will allow you to capture standard and extended VGA text modes and standard VGA graphics modes. DosCapture images are saved as PCX files. Requires 222k hard disk space. $39. JASC Inc.

## QuickShow ★★★★

qshow.exe

http://www.north.net/alchemy

Windows

This Windows slide show package has been designed to be exceptionally easy to use. Incorporating much the same point-and-shoot interface that Graphic Workshop uses, it will allow you to create slide shows which are as simple or as complicated as you like. Slide shows can include any combination of images in the still-bitmapped formats supported by Graphic Workshop, including GIF, PCX, TIFF, JPEG, PNG, and Photo-CD. Each image can have a unique caption, background color, and multimedia element, such as a WAV or MIDI file. The QuickShow package is ideal for generating fast presentations or simply for browsing through an image file collection. Its uses

198

in the classroom are many, such as displaying maps, flashcards, multiplication tables, and so on. Requires 1.82 megabytes hard disk space. Requires four megabytes of RAM. Bookware (order a copy of *The Order* by Steven William Rimmer, $6.99). Alchemy Mindworks.

## QuickTime for Windows ★★★★★

qt16inst.exe (sixteen-bit version for Windows 3.1x)

qt32inst.exe (thirty-two-bit version for Windows 95)

ftp.wuarchive.wustl.edu

Windows and Windows 95

This is *the* program for playing MOV and MPEG animation clips and viewing JPEG graphics files. Developed by Apple, it has been ported to Windows to provide the needed tool for multimedia capabilities. For those without easy access to FTP, a Windows version is also available on the World Wide Web, with the file name of qtw11.zip, at <http://www.north.net/alchemy/gww.html>. It's hard to gauge hard disk space, as it is installed in several locations of the Windows system, but figure it to use about one megabyte. Freeware. Apple.

## ThumbsPlus ★★★★★

thmpls.exe

http://www.shareware.com

Windows

This is a terrific graphic file previewer, locator, and organizer which simplifies the process of finding and maintaining graphics and clip-art files. It displays a small image (thumbnail) of each file. You can use ThumbsPlus to browse, view, crop, launch editors, and copy images to the clipboard. You can use drag-and-drop to organize graphics files by moving them to appropriate directories. ThumbsPlus will also create a slide show from selected graphics, and install bitmap files as Windows wallpaper. You can print individual graphics files or the thumbnails themselves as a catalog.

Though not designed primarily as a conversion tool, the program can convert any image that it displays to the appropriate native Windows format. ThumbsPlus will also convert metafile graphics to bitmaps. Two important features: It can make and display thumbnails from CD-ROMs and will create sample-text thumbnails of TrueType fonts. The font displays are much clearer than in other font viewers in Windows, making font choices more intelligent. All popular graphic formats are supported, including icons. Requires 1.74 megabytes hard disk space, but will expand greatly as the thumbnail database file grows. $50. Cerious Software.

## VuGrafix ★★

vugraf13.zip

http://www.shareware.com

Windows

An image viewer/thumbnail creator. You may view, convert, print, and file graphics. It has support for BMP, TIFF, GIF, JPEG, IMG, WPG, WMF, DCX, PCX, and EPS file formats. It makes thumbnails, color adjustments, does copy-and-paste, and can display multiple images on the screen. There are more complete and more versatile graphics viewers around, but this program has the added benefit that it creates thumbnails on the fly without creating those often-huge hard-disk-swallowing data files. Requires 683k hard disk space. $19. Informatik Inc.

## Electronic Text Readers

## As You Like It ★★★★★

ayli12.zip

http://www.jumbo.com/

Windows

This may be the future of literature—or not. At the very least, it is a superb source for the great literature of the English-speaking world.

As You Like It is an electronic text reader which allows the reading of a great number of renowned selections. The books for this reader can be obtained either free from the producers' Internet site, or by disk for $2 each, with each disk containing seven to ten works. The reader itself is state-of-the-art, so configurable that it can suit the needs of any reader. Requires 366k hard disk space. Freeware. Ars Longa Group, Ltd.

## Genealogy

### EZ-Tree Genealogy System ★★★

ezt230.zip

http://www.shareware.com

DOS

A genealogy program to track and report on family trees. The program records information in variable-length records and fields. Family trees can be viewed in three different formats and reports are easily printed. EZ-Tree should make it easy for students to build their own family trees. Grades 5–12. Requires 245k hard disk space. $30. MicroFox Company.

### Family History Help ★★

fhh130.zip

http://www.shareware.com

DOS

This is a text file program that shows people how to do research into their family trees. It offers guidelines on sources of genealogical data. It guides users to some of the best sources of family history, such as the huge records of the Church of the Latter Day Saints. Grades 5–12. Requires 266k hard disk space. Freeware. Steve Hayes.

## Family Tree in a Window ★★★

fmtrw106.zip

ftp://oak.oakland.edu/simtel/win3/genology

Windows

A program which allows you to enter information about your family and relatives easily and quickly. You can specify names, dates, relationships, a long biographical note—even include a scanned portrait of the person in color or black-and-white (BMP format). Six types of reports can be produced: a full detail report (including pictures) of all information and relationships for each person; a full tree chart for any selected individual, graphically showing all direct ancestors and descendants (including pictures); a life-line chart for all people with known birth dates; a birthday report organized by month; a descendants report that includes spouses; and a MOSAIC printout of any or all pictures. This is a very user-friendly genealogy program and could be of great value to children in lower grades, e.g., third through sixth, as well as to the children in middle school and high school. Requires 564k hard disk space. $29.95. C. A. Hartley.

## Pantheon! ★★

pan104.zip

ftp://oak.oakland.edu/simtel/win3/genology

Windows

A genealogy database program with easy data entry. The program allows for entry of all standard genealogical information, plus special fields for medical and biographical data. Appropriate for fifth grade through high school. The demo version of Pantheon! does not have a working "save" function, and will only allow you to open the pre-made genealogy file "sample.gen." Requires 248k hard disk space. $20. Hyperion Technologies.

202

# Typing

### Al Bunny's Typing Class ★★★

albun122.zip

http://www.shareware.com

Windows

A colorful, graphics-based, game-style typing tutor. It may have special value in that children not ordinarily drawn to enhancing their keyboard skills would find this game friendly and inviting. Multileveled and fully configurable. Grades 3–8 (older kids might be turned off by the bunny theme). Requires 590k hard disk space. $10. SUNMOON USA.

### FasType Typing Tutorial ★★★★★

fastyp50.zip

AOL

Windows

This program is a wonderfully designed typing tutorial. It guides the student through various levels, from home keys to total keyboard mastery, all the while charting progress and giving the student a clear view of goals and results. A student's history is constantly maintained and the full menu of options provides a very friendly environment for learning. The 3-D graphic interface is unsurpassed and the lessons are skillfully conceived. Middle school to adult. Requires 1.7 megabytes hard disk space. $25. Trendtech Corp.

### MasterMind Typing ★★★

mmtype04.zip

AOL

Windows

A user-friendly, step-by-step typing tutorial. Move up in speed as you control how challenging the tutorial exercises are. Middle school to adult. Requires 1.5 megabytes hard disk space. $29.95. Peter Turnquist.

### Touch Type Tutor for Windows ★★

tttwin10.zip

AOL

Windows

An easy-to-use typing tutor that teaches and tests. Simple and direct. Allows for multiple student files and is customizable to student's ability level. Middle school to adult. Requires 145k hard disk space. $20. David P. Gray.

### Typegame ★★

typegame.zip

http://www.shareware.com

Windows

A simple, yet entertaining typing game. It is not a tutorial per se, but it might be a nice break in the action for advancing students. Students are challenged to type words and letters before they fall off the screen. Middle school and high school. Requires 92k hard disk space. $5. Jon and Paul Elosegui.

### Typing Made Easy ★★★

tme.zip

CompuServe

DOS

An old but very straightforward, effective program to teach typing. Paced and well organized. Middle school to adult. Requires 138k hard disk space. $25 for unlimited site license. QED Information Sciences, Inc.

# Resumés

### 03resume or 04resume templates ★★

resume.zip

CompuServe

Windows

These are two well-designed template files for Microsoft Word for Windows 6.0. They would be effective for teaching the proper form of a simple resumé to students in high school or community college, or for helping students apply for jobs in a career guidance center. Requires 176k hard disk space. $5. David Anderson.

### Curriculum Vitae Executable ★★★

curvita.exe

CompuServe

Windows

This program is actually two programs in one: a resumé creator and a playback viewer. With the creator, you first enter your address and select a BMP photo of yourself. Then you enter your information by subject and date; you can select a BMP for each heading from a list of provided graphic images. When you've entered all the information, you can save to disk or ask the program to create a distribution floppy disk; the program will copy both the resumé and the viewer utility to the floppy disk. Any potential employer with a Windows system can play back the very attractive resumé. Although it's a little confusing to learn how to enter information, there are context-sensitive help files each step of the way. This program could be used to teach resumé-writing in high schools or colleges, or could be made available at public libraries to assist job-seekers. Requires 2.65 megabytes hard disk space. $19 (registration brings automatic posting of a resumé to Unisoft's WWW page and distribution to appropriate job agencies). Unisoft.

## Jobdisk/Resumé On Disk ★★★

jobdis.exe

CompuServe

DOS

> This is a slightly eccentric but very effective tutorial on writing resumés, job searching, filling out applications, and performing during job interviews. It is divided into sections: Resumé Guide, Prospecting for a Job, Time to Move On, Application Note, Interview How-To, Salary Negotiation, Electronic Resumé, and Floppy Instructions. Included with the program is an applet which creates an electronic resumé for the job-seeker; the resumé is copied to floppy disk for distribution to employers. This program could be very helpful in career guidance centers in high schools and community colleges, as well as at universities; it would be a valuable resource at the local public library. Requires 193k hard disk space. $19.95. Rogue Marketing.

## Looking for Work ★★★★★

work2.zip

CompuServe

DOS

> An interactive guide for professionals and managers seeking to change or find employment. It is a step-by-step aid in planning and mounting an effective marketing campaign. It contains six units and almost two dozen worksheets, checklists, and models to structure and guide the search for a new job. The program's theme is that a job search is a marketing campaign—one that requires planning, analysis, targeted markets, and commitment to a schedule of tasks and activities. The program provides an introduction to a job search, a substantial amount of guidance in analyzing one's "natural" market, and considerable direction and structure in carrying out the many tasks and activities of an efficient campaign. It shows one how to go about it through a series of exercises and worksheets, taking the user through the process. When the user completes the

program, he or she will have a list of potential employers, a resumé, a core marketing letter, and will be well prepared for job interviews. This is a solid job search tutorial and resumé creator. It can be of use in libraries, career guidance centers, computer labs, and the classroom. Requires 317k hard disk space. $29. Interdigital.

## Resumé Master Deluxe ★★★
rmd40.zip
CompuServe
DOS

An easy-to-use, menu-driven resumé creator. It prompts you to enter information about yourself, work history, education, etc. It takes this information, formats it, then prints it out to create a professional-looking customized one-page resumé. Two formats are offered: chronological or targeted resumé. The program can be used as a tutorial or to help students apply for jobs. Requires 344k hard disk space. $20. Whirlwind Technologies.

## The Right Resumé ★★★★★
trr.zip
CompuServe
Windows

This is the premier resumé creator I've evaluated. It is essentially a WYSIWYG word-processing program specifically designed for creating resumés and cover letters. The word processor enables many of the options found in powerful programs such as colored fonts, cut-and-paste, etc. Three types of resumés can be created: chronological, functional, or targeted. The registered version includes a fifty-thousand-word-plus spell checker; a contact manager to manage prospective employers, contacts, interviews, etc.; a calendar to organize your job search; a mail merge for generating multiple, personalized letters for wide distribution; and more. This program can be used in the classroom to teach resumé writing skills, in the career guidance center to help students find jobs, or in public libraries as a valuable community resource. Requires 3.15 megabytes hard disk space. $25, with a generously discounted site license schedule. Whirlwind Technologies.

### "You're Hired!" ★★★★
yhired.zip
CompuServe
DOS

This program asks the student common challenging interview questions in a lifelike simulation and records elapsed times as the student verbally responds. If help is needed answering a question, pressing a key offers professional advice and gives students an opportunity to view their own reminder notes. The user can also add or change the questions and advice, and create customized interviews that ask only select questions. Users can practice anywhere with a printed copy, and polish their interviewing skills with the help of the program's three-step training strategy. The questions asked in the simulated interview are intriguing and the advice about responses is apt. The ability to enter personal notes for each question is a plus for helping students consider the interview process more deeply. The program not only prepares the user for interviews but also serves to build confidence and a realistic view of the whole process. Requires 343k hard disk space. $26.95. DataWell.

## Word Processing

### Japanese Word Processor ★★★★★
download all files beginning with "jwp"
ftp.cc.monash.edu.au/pub/nihongo/
Windows

This outstanding freeware word processor has complete online English-Japanese and Japanese-English dictionaries. It is very user-friendly and can mix English with Japanese word processing. You'll find it excellent in all ways. It's also a very good Japanese-language learning tool. Runs best with 486 or better. Requires 11.3 megabytes hard disk space. Freeware. Stephen Chung.

## Word Easy ★★★

wordeasy.zip

http://shareware.com/

Windows

There is much to recommend this word-processing program, especially the online spell-checker that catches mistakes as you make them; also, the search line locates words you're unsure of and allows the use of wild cards. Other features include built-in character map for instant insertion of symbols and foreign characters, multiple document windows, and handy tabs for switching between pages of a document. The program is rather intuitive and the learning curve should be less steep than for many similar programs. Requires 1.3 megabytes hard disk space. $30. Rong De Lu.

## Spreadsheet Applications

## Spread Em Out ★★★★

spread.zip

CompuServe

Windows

Though this full-functioned spreadsheet application runs well on PCs, the developers point out that it is a spreadsheet of choice for notebook computers running Windows. Spread Em Out packs the most useful functions in a small, simple package rather than adding complex features you never need and usually can't understand. Features include OLE support, charting (various types), multiple documents (MDI), TrueType support, importing of various formats,

and high accuracy. Requires a 386-SX or higher with two megabytes of RAM. Requires 1.66 megabytes hard disk space. $35.
amitySoftware.

## VistaCalc ★★★

vista.zip

CompuServe

Windows

A fast, powerful, and easy-to-use spreadsheet program for the home
and office. VistaCalc's user-friendly interface enables you to create
a wide range of documents, from your own personalized budget
plan to financial and accounting presentations. It is a full spreadsheet program with many special features and functions that only
programs such as Excel can offer. Requires 748k hard disk space.
$29.95. Brandon Fridley.

# Chapter Eight

# World Wide Web, Gopher, and FTP Sites

The more I explore the World Wide Web, the more I am thrilled to discover how many sites are dedicated to areas of interest to librarians, library media specialists, educators, and administrators. I've included in this list sites that are particularly germane to these professions and tried to avoid listing sites that were merely of tangential interest. I also spent considerable time in e-mail discussion groups listening to just what you've all been looking for on the Web. As many of you conversed via e-mail, you shared Web sites with each other. I checked your offerings and evaluated them to see if they were of broad appeal. In most cases they were and are included in this list. Other sites are included because they address the kinds of needs you expressed. Many of you worried, for example, about copyright and fair use questions. So I found sites that may set these worries to rest. Others were in search of keypals or listservs; I plugged the appropriate keywords into Yahoo! or WebCrawler and found sites to fill those needs.

I hope this list will keep you occupied for a while and take care of a myriad of your needs. But whatever I can do, you can do as well. I've included Web addresses for all the major Web search engines; learn to use these to meet your future needs and to find the numerous sites that will be coming online in the impending days. These search engines are fairly easy to use and many of them provide helpful advice on how best to use them.

There is great frugality inherent in utilizing the World Wide Web as the wonderfully vast set of reference works that it is. Some of you cannot possibly afford the cost of procuring many newspaper and magazine index and article database CD-ROMs at the present time. You may be able to get along quite nicely with the World Wide Web online newspaper sites and the archives they provide for free or moderate fees. Once you've explored the resources listed in this book and mastered the use of Web search engines, you'll have a feel for finding resources on your own. As the Web evolves (and it will do so at amazing speed), more and more resources and for-fee newspaper and magazine databases will be coming online. You'll know how to keep an eye out for these wonderful resources to extend the services in your library or classroom.

The World Wide Web is the largest and most alive reference document in history. Enjoy it and profit by it. It's a brave new world indeed. Good luck.

Note: You'll find several valuable gopher sites among the World Wide Web listings. The small number of these sites does not warrant a separate section and, since most of you will access them through a Web browser, they have been included here for your convenience. FTP sites, however, are presented separately at the end of this chapter. Most of the current Web browsers will easily access these FTP sites, though many of you will access them through separate FTP applications, such as Fetch, or through direct FTP connections provided by online services.

# Professional/Librarian

## American Library Association

http://www.ala.org/

Every librarian in the country should be familiar with the Web site of their very own association. Here you will find information on its services and its extensive array of programs, educational opportunities, conferences, and publications for librarians and the general public interested in library issues. Stay in tune with current activities, events, publications, and initiatives with frequent visits, and take advantage of the links to library-related resources.

## Back to School: Electronic Library Classroom 101

http://web.csd.sc.edu/bck2skol/bck2skol.html

This page offers a course on Internet use. "Bck2Skol" represents a beginner's course on the Internet and its various tools targeted toward librarians and other information professionals. Lessons include information on participating in mailing lists and USENET newsgroups, and cover basic Internet tools including telnet, FTP, gopher, Archie, Veronica, and the World Wide Web. Also provided are pointers to librarians on how best to use the Internet to research eight basic academic subject areas.

## Big 6 Information Problem-Solving

http://edweb.sdsu.edu/edfirst/bigsix/bigsix.html

This site, by Mike Eisenberg and Bob Berkowitz, presents an organized approach for both teaching and learning information problem solving with an emphasis on critical thinking skills. It is geared toward librarians, teachers, and information specialists for use in helping learners acquire information literacy.

## CD-ROMs

http://www.awa.com/nct/cds/cdlead.html

A site for CD-ROM reviews. They only list titles they like, saving you from learning more about junk.

## Children's Literature: A Newsletter for Adults

http://www.parentsplace.com/readroom/childnew/index.html

ParentsPlace.com presents a newsletter with hundreds of online reviews of chidren's books.

## Children's Literature Web Guide

http://www.ucalgary.ca/~dkbrown/

This Web site gathers and categorizes the growing number of Internet resources related to books for children and young adults. There are compilations of book awards lists, information on children's bestsellers, authors, and links to children's literary resources for parents, teachers, and librarians. Of special interest are the links to discussion groups on the topic, as well as links to electronic text collections for children. This is an outstanding site for children's literature.

## Children's Software Reviews

http://qv3pluto.leidenuniv.nl/steve/reviews/welcome.htm

This collection of WWW documents is intended as a repository for volunteer reviews of children's software produced by the users of the newsgroup <misc.kids.computer>.

## Copyright

http://www.chem.lsu.edu/htdocs/conferences/copyright/copyref.html

This Web site is a group of links to sites with information concerning the bedeviling issue of copyright law and policy. There are links to the U.S. Copyright Office Home Page, the U.S. Patent and Trademark Office, the Copyright Website, Supreme Court Decisions on copyright from Cornell Law Center, and many, many more. Surely those at libraries and schools will have the question "to use or not to use" answered here.

## Engines for Education

http://www.ils.nwu.edu/~e_for_e/index.html

This Web site is sponsored by the Institute for the Learning Sciences at Northwestern University. Its objective is developing and transferring innovative educational technology from the laboratory to practical applications in businesses, schools, government agencies, and the community. This site may be of general interest to librarians and educators.

## Fair Use Web Site

http://www.benedict.com/fair.htm#fair

A site dedicated to the intricacies of the "fair use" concept involving copyright law. This is an important topic for librarians and other educators.

## *From Now On: The Educational Technology Journal*

http://www.pacificrim.net/~mckenzie/

This online magazine discusses issues and ideas in the rapidly growing technological fields as they impact education and affect educators and families. Come here to stay current with trends in the virtual world. A sampling of articles revealed discussions of issues of importance to librarians such as AUPs, censorship, and information skills.

## The GSLIS Multimedia Product Reviews

http://volvo.gslis.utexas.edu/~reviews/index.html

Here you'll find reviews of current multimedia products by graduate students at the University of Texas, neatly divided into categories.

## IFLANET Quotations About Libraries and Librarians

http://www.nlc-bnc.ca/ifla/I/humour/subj.htm

Come here to read what they've been saying about you over the years. Some of it is humorous, and some of it deadly serious; you'll nonetheless appreciate the warmth and wisdom.

## Innovative Internet Applications in Libraries

http://www.mtsu.edu/~kmiddlet/libweb/innovate.html

This site offers a comprehensive view of how libraries today are using the Internet to expand their services. Topics include bibliographic instruction, cataloging, collection management, digital library projects, library research guides, and electronic publishing. Here you'll find an open window to the libraries of today and tomorrow.

## International Federation of Library Associations and Institutions

http://www.nlc-bnc.ca/ifla/

This organization was created to provide librarians around the world with a forum for exchanging ideas and promoting international cooperation, research, and development in all fields of library activity. Its Web site will keep you in touch with conference information, publications, IFLANET Electronic Information Services, and more.

## Internet Public Library

http://ipl.sils.umich.edu/

I was thrilled to find this huge Web site from the School of Information and Library Studies at the University of Michigan. It is a virtual construction of an actual library, with "rooms" and such. There is a reference desk which leads to extensive reference works such as dictionaries, atlases, and encyclopedias, and links to sites to support science, business and economics, education, environment, government and law, health and nutrition, social issues and

216

services, and computers and the Internet. There are divisions for youth, teens, and MOO (Multi-User Object-Oriented environment, an interactive system accessible through telnet by many users at the same time). The library also has rooms called Classroom (with tutorials related to using the Internet, including interactive classroom lessons), Exhibit Hall (exhibits of art, photography, etc.), and the Reading Room (books in text and HTML, and magazines, journals, and newspapers from around the world). There are services for librarians and help with Web searching. This is the kind of site that can easily make a top-ten list.

## Internet Source Validation Project

http://calvin.stemnet.nf.ca/~dfurey/validate/

Here's some valuable help on the important subject of Internet source validation. The site is aimed at both students and teachers. The material here can help librarians develop guidelines for those who want to use the Internet as a source of information for research papers.

## Jenny's Cybrary to the Stars

http://sashimi.wwa.com/~jayhawk/

This refreshing and innovative Web site will lift your spirits while keeping you abreast of information resources on the World Wide Web. Especially valuable is the feature "Librarians' Site du Jour," where you'll be introduced to new resources you may not have discovered yet. There also are links to library-related sites, Internet help sites, Windows 95 resources, and Jenny's offbeat personal favorites.

## Karen's Kitchen: The Freedom Pages

http://www.intac.com/~kgs/freedom/

This site is dedicated to library policies (AUPs and the like) and provides pointers to collections of library policies, including the ERIC Archive of Acceptable Use Policies, the California Department of Education, and Rice University's education gopher.

## Lex Systems—Library Automation Services

http://www.link.ca/~lex/

This is a commercial site for Lexifile, a full-featured OPAC/CIRC system for PC-compatible computers. According to Lex Systems, Lexifile "is fast, easy to use, and less expensive to learn than most similar programs." You can download a sample program (sample.exe) which can build MARC records, print spine label sets, cards, lists, etc. The company also offers to contract to convert your data to MARC (machine readable) form.

## Library and Information Science Resources

http://www.loc.gov/global/library/library.html

An important Library of Congress offering. They've put together a page of links to some of the most vital WWW sites for the library and information world. You'll find access to national, state, and foreign library sites, as well as links grouped by special interest or type. Use the links to online library catalogs and to the research and reference services.

## LION: Librarian Information Online Network

http://libertynet.org/~lion/lion.html

This site is an information resource for K–12 school librarians. You'll find a wonderfully diverse set of resources.

## LM_NET Archives

gopher://ericir.syr.edu:70/11/Listservs/LM_NET

Of great value to all school librarians is the LM_NET discussion group on school library media topics. This gopher site contains the archives of past discussions, organized into the past month's messages, and messages by year back to 1993. You'll find a convenient subject-line search of the archive. Also of interest is a directory of the discussion group's members.

## Mansfield Cybrarian

http://www.mnsfld.edu/~library/#contents

The Mansfield University Library Web site offers a vast array of links to library catalogs, as well as links to information resources on the WWW. This well-organized site provides research Web pointers by subject, links to reference works, guides to learning the Internet, Internet guides and lists of lists, search engines for navigating the Net, and software for downloading.

## MARCmaker and MARCbreaker

gopher://marvel.loc.gov:2069/7?MARC
gopher://marvel.loc.gov:70/11/.ftppub/marc

These are the addresses for obtaining two freeware programs for working with MARC records.

## The Public Service Librarian's Professional Guide to Internet Resources

http://k12.oit.umass.edu/libguide.html

The title of this Web site says it all. Resources you'll find here include listservs, library catalogs, Internet lessons, resource lists and subject guides, indexes to the Internet, multipurpose sites for librarians, book reviews and literature, and discussions about copyright and censorship.

## School Library Hotspots

http://www.mbnet.mb.ca/~mstimson/text/hotspots.html

This is a comprehensive site for library resources, focusing on core issues and needs, such as AUPs, information services, reference, materials sources and reviews, lesson plans, and more. There are links to many often-visited, highly valuable Web sites, including Kidopedia, LM_NET archives, and EdWeb, and links to a host of print and nonprint materials. This is another "one-stop-shopping" site for librarians.

## Superkids Educational Software Review

http://www.superkids.com/

The goal of this site is to present unbiased reviews of children's software by parents, teachers, and kids.

## Ten Big Myths About Copyright Explained

http://www.clari.net/brad/copymyths.html

A Web page delving into a complicated issue for librarians, teachers, and all those who can get snared by the labyrinth of copyright law.

## Welcome to Gale

http://www.gale.com/gale.html

The home page for Gale, a provider of CD-ROM, online, and book databases. Of special value here is the "Celebrate Libraries" page. It's a nice place for a daily coffee break to stay in the know.

## Young Adult Librarian's Help/Homepage

http://www.acpl.lib.in.us/young_adult_lib_ass/yaweb.html#

This site can be of special interest to middle school and high school librarians as well as public librarians with extensive young adult collections and services. It provides links to school and public libraries, electronic literature resources such as teen-oriented "e-zines," and discussions relevant to professional issues for librarians. The resources here are designed for use by both young adult librarians and the patrons they serve. There are more than two hundred fifty links to relevant resources on the Web.

## Acceptable Use Policies

The following sites are excellent for helping librarians of all stripes to put together a sensible policy for their particular situations.

### Acceptable Use Policy—Greenfield-Central High School
http://gcsc.k12.in.us/AUP/AUP.html

### Classroom Connect AUP FAQ Page
ftp://ftp.classroom.net/wentworth/Classroom-Connect/aup-faq.txt

### ERIC Archive of AUPS
gopher://ericir.syr.edu:70/11/Guides/Agreements

### Indiana Public School Internet Acceptable Use Policies and Guidelines
http://doe.state.in.us/LearningResources/aup123

### The Internet Advocate
http://silver.ucs.indiana.edu/%7Elchampel/netadv.htm

### K–12 Acceptable Use Policies
http://www.erehwon.com/k12aup/

### Rice University
gopher://riceinfo.rice.edu:1170/11/More/Acceptable

### Writing Acceptable Use Policies
http://mercury.esc.k12.in.us/aup/1.html

## MLA Style

### Citation Guide

gopher://gopher.uiuc.edu/11/Libraries/writers/i/im

This is a subdirectory of guidelines for electronic source citations from the University of Illinois at Urbana-Champaign gopher.

### Electronic Sources: MLA Style of Citation

http://www.uvm.edu/~xli/reference/mla.html

A straightforward site of examples of citations of electronic sources for individual works, journal articles, newspaper articles, magazine articles, discussion list messages, and e-mail.

### MLA-Style Citations of Electronic Sources

http://www.cas.usf.edu/english/walker/mla.html

This site, by Janice R. Walker of the University of South Florida, offers style guidelines for citing a variety of electronic sources. It is endorsed by the Alliance for Computers and Writing.

## Teachers' Resources, K–12 Curricula, and Lesson Plans

### A Teacher's Home Page

http://pluto.njcc.com/~harris/

This Web page is full of links to many resources helpful to teachers of almost any subject. It is well organized, with different categories, e.g., teachers, parents, kids, news, and links to different subjects. Included is a virtual field trip. There is even a list of lists. So many places to go, with a special accent on current events.

## Apple Education Page

http://www.info.apple.com/education/

This Web page from Apple is dedicated to preschool through high school educators, with links to teacher training, special offers to educators, and educational products. Along with the commercialism are some fine aids and links for educators.

## AskERIC

http://ericir.sunsite.syr.edu/

The well-known Syracuse University–created clearinghouse for educational resources. Here you will find ERIC's Lesson Plans, AskERIC's Collections, Search ERIC's Database, and AskERIC Toolbox. This may be the richest site on the Internet for educational purposes. It has links to links to links!

## @School

http://www.atschool.com/

This creative virtual schoolhouse offers a vast set of resources for K–12 learning and teaching. Among its great features are: an interactive map of the U.S., Canada and Mexico, with pages and pages of links to online schools on the continent; a pageful of K–12 USENET discussion group addresses for engaging in useful educational dialogue; a five-megabyte place for your school's own Web page; links to ongoing online projects for the classroom; links to "virtual classrooms" organized by subject which contain a series of links to relevant educational resources (subdivided into sections so that locating a resource for a specific subject can be accomplished in a relatively short time); a library of links to electronic libraries throughout the Internet for reference, newspapers, periodicals, audiovisuals, fiction, and nonfiction; links to interactive teaching resources, allowing students instant access to scientific instruments, map servers, live discussion groups, and much more; and, finally, an "Educator's Desk" that serves as a set of links of benefit to educators, including lesson plans, online education magazines, and support for implementation of technology. This may be the epitome of one-stop educational shopping.

## Bright Kids Home Page

http://granite.sentex.net/~brightkd/britep1.html

A Web site for K–6 activity sheets. These look good!

## Busy Teachers' WebSite K–12

http://www.gatech.edu/lcc/idt/Students/Cole/Proj/K-12/
TOC.html

Carolyn Cole of Georgia Tech University has created this Web site to "provide teachers with direct source materials, lesson plans, and classroom activities with a minimum of site-to-site linking, and to provide an enjoyable and rewarding experience for the teacher who is learning to use the Internet." The site is neatly designed as a table of contents by subject and educational area. A quick browse through the table of contents reveals a well-researched set of resources that can indeed help the busy teacher find it fast, whatever "it" is.

## Classroom Connect Web Site

http://www.classroom.net

This Web site for Classroom Connect hosts a myriad of resources and links for K–12 educators. You can download Web browsers and tools for making Internet travel more profitable and interesting. You can "talk" to the WebMaster, who will give you advice concerning the building of Web pages. You'll find access to ClassroomWeb, a database of hundreds of schools that are on the Web; here, Classroom Connect will put school Web pages on its server for free if you do not have access to a server of your own. On the Conference Web, it posts current educational conference information to make it easier for you to find the conferences that you would like to attend. All in all, this is a good resource for educators.

## Collaborative Lesson Archive

http://faldo.atmos.uiuc.edu/TUA_Home.html

This page contains an extensive lesson plan database with plans for use from preschool to twelfth grade. Lessons from this database are intended for distribution to other educators on a nonprofit basis.

## Common Knowledge: Pittsburgh

gopher://pps.pgh.pa.us/

This gopher site is a collaboration among the Pittsburgh Public Schools, the University of Pittsburgh, and the Pittsburgh Supercomputing Center. It has menus leading to a large set of resources on K–12 subject matter, including lesson plans and general information that can help in creating study units.

## Cool School Tools!

http://www.bham.lib.al.us/cooltools/

Cool School Tools!, a service of the Birmingham Public Library, is an index to World Wide Web and other Internet resources for children and teenagers in grades K–12.

## David Bower's Educational Marketplace

http://www.io.org/~dbower/Home.html

A Web site managed by David Bower, a physics teacher in Ontario, Canada, it is a series of pages of diverse educational resources, including lesson plan banks, software for teaching, templates for testing, and lots of other resources.

## Global Network Navigator Education Page

http://gnn.com/gnn/meta/edu/index.html

This is the education page of GNN, an Internet service provider. Anyone can go there, whether a member or not. It is full of curriculum aids; lesson plans; online games; resources in language arts, mathematics, social studies, and American history; and links to other educational sites on the Web. There are many other things, such as a site for online publishing for kids, but they're too numerous to mention. A great set of resources and links.

## Gopher Menu, Michigan Department of Education K–12 Lesson Plans

gopher://gopher.mde.state.mi.us/11/class/lesson

A menu full of links to lesson plans for K–12.

## Heritage Online Courses for Teachers

http://www.hol.edu

This is the home page for an excellent program offered by Antioch University. Antioch offers regular and graduate education courses for teachers using the Internet. The courses are highly interactive with a listserv for each class. And the syllabi have links to various resources on the WWW that facilitate course completion. As many as fifteen course are available per term and all courses are available for Antioch University credit. Examples of course titles: Using Technology to Integrate Art into the K–12 Curriculum, Foreign Language Learning with the Internet, Real World Math via the Internet, Science Study on the World Wide Web, Grant and Proposal Writing for Technology Enhancement, and Using the World Wide Web to Enhance Student Writing and Publication.

## International Center for Leadership in Education

http://www.daggett.com

This site provides access to the works of Dr. Willard Daggett and the general topic of school reform.

## Kathy Schrock's Guide for Educators

http://www.capecod.net/Wixon/wixon.htm

This Web site, brought to you by a library media specialist from Maine, provides a wealth of resources to enhance curriculum and

226

provide professional growth to teachers. The list of site links is well crafted.

## Lesson Plans and Resources for ESL and Bilingual Teachers

http://www.csun.edu/~hcedu013/eslindex.html

This page, from Marty Levine of California State University at Northridge, offers links to lesson plans for ESL and bilingual education, with a tilt toward Spanish, but helpful to all in bilingual education.

## Microsoft's Focus on K–12

http://198.105.232.6:80/k-12/

It's hard to know where to list this Microsoft site. Sure, it promotes Microsoft's educational product lines, but there's so very much more in resources available here to help the K–12 technology-based curriculum.

## The Music Educator's Home Page

http://www.athenet.net/~wslow/

This site is an Internet resource for music educators, with curriculum documents, lesson plans, and music. There are also links to other sites that can benefit the classroom music teacher. The downloadable material may support this extracurricular activity that often suffers from underfunding.

## New Jersey Networking Infrastructure in Education

http://njnie.dl.stevens-tech.edu/

The lesson plans Web page of the New Jersey State Department of Education. As they put it, "Lesson plans, lesson plans, lesson plans, get your lesson plans here!!!" The NIE (Networking Infrastructure in Education) curriculum modules are lesson plans which allow students to use real-time data gathered from the Internet to participate in exciting and real scientific analysis and discovery on a variety of topics ranging from the aurora borealis to earthquakes. This page links you to other pages full of information about schools on the Internet, Internet connectivity, and Internet software.

## Pathways to School Improvement

http://www.ncrel.org/ncrel/sdrs/pathwayg.htm

This site is a product of the North Central Regional Educational Laboratory in cooperation with the Regional Educational Laboratory network. Covered topics: Assessment, School to Work, Math, Science, Leadership, Professional Development, Learning, and Governance. Each topic's page offers discussions of issues, essays, and subject-related Internet links.

## Poor Richard's Publishing

http://www.tiac.net/users/poorrich/

This site contains a variety of resources for the learning-disabled community. There are also links to Macintosh shareware and freeware.

## Princeton Regional Schools

http://www.prs.k12.nj.us/

This site is worth a visit because of its great links to K–12 educational material. Also of great service is the link to Yale University's "Macintosh Guide," which can be found at <http://www.yale.edu/macguide/>; it seems a very handy resource for solving your Mac-related problems.

## Tigger's Home

http://remarque.berkeley.edu/~tigger/

Grace Sylvan's Web site dedicated to her interests, which include kids' shareware, sewing, quilting, parenting, shareware and Web page development, and home-schooling. Her varying interests provide a rich set of resources for educators, including how to creatively use SuperCard, HyperCard, and other multimedia programs and development tools. Learn how to build a Web page and download some shareware to help you do it. Her "Children's Shareware Page" at <http://remarque.berkeley.edu/~tigger/sw-kids.html> has links to getting some of the best shareware and freeware educational programs today for Windows, DOS, and Macintosh. Many programs have been prescreened and are organized by age group for direct download, or you may search any of the many recommended sites for more shareware programs. Her personal selections are aimed at K–6 children. As usual, there are links to many great resources on the Internet. This is all accompanied by valuable and insightful advice about shareware and freeware. A top-flight Web site.

### Yahoo! Web Searcher Education Page

http://www.yahoo.com/Education/tree.html

Yikes! If you thought there wasn't much on the Internet for teachers, librarians, or anyone involved in education, then type this address into your URL. It might take a year to follow where it will lead you.

## Projects and Mentors

### Academy One

http://www.nptn.org/cyber.serv/AOneP/academy_one/menu.html

Here you can find ongoing projects and events, exchange ideas with librarians and teachers, and locate keypals.

### adventure.online

http://www.adventureonline.com/about.html

Looking for something to do online with your students or patrons? "adventure.online is dedicated to bringing adventure and adventure learning to K–12 classrooms and Internet explorers. Serving as a guide to adventure-related projects, adventure.online features exclusive expeditions, adventure news, entertaining games, and highlights from the best gear companies in the field."

## Aunt Annie's Crafts Page

http://www.coax.net/annie/

This page is dedicated to crafts projects for kids. There's a project of the week, last week's project, a craft exchange where visitors can submit new craft projects or find recent submissions (I was checking before Easter and found many Easter egg and bunny projects), tips for reusing or recycling paper scraps, and lots more. Get your scissors and paper ready!

## The National Genealogical Society's List
## of Genealogy BBSs

http://genealogy.org/PAF/www/gbbs/welcome.html

GBBS is published monthly and includes more than one thousand computer bulletin board systems around the world that support genealogists.

## New Jersey Online's Learning Center

http://www.nj.com/education

New Jersey Online makes it easy and free for schools, classes, and educators to have home pages on the World Wide Web. NJO's easy forms provide everything you need to create and update a simple, informative Web site. Build a strong home-school connection by listing your school or class here. Also, every month a member of New Jersey Online's Who's Who Online in NJ Education will review a site that he or she feels has educational merit. Check out the best site for kids this month.

## Official Homepage of the Birmingham Zoo

http://www.bhm.tis.net/zoo/

You can take a virtual safari to view pictures of animals and read all about them. This Web site is a wonderful way to introduce animals to children and encourage them to support the protection of endangered species. The safari could be a great children's library or classroom activity.


## The Promised Land: Contemporary Leaders Keypal Project

http://school.discovery.com/learningcomm/promisedland/
teachandlearn/leaders/

This project, sponsored by the Discovery Channel, offers children and teachers a chance to find out the answer to "What makes a leader?" by submitting questions via e-mail to a panel of six nationally recognized leaders. The site welcomes teachers to use this service for class projects.


## The Web of Culture

http://www.worldculture.com/

The Web of Culture is dedicated to educating and entertaining the visitor on the topic of cross-cultural communications. It presents a virtual atlas of the world, with a section on each continent and information about each country, such as population and capital. There are pages featuring languages, gestures, religions, embassies, currency, and cross-cultural quizzes. You'll find resources and links to other sites on the Web for cross-cultural interests.

# Internet Resources

## AskERIC

http://ericir.syr.edu/

AskERIC is the Internet-based education information service of the ERIC System, headquartered at the ERIC Clearinghouse on Information & Technology at Syracuse University. It, of course, has links to the Educational Resources Information Center (ERIC) national information system, supported by the U.S. Department of Education. AskERIC key areas include ERIC's Lesson Plans, AskERIC's Collections, Search ERIC's Database, AskERIC Toolbox. Go to <gopher://ericir.syr.edu/11/Lesson> from the home page and you will find an extensive menu of lesson plans, including CNN Newsroom Daily Lesson Plans, Newton's Apple Educational Materials, Discovery Network's Educator Guide, NASA's SIR-CED Education Program, and many subject-specific lesson plans. There are extensive worldwide links to SunSITE, a major access point for shareware and freeware programs. AskERIC was named best professional K–12 Educational Web site by GNN, the first fully integrated and consumer-oriented Internet service. It is no doubt a powerhouse educational WWW site.

## The Awesome Lists

http://www.clark.net/pub/journalism/awesome.html#a

Internet trainer, columnist, and consultant John S. Makulowich has put together something "truly awesome" in terms of Internet resources: two A-to-Z lists of top Internet sites, plus a Lycos search engine. A great place to start your Internet search.

## CU-SeeMe Welcome Page

http://cu-seeme.cornell.edu/

CU-SeeMe is a free videoconferencing program (under copyright of Cornell University and its collaborators) available to anyone with a Macintosh or Windows and a connection to the Internet. With

CU-SeeMe, you can videoconference with another site located anywhere in the world. By using a reflector, multiple parties at different locations can participate in a CU-SeeMe conference, each from his or her own desktop computer. Though there are certain system requirements in order to do videoconferencing, they are not as demanding as one might think. These requirements are explained at length at this Web site. It is possible to be videoconferencing with as little an investment as $100!

## The EdWeb K–12 Resource Guide

http://k12.cnidr.org:90/k12.html

This Web page offers a collection of the best online educational resources available, including teacher discussion groups and administrative services, as well as lesson plans, interactive projects, and interesting places for kids to explore. Most of these services are available for free over the Internet, and whenever possible you will be able to connect to the service simply by clicking on to its Internet address. You can also learn about commercial services which require a registration fee. The diverse set of subjects includes:

Gopher and the World-Wide Web
Listserv Discussion Groups and E-Journals
USENET News Groups
Commercial Collaborative Learning Services
Chat Forums for Kids
Educational Gateways
General Educational Networks
State-Sponsored Education Networks
Question & Answer Services

## The Eight Minute HTML Primer

http://web66.coled.umn.edu/Cookbook/HTML/MinutePrimer.html

If you're setting up a Web site, this tutorial on using HyperText Markup Language should help you get off to a quick start.

## The ERIC Database

http://ericir.syr.edu/ERIC/eric.html

The Educational Resources Information Center (ERIC) is a national information system designed to provide users with ready access to an extensive body of education-related literature. The ERIC database, the world's largest source of education information, contains more than eight hundred thousand abstracts of documents and journal articles on education research and practice. Here at the Web site, a search engine is provided to give you access to the database, making it a smooth and easy interface to this fantastic set of resources.

## Gopher

http://gagme.wwa.com/~boba/gopher.html

Bob Allison (of Spider Web) maintains a collection of top gopher sites for software, children's literature, school computing, and much, much more. A look at this list will have you thinking that gopher is the way to go on the Internet. As an added bonus, click on Bob's FTP sites link at the top of the page to find some pretty diverse stuff, including links to book reviews on the Internet.

## Gopher Jewels

http://galaxy.einet.net/GJ/

Gopher Jewels is a moderated list service for the sharing of interesting gopher finds. You're even invited to join their discussion forum on gopher topics. The resources themselves are an A-to-Z list of top-rated gopher sites, full of resources on dozens of topics including library information and catalogs as well as K–12 education. There is a handy key-word search at the bottom of the page.

## Guidelines for Creating Mesa Web Pages

http://www.ci.mesa.az.us/manuals/user/guidelin.htm

These guidelines were written for Mesa, Arizona, employees, but they could be used for the basis of one's own Web page policy. A good jumping-off point if nothing else.

## ICONnect

http://ericir.syr.edu/ICONN/ihome.html

ICONect, from the American Association of School Librarians (a division of the American Library Association), offers school library media specialists, teachers, and students the opportunity to learn the skills necessary to navigate the Information Superhighway. It has online courses on Internet basics, strategies for integrating the Internet into the curriculum, and mini-grants that encourage the use of Internet resources to develop meaningful curriculum connections, and it offers an Internet Q&A service called KidsConnect. Lastly, it offers the ICONnect Publication Series, which is geared to school library media specialists, classroom teachers, and school administrators.

## NETCOM

http://www.netcom.com/

This major Internet service provider offers special programs and price breaks to libraries and schools. NETCOM will wire your school for the Internet if it isn't already so. They have special programs for K–12 library research, K–12 staff development, and other Internet incentive programs. They truly seem ready to assist libraries and education.

## Pitsco Technology Education

http://www.pitsco.com

This is the home page for Pitsco, a commercial supplier of educational products and activities for students. Pitsco has put together a WWW site to help educators in many ways and intends to be a one-stop Internet resource for teachers. Of great value most certainly will be its Primary and Secondary School Internet User Questions page, which is a comprehensive online guide for users new to the Internet, with a slant toward public institutions such as libraries and schools. Of equal value are its lists for listservs, keypals, and online collaborative projects. Pitsco's Launch to Educational Resources is a comprehensive set of links to many areas of interest to librarians and educators. There are links to the following vital subjects:

| | |
|---|---|
| Acceptable Use Policies | Journals & Publications |
| Activities | KeyPals |
| Aeronautics | Lesson Plans |
| Art & Exhibitions | List of Listservs for Educators |
| Ask an Expert | Listservs: Everything You Want |
| AT&T Learning Network | to Know and More |
| Citing WWW Resources | Math |
| Contests for Educators | Multimedia |
| Copyright and Fair Use | Organizations |
| Curricula | Projects Online |
| CU-SeeMe | Recycling Old Computers |
| Dictionaries | References for the Classroom |
| Dragster Web Sites | Reform Movements |
| Employment | Rural Schools |
| English | Schools on the Net |
| Environment | Science |
| Find People on the Internet | Science Fair Resources |
| General References | Search Engines |
| Government | Software |
| Grants & Funding | Special Education |
| History | Technology Plans |
| Icon Resources | Television News on the Net |
| Inclusion | Current Event Info |
| Internet Access Software | Weather |
| Inventions/Inventors | Your School and the Web |

## Pitsco's Launch to Safe Internet Access

http://www.usa.net/~pitsco/pitsco/safe.html

Here is a site for obtaining many safeguarding programs such as CYBERsitter for Windows, Cyber Patrol for Macintosh and Windows, the Internet Filter for Windows, InterGo for Windows 95, NetNanny for Windows and Windows 95, NetShepherd for Windows/Windows 95 and Macintosh, ProGuard for the PC, SurfWatch for Windows/Windows 95 and Macintosh, and TattleTale for Windows.

## Point

http://www.pointcom.com/cgi-bin/pursuit-form-gif

Point's staff of reviewers surfs the Web daily looking for the best, smartest, and most entertaining sites around (they also look at suggestions they receive in their submit box). If they review a page, it means they think it is among the best 5 percent of all Web sites in content, presentation, and/or experience. Some sites are tops in all three categories; others qualify due to fabulous content or exceptional presentation. Some, they say, make it in just because "they're so deliciously silly." For unreviewed, wider searches, the site offers access to the Lycos search engine.

## *The Scout Report*

http://rs.internic.net/scout_report-index.html/

*The Scout Report* is a weekly Web newsletter (you can also receive it by e-mail) and specializes in providing a fast, convenient way to stay informed about valuable resources on the Internet. It combines in one place information about new and newly discovered Internet resources, especially those of interest to researchers and educators. The articles are stimulating and vital, and the pointers to new Web sites will keep you current on the ever-evolving Web.

## Seattle University World Wide Web Policy and Guidelines

http://www2.seattleu.edu/general/policy.html

Here is some help in formulating guidelines for WWW pages.

## Shirl's Internet Toolbox

http://www.bcr.org/garden.html

Shirl Kennedy of the Bibliographical Center for Research has put together this very useful and comprehensive site to help people accomplish things on the Internet. Here are fabulous resources for librarians and educators. The headings show the areas of value:

Searching the Web

Searching Gopherspace, Telnet Sites, and WAIS Databases

Finding People
Locating Software
Searching for Electronic Mailing Lists
Searching USENET Postings and FAQs
Specific Types of Information
    Computer Information
    Government Information
    Internet Information
The Electronic Ready-Reference Collection
New and Noteworthy
The Librarians' Lounge

Of special interest to librarians and educators are the vast array of search engines, access to lists of listservs, the electronic reference section, and the Librarian's Lounge, which has literally dozens and dozens of links of great value to librarians across the country.

## South Point University Style Guidelines (Great Britain)

http://www.sbu.ac.uk/cop/style_guide.html

Another set of Web page guidelines, this time from a university in Great Britain. Food for thought for your own guidelines.

## Tips for Web Spinners

http://gagme.wwa.com/~boba/tips1.html

If you want what appears to be the most comprehensive site on the World Wide Web about the World Wide Web, you should come here. There's a major emphasis on how to put together a great Web page or site and why. You'll find links to dozens and dozens of tools to design and build your own Web page. Additionally, there's a whole host of information about what the WWW is, what it's doing now, and where it's going to go. Bob Allison doesn't stop there. Want to know about graphics and where to get them? Web browsers and where to get them? Come to Bob's site. He'll explain everything you need to know about the World Wide Web: how to view it, use it, and do it. He gives you links to USENET groups involved with Web page subject matter. Plus, he throws in links to resources around the Web that will take you to great places while demonstrating how to include the same links on your page. Last, he introduces the notion of random Web browsing, offering four engines for landing on random Web pages.

## VNewsPaper

http://aristotle.isu.edu/vnewspaper.html

Called "real news on virtual paper," this online newspaper is maintained by Idaho State University. A good example of the new method of distribution of information in the Information Age, *VNewsPaper* features current events, sports, business, technology, and education. A must visit is the Kid's Clubhouse, where you'll find fabulous links to dozens of great reference works and electronic texts of novels; a math page with an "Ask Dr. Math" feature; a geography and social studies page with an online atlas and links to home pages of countries throughout the world and to schools on the Internet; a history page full of links to sites on the subject including the History Computerization page; a science page covering general science resources, astronomy, biology, chemistry, geology, oceanography, paleontology (dinosaurs), physics, science museums, weather (meteorology), and wildlife; and pages on communications and computers. Last, teachers will find their fill of resources at the Teacher's Apple page with links to teacher's discussion groups, search engines for teachers, lesson plans, and much more.

## The Web as a Learning Tool

http://www.cs.uidaho.edu/~connie/interests.html

This site is a guide dedicated to ongoing learning on the Web, containing a rich set of links to the following categories: creating your own Web pages, literature, art, music, theatre, science, math, medicine, geography, cultures, people, history, world news, education, schools, children, animals and ecosystems, Web cities and commercial sites, recreation, entertainment, and gateways to the Web.

## World Link

http://www.smartpages.com/worldlink/worldlink.html

This newsletter is designed to help educators navigate the Net, with tips, projects, and pointers to Internet sites.

## World Village School House

http://www.worldvillage.com/wv/school/html/school.htm

This site, sponsored by InfoMedia, offers resources for educators and parents. There are software reviews, articles, cartoons, links to cool sites, direct downloads of shareware and freeware, and live chat. They're careful to offer "family-safe software" and help for parental (read teacher or librarian) control. They graciously offer the "Yahooligans!" search engine from Yahoo! to facilitate location of things of interest to children.

## The WWW Virtual Library

http://www.w3.org/hypertext/DataSources/bySubject/Overview.html

This is a distributed subject catalog, using a variety of ways to take you to Web sites on a great variety of subjects.

# Search Engines

## Alta Vista

http://www.altavista.digital.com/

With this search engine, operated by Digital Equipment Corporation, you have access to nearly eleven billion words found on nearly twenty-two million Web pages. If you wish to search the newsgroups of USENET for pertinent information, there is a full-text index of over thirteen thousand newsgroups updated in real-time. They'll deliver the articles to you too.

## c l net's search.com

http://www.search.com/

> c l net, always innovative, here provides what may best be described as the mother of all Internet search sites. In addition to a number of search engines on the home page, you'll find A-to-Z listings and links to dozens of other more narrowly focused search engines.

## Excite

http://www.excite.com/

> Yet another search engine with a large searchable database. Here are the features it offers:
>
> Web documents—Search the large Web database of more than 11.5 million pages
>
> Reviews—Search a database of over fifty thousand Web site reviews
>
> USENET—Search more than one million articles from ten thousand newsgroups
>
> Classified—Search USENET classified advertisements from the past two weeks.

## Galaxy

http://galaxy.einet.net/www/www.html

> TradeWave Corporation provides a variety of ways to search the World Wide Web. An extensive page of Web topics appears on Galaxy's page at <http://galaxy.einet.net/galaxy.html>. Its more powerful search engine appears at <http://galaxy.einet.net/cgi-bin/wais-text-multi?>. You'll also have a very helpful page full of searchable reference works such as a dictionary, thesaurus, fact book, and links to other search engines and clearinghouses at <http://galaxy.einet.net/search-other.html>.

## Infoseek

http://www.infoseek.com/

Infoseek allows you to browse Web pages, USENET newsgroups, FTP and gopher sites, and more. It offers convenient topic areas to limit the scope of your search and it has graciously provided links to downloading Netscape Navigator, Microsoft Internet Explorer, and Websurfer. It also provides a subscriber service called Infoseek Professional by which you may search through a comprehensive selection of business, computer, and medical information.

## Inktomi

http://inktomi.berkeley.edu/

The Inktomi search engine is "the first fast Web indexer with a large database. Inktomi uses parallel computing technology to build a scalable Web server using commodity workstations; we currently use four SparcStation 10s." Inktomi is part of the Network of Workstations (NOW) project at the University of California at Berkeley.

## Lycos

http://lycos.cs.cmu.edu/

This search engine, operated by Lycos, Inc., claims to have the largest catalog of URLs. It has a directory of the Web's most popular sites, a feature called New2Net, and real-time news links. It is well organized with a list of popular categories to streamline your search.

## Magellan

http://www.mckinley.com/

This search engine is an online directory of reviewed and rated Internet sites. Magellan's reviewers evaluate each site for depth, ease of exploration, and net appeal, and Magellan awards an overall rating of from one to four stars. By performing a search or exploring Magellan topics you can instantly go to a list of sites in your area of interest. Of special value to many of you may be

242

Magellan's "Green Light." A green light appears next to reviewed sites that, at the time of review, contained no content apparently intended for mature audiences.

## MetaCrawler

http://metacrawler.cs.washington.edu:8080/index.html

This may be the most powerful search engine on the Web. The MetaCrawler works by querying a number of existing free search engines, organizes the results into a uniform format, and displays them. With the MetaCrawler, you also have the option of scoring the hits, so that the list displayed can be sorted by a number of different ways, such as by locality, region, and organization. It searches the databases of Open Text, Lycos, WebCrawler, InfoSeek, Excite, Inktomi, Alta Vista, Yahoo!, and Galaxy.

## New Rider's World Wide Web Yellow Pages

http://www.mcp.com/newriders/wwwyp/

This WWW search engine is very efficient and has very good descriptions in its listings.

## Open Text Index

http://www.opentext.com/

Open Text Corporation offers the Open Text Index Internet search engine. You type a word, or a group of words, or a phrase of any length, into a search form. Then the Open Text Index searches every word of every page of the World Wide Web for occurrences of your search terms, and shows you a list of pages that include them. It also lets you link to those pages.

## Starting Point

http://stpt.com/

A Web search engine designed to make your Web experience more productive. It has a well-organized interface for rapid access.

## WebCrawler

http://webcrawler.com

This search tool is one of the best. Type in keywords and let it do the rest. Example: Type "The Civil War" or "home schooling" and watch what happens!

## World Wide Web Worm

http://guano.cs.colorado.edu/wwww/

This search engine at the University of Colorado is well crafted for multiple keyword searches. You can also limit your search to all URL references, URL addresses only, document titles only, or document addresses. Pinpoint location of resources should be easy through the World Wide Web Worm.

## Yahoo!

http://www.yahoo.com

This is one of the first and best-known search engines on the WWW. On its home page, it has a large, well-organized index of areas of interest to allow limited subject-oriented searches. Much can be accomplished with Yahoo! It'll take you there.

## Yahooligans!

http://www.yahooligans.com/

Yahoo! has developed a search engine just for eight- to fourteen-year-olds. The categories on this page are Around the World; School Bell; Art Soup; Science and Oddities; Computers, Games, and Online; Sports and Recreation; Entertainment; and The Scoop.

# Directories: Zip Codes, E-mail, Telephone, 800 Numbers

## AT&T Toll-Free 800 Directory

http://att.net/dir800

A Web page to locate any listed 800 telephone number.

## BigBook

http://www.bigbook.com/

This Web lookup service for businesses is fast and easy to use. Its special feature is its street-level maps, showing the location of the listed business. The maps allow you to zoom in and zoom out, making it easy to plan your route. Very convenient.

## BigYellow

http://s18.bigyellow.com/home_philly.html

This lockup service is provided by NYNEX and contains a database of over sixteen million businesses nationwide.

## Four11 Directory Services

http://www.four11.com/

An e-mail address directory.

## LookUp! Searching

http://www.lookup.com/lookup/search.html

An e-mail address directory.

## LookupUSA

http://www.abii.com/

Throw away the telephone books! At LookupUSA, just type in the name of the business or the person you're looking for into the search engine, select the city and state, and wait a few seconds. I typed

"Waldenbooks," selected Pennsylvania, and got the full addresses and phone numbers for fifty-six stores!

## Switchboard

http://www.switchboard.com/
> A free service of Coordinate.com, Switchboard can be used to look up numbers for people or businesses. Easy, efficient interface.

## U.S. Postal Service ZIP Code Lookup
## and Address Information

http://www.usps.gov/ncsc/
> The U.S. Postal Service does deliver with this efficient ZIP code search form.

# Listservs and Newsgroups

## Deja News

http://www.dejanews.com
> This is the largest collection of indexed archived USENET news anywhere. It has archived the entire USENET. Every post (i.e., item posted on USENET) and follow-up to every newsgroup now resides on fifteen computers. Their search engine allows for comprehensive searches in seconds. I typed in "library" and got 134,917 hits in about two seconds! It's a great way to access information and opinion, and in general get acquainted with USENET.

## Liszt

http://www.liszt.com
> This is a search engine dedicated to finding e-mail discussion groups for every conceivable subject area. Liszt boasts of having 28,643 listserv, listproc, majordomo, and independently managed lists from 757 sites.

## Online Discussion Groups and Electronic Journals

http://k12.cnidr.org:90/lists.html

A gentleman by the name of Andy Carvin has put together a Web page that clearly appears to be the mother lode of addresses for listservs for groups dedicated to education. My evaluation is that if you're into education and you can't find it here, you're too darned particular. Included is a brief tutorial on joining a special interest discussion group mailing list.

## Tile.Net/Lists

http://tile.net/listserv/

This WWW site is a reference to all the listserv discussion groups on the Internet. Please note that tile.net/listserv only contains lists run by listserv. Listproc and majordomo lists are not included, but work is now proceeding to add them.

## USENET Info Center Launch Pad

http://sunsite.unc.edu/usenet-i/

For those wanting to join newsgroups, this is a great place to start. It not only serves as a primer to USENET but also provides vital links to sites everywhere to further your productive use of USENET.

# Reference

## Berkeley Digital Library SunSITE

http://sunsite.berkeley.edu/

This Web site could be a bonanza for librarians and educators of all stripes. The Berkeley Digital Library's stated goal is to provide information and support for those building digital libraries, museums, and archives. It functions as a clearinghouse for texts and graphics in digital form; you can thus access from these pages hundreds if not thousands of electronic texts and graphic images. You will find links to major providers of works of literature in digital form, including great works of poetry, fiction, drama, and philosophy from all eras of human history, from ancient Greece through Chaucer, Shakespeare, on up to today. On their Digital Collections page, there is an entry entitled "Current Cities," which is the complete collection of an annotated monthly bibliography of selected articles, books, and electronic documents on information technology. There seems to be a nearly inexhaustible supply of literature and access to supporting scholarship. The Image Collections contain links to sites for downloading art of all kinds, links to virtual tours of the great art galleries of the world, and information of all kinds on the world of art and graphics. This site is too dense with material to give a proper overview. Go there and spend a few months. As you do, check out the Tools page for downloading software for building electronic libraries. There you will find electronic text readers, utilities, and software for network servers.

## *The Free On-line Dictionary of Computing*

http://wombat.doc.ic.ac.uk/

Here is a dictionary dedicated to every aspect of computing, including its history, jargon, projects, architecture, operating systems, theory, companies, products, and more. If it's about computers and you don't know it, find it out here. Entries typed into the search line yield fast results and the "previous" and "next" words listed with each search will whet your appetite for more knowledge about the intricacies of computing. There is a button on the search bar called "random." Press it to find an explanation of a random word in the dictionary. This may be the equivalent of the chaos theory of education.

## The Homework Page

http://www.tpoint.net/Users/jewels//homework.html

Students shouldn't be disappointed by the title of this page: It won't do your homework for you. It should, however, provide an excellent series of links of value when researching school projects. The collection organizes pointers by category and primarily uses the services of Galaxy, Yahoo!, and the WWW Virtual Library. Consider this a top-flight reference page.

## Internet Public Library

http://ipl.sils.umich.edu/

I was thrilled to find this huge Web site from the School of Information and Library Studies at the University of Michigan. It is a virtual construction of an actual library, with "rooms" and such. There is a reference desk which leads to extensive reference works such as dictionaries, atlases, and encyclopedias, and links to sites to support science, business and economics, education, environment, government and law, health and nutrition, social issues and services, and computers and the Internet. There are divisions for youth, teens, and MOO (Multi-User Object-Oriented environment, an interactive system accessible through telnet by many users at the same time). The library also has rooms called Classroom (with tutorials related to using the Internet including interactive classroom lessons), Exhibit Hall (exhibits of art, photography, etc.), and the Reading Room (books in text and HTML, and magazines, journals, newspapers from around the world). There are services for librarians and help with Web searching. This is the kind of site that can easily make a top-ten list.

## Learning Community

http://www.eworld.com/education/resources/

The Learning Community Web page is a resource for educators, parents, and students. It contains a wide variety of pointers to educational resources across the Internet. This site is a bit commercial, but it offers many fine resources. Its library contains many online reference works, including dictionaries in English, French, German, and Spanish, plus many well-known works such as *Roget's Thesaurus*. There are links to schools and colleges throughout the world.

### Ready Reference Using The Internet

http://k12.oit.umass.edu/rref.html

> This is an A-to-Z guide to full-text and data on the Internet. Librarians and teachers could use this to help patrons and students quickly find information on specified topics.

## Pay Services

### Britannica Online

http://www.eb.com/

> *Encyclopaedia Britannica* is available online on a subscription basis. First, take a guided tour and have a seven-day free trial.

### Electric Library

http://www.elibrary.com

> Here is this commercial venture's own description: "The Electric Library makes it possible to conduct real research over the Internet, using a deep database of reliable sources. Never before has finding the information you need been so fast and so easy! With the Electric Library, any person can pose a question in plain English and launch a comprehensive, simultaneous search through more than one hundred fifty full-text newspapers, nearly eight hundred full-text magazines, two international newswires, two thousand classic books, hundreds of maps, thousands of photographs, as well as major works of literature and art." With access to over one billion words and over twenty-one thousand images, the Electric Library may be a valuable and affordable extension to a library's resources. Before joining the service you can get a free trial which allows one hundred free searches and retrievals over a two-week period.

# Electronic Texts

## Bartleby Library

http://www.columbia.edu/acis/bartleby/

At Columbia University's Web site you'll find another wonderful electronic library. Here are works by celebrated writers such as Dickinson, Shelley, Yeats, Frost, Sandberg, Keats, Wordsworth, Whitman, Melville, D. H. Lawrence, Wilde, Hardy, etc., plus luminaries such as William Strunk and Gertrude Stein. A truly wonderful place.

## Cyber-Seuss

http://www.freenet.ufl.edu/~afn15301/drseuss.html

This Web site is dedicated to Dr. Seuss, his life, and writings. Many of his stories and poems are available in electronic text form, thus providing quick and easy access to a great deal of his work. Some links are provided.

## The Global Electronic Library

gopher://marvel.loc.gov:70/11/global

This gopher menu (accessible via most Web browsers) directs us to extensive collections of electronic text resources around the Internet. The categories include:

Reference
Library Science
Philosophy and Religion
Language, Linguistics, and Literature
The Arts
Social Sciences
Law
Economics and Business
History and Geography
Medicine and Psychology
Natural Science

Mathematics
Applied Science and Technology
Sports and Recreation

Each category takes you to another menu that offers a host of resources on the subject, plus menu links to e-text versions of famous works. You will find a lifetime of reading here without leaving your seat at the computer. Small libraries could double their collections by making this site available to patrons. Teachers on all levels could direct their students to resources on the pertinent subject.

## The Internet Wiretap Directory of Classics

http://wiretap.spies.com/ftp.items/Library/Classic/

Here is a directory full of hundreds of classic works of literature in electronic text form. Download and enjoy. Go back up the directory tree to <http://wiretap.spies.com/> to discover what else is available at this site, formerly called the Wiretap Electronic Text Archive. It has links to other e-text archives.

## The On-line Books Page

http://www.cs.cmu.edu/Web/books.html

Look here for an index of over fifteen hundred online books, and for common repositories of online books and other documents.

## Project Gutenberg

http://miso.wwa.com/~boba/gutenberg.html

There are many ways to get to a site to reach this most extensive of e-text projects; this WWW address was quite reliable. Project Gutenberg has been working on electronic text versions of literary classics for some time now. Search their incredible collection. Project Gutenberg turns any computer into a virtual library.

**Project Gutenberg** (alternate link plus links to other e-text sites)

http://gagme.wwa.com/%7Eboba/gutenberg.html

Project Gutenberg, the original and most prolific of the projects to translate the great literary works of humankind into electronic text format, is a widespread resource. It is available at many places on the Internet, though not every site is well managed or accessible, perhaps due to unreliable servers. Just plug the name into a Web search engine and you'll find many ways to Project Gutenberg. This site was the most functional and organized the last time I looked. Also available at this site is a monster list of sites for electronic text sites all over the place. Go here!

**Spider's Web Etext Page**

http://miso.wwa.com/~boba/etext.html

This is the most extensive, most impressive set of links to electronic texts I've ever seen or can ever imagine. Entering this page is like walking into a library the size of a continent. Bring your reading glasses and a thermos of coffee. This is a must-have bookmark for libraries.

**The WWW Virtual Library**

http://www.w3.org/hypertext/DataSources/bySubject/Literature/
Gutenberg/Overview.html

This site is a series of hypertext links to the ever-expanding collection of electronic texts on the Internet. It's a little overwhelming, but after you begin to surf from this site you won't believe what you can find.

## News/Broadcast

### A&E

http://www.aetv.com

Besides the more mundane resources like TV listings, Biography, Mystery, and the A&E Store, perhaps the most valuable sections of the Arts & Entertainment Network Web site are A&E Classroom at <http://www.aetv.com/aeclassroom/classroom.html> and the History Channel. A&E says: "Programs from A&E make exciting and useful additions to middle school, junior high, and high school curricula. To find out how, follow the links...they lead to resources to help teachers plan classroom discussions and research projects based on A&E's shows. The network also sponsors awards and other programs designed to support quality history education in America's schools." In an area called the History Classroom, links are provided to a host of classroom materials tailored to go along with the programs of the History Channel (they'll gladly mail you teacher's packets if you request them by filling out a simple form on the appropriate Web page). Also available is an extensive calendar of A&E Classroom events throughout the year.

### AP on the Globe Online

http://www.globe.com/globe/cgi-bin/globe.cgi?ap/apnat.htm

Here is a source of stories from the Associated Press, updated hourly.

### Bravo

http://www.bravotv.com

There is more to this site operated by Bravo, "The Film and Arts Network," than just program listings. Especially valuable to English teachers are presentations such as Patrick Stewart (of *Star Trek: The Next Generation*) sharing his thoughts about Shakespeare, or the many offerings in the area of theater and the arts. Also of interest to teachers at the high school level is Bravo in the Classroom, a daily, commercial-free program designed for high school teachers and their classes. Bravo in the Classroom brings you programming and resource material intended to enhance arts and humanities studies for students at the secondary school level. Study guides and classroom materials are available.

## CNN Interactive

http://www.cnn.com

CNN Interactive is just like having a newspaper on a computer in your library or classroom, only this one is updated far more often. There would be no end to current event discussion in any class-room with CNN Interactive available online. There are, however, no specific lesson plans available as with many other network Web sites. But, after all, this is a news network, and almost all of us know how it works and how to use it for best educational advantage. It's important to note that this Web site is available in a text-only version for those without graphical Web browsing ability. Also, there is a search function for older news articles in the CNN database; this would be a boon to students researching current or recent news topics.

## Court TV Law Center

http.//www.courttv.com

Court TV serves as a discussion of legal issues, especially as they impact courtrooms today. Of special interest to librarians and teach-ers is Court TV Kids at <http://www.courttv.com/kids/>. On this page, Court TV provides a legal dictionary, the complete U.S. Con-stitution, and a variety of files on the legal system to give kids a better understanding of the law, including "The Law: What It Is and Where It Comes From," and "How the Courts Are Structured." Of additional interest is a page dedicated to legal topics directly affecting kids at <http://www.courttv.com/kids/law/>. Topics included are "How the Law Treats Kids," "Entering Contracts," "Parental Consent," "Babysitting," "Getting a Job," and "Your Rights at School."

## C-SPAN

http.//www.c-span.org

This Web site keeps you in touch with the goings-on of C-SPAN, the network best known for its coverage of the U.S. Congress, the judiciary, and other political and government matters. Of special interest to educators (mostly on the high school level, but some grade school and middle school teachers may be interested too) is "C-SPAN in the Classroom" at <http://www.c-span.org/ cinc.html>. As the Web page says, "In addition to live, gavel-to-gavel coverage of the U.S. House of Representatives on C-SPAN and the U.S. Senate on C-SPAN 2, both networks offer a variety of other educational programming. Regular programming includes congressional hearings, White House press briefings, National Press Club speeches, 'Booknotes' author interview programs, and the 'Washington Journal,' featuring live viewer call-ins with journalists and public policy-makers." Lesson plans for utilizing C-SPAN are available at <http://www.c-span.org/classroo/lessons.html>.

## Discovery Channel Online

http://www.discovery.com

The Discovery Channel, which has recently been rivaling PBS for educational content in nature, science, history, and military and aviation, maintains this site to provide information on its programming. There's a host of information and articles on its programs which may have direct educational value. In addition, it promotes its catalog of CD-ROM products that could be of great interest to librarians and educators. At Discovery Channel School at <http://school.discovery.com/> you'll find an area devoted to K–12 educational resources and experiences.

## ESPN

http://espnet.sportszone.com/

The well-known sports network provides a very good daily updated sports-oriented Web news magazine.

**The Gate** (*The San Francisco Examiner*
and *The San Francisco Chronicle*)
http://www.sfgate.com/
>The two great dailies of San Francisco team up for one hot site of news, columns, and stories. There are searchable archives of past issues, and all of the things one expects from a quality newspaper.

## History Channel

http://www.historychannel.com/
>This is the home page for the History Channel, an A&E Network enterprise. Of great value is the "Today in History" page at <http://www.historychannel.com/today/>. Also of interest is "Living History" at <http://www.historychannel.com/calendar/calendar.html>, and "History for Kids" at <http://www.historychannel.com/kids/kids.html>.

## *The New York Times* on the Web

http://www.nytimes.com/mhome.html
>Well, it's the *New York Times*.

## News from Reuters Online

http://www.yahoo.com/headlines/
>Read the most recent news stories from Reuters, updated hourly.

## PBS

http://www.pbs.org
>The Web site for the Public Broadcasting System has a very unique feature: a search engine for locating information about a particular series or special. You locate the series or special in the pop-out lists, whether it's "Bill Nye the Science Guy," "Newton's Apple," or "Reading Rainbow," then click; you are taken to the page for that series or special. This Web site can be of help in using PBS programming with your curricula. Also of interest is the PBS Learning Services Page.

## USA Today

http://www.usatoday.com/

USA Today not only provides a top-notch online newspaper, complete with articles and pictures that are updated often, but also provides an articles database search engine which brings up articles on the entered subject and often includes a set of links to other sites on the Internet with information on that subject. This is one great resource for current events research.

# For Kids

### Berit's Best Sites for Children

http://www.cochran.com/theosite/ksites.html

A well-organized set of links for kids, rated for content and suitability for a young audience.

### The Best of Kidopedia

http://rdz.stjohns.edu/kidopedia/

As defined by this site's home page, a "kidopedia is an encyclopedia written by children for children." This site has collected the best articles from kidopedias around the world. A very touching example is an article written by a Kobe High School student a week after the Kobe earthquake. That kind of information isn't always in the dailies.

### CyberKids

http://www.CyberKids.com/

CyberKids, published by Mountain Lake Software, has a kids' art gallery, e-magazine, activities and games sections, music, kids' bulletin board, and a large set of links to other kids' sites on the Web. CyberKids uses a new Netscape plug-in, Shockwave, to play animations and sounds on interactive pages. CyberTeens, a site for older kids, is also headquartered here. Download both Netscape and Shockwave here.

## Interesting Places for Kids

http://www.crc.ricoh.com/people/steve/kids.html

This top-rated site might serve well as a hub for sending children out onto the World Wide Web. Beyond extensive links to sites of interest to kids you'll find advice for parents and all the popular search engines.

## The International Kids' Space

http://plaza.interport.net/kids_space/

This is one delightful site for kids and should be available at every terminal in every children's library. A reassuring note at the top of the home page is: "This site is rated G." You'll find a children's art gallery (where children can submit their own work); a "Story Book" which is "of the Kids, by the Kids, for the Kids"; an On Air Concert where kids can listen to real audio of kids' musical performances from around the world (they can submit their own); a Mail Office to find keypals all over the world and to post questions for other kids to answer (there's even a message box for adults to post their messages); a Web Kids' Village to find kids' home pages; and a set of links called "Kids' Places in Internet." Take your children to the Kids' Place and drop 'em off. They'll be safe here.

## The Internet Explorer...Steve Davidson

http://www.teleport.com/~stdavid/nov2095.shtml

Steve Davidson is a Netscape development partner, senior systems analyst, columnist, and consultant in Salem, Oregon. He has graciously put together a Web site for the sole purpose of alerting everyone to all the fabulous Web sites dedicated to kids and their interests. It's very inviting, with a wide and very childlike selection of sites to explore. I envision a librarian hosting a Saturday afternoon of Internet exploration, or a teacher in some K–6 classroom spending a week of Internet navigation, originating from this singular and loving page. The variety of links is cunning and imaginative: links to dinosaurs, volcanoes, insects, traditional children's stories, space exploration and astronomy sites, games of all kinds, hundreds of schools around the world, and science museums all over the country such as the brilliant Exploratorium in San Francisco.

## Internet for Kids

http://www.internet-for-kids.com/

Take the kids here for a great introduction to the Internet. Children, from babies on up, can learn how to travel the World Wide Web, participate in ongoing story-writing, find keypals, join in fantasy adventures, go to schools on the Net, and have fun with science. Follow the links to game sites, kids' home pages, and many places for kids' learning and enjoyment.

## Kids Internet Delight

http://www.clark.net/pub/journalism/kid.html

This Web site is simply 108 links to sites for kids, plus a Lycos search engine at the bottom of the page for your convenience. For a library or K-6 classroom, this can be a launching page for children's exploration of the Web.

## Kids Web

http://www.npac.syr.edu/textbook/kidsweb/

This page, maintained by Paul Coddington, Northeast Parallel Architectures Center at Syracuse University, is a vast set of resources in the arts (art, drama, literature, music), science (astronomy and space, biology and life sciences, chemistry, computers, environmental science, geology and earth sciences, mathematics, physics, technology, weather and meteorology), and social studies (geography, government, history), with special sections for fun and games, reference materials and sports.

## Oz Kidz Internaut Cyber Centre

http://iccu6.ipswich.gil.com.au/ozkidz/

This great Australian Web site, supported by Ipswich City Council and Global Info-Links, is designed for and by Australian students. As they describe it on their "about" page, "Oz Kidz is an ambitious project geared to allow local, state and national students and teachers the opportunity to access and participate actively in the Digital Information and Communications Revolution currently sweeping the world." There are sections on Australian children's literature and students' writing, and those doing research assignments on Australia will find lots of links to all things Australian. Here we have an inexpensive way to visit Down Under!

## Rad Sites for Young Adults

http://cga.mdpls.lib.fl.us/ya.htm

The Miami-Dade Public Library has organized a page specifically for teens, with links to information on colleges, online books, NASA, sports, computer games, the Teen Page Web site, and literature of all kinds from Shakespeare to science fiction. This might be a great, safe starting point for school librarians to offer their teen patrons.

## Special Sites for Kids

http://www.ipswichcity.qld.gov.au:80/eetint1a.html

This page, hosted by the Information Support Librarian, Ipswich City Council, in Ipswich, Australia, gives a set of links to WWW sites especially of interest to kids. There's a fabulous grab bag of goodies, from Kidopedia to Calvin and Hobbes.

## Uncle Bob's Kids' Page

http://miso.wwa.com/~boba/kidsi.html

This is a page of annotated links, with spotlights on special subjects. It places a special emphasis on "safe surfing," with links to many sites for blocking software, before you get to the actual listings.

# Storytelling

### Jim Maroon's National Storytelling Resources

http://members.aol.com/storypage/index.htm

This home page is dedicated to the art of storytelling, emphasizing the oral tradition where a teller imparts a story to one or more listeners. There's a link to the StoryTell listserv archive, a chat room for storytellers, and resources for storytelling and puppetry.

### Story Resources Available on the Web

http://www.swarthmore.edu/~sjohnson/stories/

In addition to the resources for storytelling, you'll find good links to storytelling organizations and tales from other cultures around the world.

### Tales of Wonder: Folk and Fairy Tales from Around the World

http://www.ece.ucdavis.edu/~darsie/tales.html

This charming site has dozens of tales from Russia, Siberia, Central Asia, China, Japan, the Middle East, Scandinavia, Scotland, England, Africa, and India, as well as Native American tales.

# Keypals

### CyberFriends

http://www.dare.com/fr_main.htm

CyberFriends is the electronic version of traditional pen friendship service, allowing you to find people of your profession and interests and contact them for personal or professional friendship. Lists are maintained by age, gender, nationality, and ethnicity.

## The E-Mail Key Pal Connection

http://www.comenius.com/keypal/index.html

Service matches people all over the world with others who want to exchange mail. Within a week of filling out the survey, you should receive a list of several potential keypals.

## Heinemann Keypal Contacts

http://www.reedbooks.com.au/heinemann/global/keypal.html

At this Web site, you can find keypals from around the world. You can also post a message so that people can seek you out. Nicely divided into different sections: individuals, teachers, and classes, grades K–8; and teachers and classes, grades 9–12.

## Keypals International

http://www.collegebound.com/keypals/

This service is focused on connecting high-school-aged children to international keypals.

## Looking for Keypals

http://ietn.snunit.k12.il/keypals.htm

Links to Israeli keypals.

## Pitsco Launch to Keypals

http://www.pitsco.com/pitsco/keypals.html

Pitsco offers listservs and WWW sites for keypals.

## Rigby Keypal Contacts

http://www.reedbooks.com.au/rigby/global/keypal.html#individ

This Web site is organized very much like the Heinemann pages. There are scores of listings for locating keypals around the world. You may also post your own messages.

# Arts

## The Arts Archive

http://pmwww.cs.vu.nl/archive/images/arts/.html/

A site of fine art to rival WebMuseum. It is maintained by Vrije University in the Netherlands.

## Asian Arts

http://www.webart.com/asianart/index.html

This is an extraordinary site for the appreciation of Asian art. There are current exhibits from countries of Asia, articles to read on the subject of Asian art, online Asian art galleries, a set of links to other sites on the subject, and an Internet Relay Chat with site editors and visitors. Here you'll find a rich and warm experience.

## Paintings of Vermeer

http://www.ccsf.caltech.edu/~roy/vermeer/index.html

Here is the largest collection of the paintings of Vermeer I've yet found on the Web. Along with some history of the famous Dutch painter, you'll be able to view and download an exceptional variety of images of his paintings. A nice feature of this site is a clickable map that will tell you the locations of museums where you can go to see the real thing.

## WebMuseum

http://www.emf.net/wm/

The WebMuseum, coordinated from Paris by Nicholas Pioch, brings us the art of the world in one unbelievable site. It's absolutely astounding. There are special exhibits from time to time on all kinds of art from around the world and throughout history, as well as the vast collection of the famous paintings of Europe and America. This is a must-visit site, if there is one, on the Internet.

## World Art Treasures

http://sgwww.epfl.ch/berger/intro.html

Here you'll find a Web site in Lausanne, Switzerland, dedicated to art and beauty. The one hundred thousand slides belonging to the Jacques-Edouard Berger Foundation, which come from Egypt, China, Japan, India, and Europe, provide wonderful, rotating resources to browse, download, and enjoy. There is more than just a representation of the fine arts here, for you'll find photographic representation of the great historical cultures of the world as well. In addition to the featured programs, the site has a convenient search engine to locate the subject area you're most interested in. The site also has a French-language version.

## World Wide Arts Resources

http://wwar.com/default.html

The art and art information available at this site is astounding. Its best feature may be its search engine. I typed in "japan" and received dozens of links including some to online art galleries in Japan. Next of great interest is the artists' index which contains over six thousand names with links to their history and works. Here you will also find current information on art exhibitions and festivals, U.S. museums, performance art, arts education, art agencies, commercial art, and all the links you need to keep you, your patrons or students busy in pursuit of the artistic for days to come.

# Language Arts

## The Allan K. Smith Writing Center

http://www.trincoll.edu/writcent/aksmith.html

If writing well is the goal, this Web site run by Trinity College in Hartford, Connecticut, is well constructed to help meet that goal. The writing resources available run the gamut: *Roget's Thesaurus*,

Strunk's *Elements of Style*, *Bartlett's Familiar Quotations*, Literary and Rhetorical Terms, Writers' Workshop On-Line Handbook (Bibliography Styles and Grammar), Technical Writing Online Textbook, English as a Second Language Home Page, the Human-Languages Page, and How to Cite Electronic Sources. Their research tools provide links to many great online electronic libraries. There are teaching resources and the usual links to other subject-related Web sites.

## *Bartlett's Familiar Quotations*

http://www.columbia.edu/acis/bartleby/bartlett/

The famous book of quotations has been turned into a searchable database of hundreds of famous authors. A marvelous feature is its list of primary authors. Click on a name and you're taken to a page of that author's familiar quotations. Then, in many cases, you can click on the title of the work the quotation is drawn from and get the full text of the work.

## *The Elements of Style*

http://www.cc.columbia.edu/acis/bartleby/strunk/

This seminal treatise on the correct use of English lives on, this time in complete online form. A rich resource to introduce to your patrons or students. Click anywhere on the HyperText of the table of contents and find out how not to abuse the English language.

## "A Funeral Elegy," newly discovered work by William Shakespeare

http://mbhs.bergtraum.k12.ny.us/cybereng/ebooks/elegy.htm

This site presents the newly discovered poem by Shakespeare, found thirteen years ago but just now being accepted by scholars. The full text is here, plus a very interesting discussion on the *Newshour* about the find. Also, there is a link to critical analysis. This page would be of interest to any teacher or admirer of Shakespeare and could make an interesting unit for a high school English class.

## On-line English Grammar

http://www.edunet.com/english/grammar/index.html

Here we have an online grammar and style guide. You can look through the various topics to find the answer to that obscure point of grammar or you may submit a question to be answered by a professional teacher from the Lydbury English Centre. By all accounts, there is an exhaustive presentation of the elements of English grammar, designed for ease of use. Don't wonder if you're right, come here and find out.


## Quotations

http://www.lexmark.com/data/quote.html

If you're looking for an amusing or edifying quote, you will no doubt find one here. Though the site contains 5,305 quotations at present, there's no apparent search engine for specific quotations. But the handy categorization will lead you closer to what you're looking for. Just browsing could stimulate many a dull class or help you locate essay or discussion topics. Also, the links to other sources of quotations around the Web will take you to places that can help you locate that long-lost quote you've been trying to remember.


## The Works of the Bard

http://www.gh.cs.usyd.edu.au/~matty/Shakespeare/

Matty Farrow of Australia has graciously constructed a search facility that allows the location of words and lines from any of the works of William Shakespeare. He also provides e-text and HTML versions of the Bard's plays and poetry, plus links to other Shakespeare Web sites.

# History

## Gateway to World History

http://neal.ctstateu.edu/history/world_history/index.html

Gateway to World History provides resources to support the study and teaching of world history and history in general. It has archives of documents relevant to the study of history, search engines to locate Internet resources, a topically and geographically organized tree of links for history, a list of e-mail discussion groups dedicated to history, an online reference section, and much more.

## History (Social Studies)

http://galaxy.einet.net/galaxy/Social-Sciences/History.html

A Web page set up with dozens of links for the study of history.

## Monticello

http://www.monticello.org

This Web site, managed by the Thomas Jefferson Memorial Foundation, Inc., takes you through "A Day in the Life" of Jefferson at his beloved home, Monticello. In "Matters of Fact," older students and adults can browse a clickable index to find information on a variety of matters relating to Jefferson. There is also a page on how to plan a visit to the famous memorial in Virginia.

## Notable Citizens of Planet Earth

http://www.tiac.net/users/parallax/

This Web site hosts biographical information on over eighteen thousand people from ancient times to the present day. These are the notable men and women who have shaped our world. Information contained in the site's dictionary includes birth and death years, professions, positions held, literary and artistic works, awards, and other achievements.

## Today in History

http://www.unison.com/wantinfo/today

A nice little site for getting "today in history" facts, useful in providing students with journal or other writing projects. A link allows you to arrange to receive "Today in History" daily via e-mail.

## The United States Civil War Center

http://www.cwc.lsu.edu

This Web site is the only comprehensive Civil War research center in existence. Its area of interest includes all aspects of the Civil War and Reconstruction. Its stated mission is to locate, index, and/or make available all appropriate private and public data regarding the Civil War, and to promote the study of the Civil War from the perspectives of all academic disciplines, professions, and occupations. The following are additional Civil War sites, not connected with the above center, but listed here for your convenience:

http://www.acess.digex.net/~bdboyle/cw.htm

http://cobweb.utcc.utk.edu/~hoemanm/warweb.html

http://esu3.esu3.K12.ne.us/districts/millard/centmidd/
     central.html

http://rs6loc.gov/timeline.html

# Mathematics

## Eisenhower National Clearinghouse

http://enc.org/

The Eisenhower National Clearinghouse sponsors this site designed to help K–12 educators improve teaching and learning in science and mathematics education. The monthly "Digital Dozen" highlights the latest and best resources in these subject areas, and there's a huge array of links to interesting spots all over the Web.

## The Math Forum

http://forum.swarthmore.edu

The hosts of this site at Swarthmore University describe it as "a virtual center for math education on the Internet," and they are not incorrect in their description. This site is a well-organized set of resources for mathematics from kindergarten through college. In each of twenty-three categories of math subjects, the Forum presents classroom materials for teachers and students, software for each subject (sometimes downloadable, sometimes in review form), Internet projects, and public forum links for the discussion of each subject. There is also an "Ask Dr. Math" connection, in which K–12 teachers and students can submit problems to experts and receive personal answers. The Math Forum has pages dedicated to discussion and analysis of the major innovations and concerns in the math world today. As with any top site, there are links to subject-related resources all over the Internet, and subject-dedicated search tools.

## Mathematics Archives WWW server

http://archives.math.utk.edu/

A set of links to mathematics shareware (both Mac and PC) and teaching materials sites. The primary emphasis is on materials which are used in the teaching of mathematics. Currently, the Archives is particularly strong in its collection of educational software. Other areas, ranging from laboratory notebooks and problem sets to lecture notes and reports on innovative methods, are growing. This is the strongest site for mathematics yet found, with materials from kindergarten to college. It also offers a powerful search engine to locate shareware programs.

# Science

## Dino Russ's Collection of Dino GIFs

http://denr1.igis.uiuc.edu:/isgsroot/dinos/GIFs_path.html

A site with dozens of high-quality dinosaur graphics to download.

## The Dinosauria: Truth Is Stranger Than Fiction

http://ucmp1.berkeley.edu/diapsids/dinosaur.html

A Web site operated by the University of California at Berkeley. This site is mostly informational, but what great information it is! And the organization of the information is great, too, as it both explains what dinosaurs are and explores the myths surrounding dinosaurs from a scientific rather than a cultist view. As with many good sites, this has a great set of links to other dinosaur sites as well as ones relating to geology. There's even a search engine to look through their vertebrate catalog of dinosaur holdings.

## Dino-Trekking: The Ultimate Dinosaur Lover's Travel Guide

http://www.bridge.net/~gryphon/dino/

This is a Web page to advertise the above-entitled book. Though it may be a worthy title, the best thing about this page is its list of links to interesting dinosaur sites. It may be a good starting point for info, activities, lesson plans, and units about dinosaurs.

## The Earth Times

http://www.igc.apc.org/earthtimes/

This is the Web site for a newspaper concerned with environmental and population issues. You can browse recent issues. It has a full-text search of its library. The entry "population" turned up ninety-seven articles in about three seconds. A great site for researching and teaching environmental issues. It can be a rich resource on current trends in the field.

## Eisenhower National Clearinghouse

http://enc.org/

> The Eisenhower National Clearinghouse sponsors this site designed to help K–12 educators improve teaching and learning in science and mathematics education. The monthly "Digital Dozen" highlights the latest and best resources in these subject areas, and there's a huge array of links to interesting spots all over the Web.

## Funky Dinosaur Land

http://www.comet.net/dinosaur/

> This Web site is dedicated to dinosaur lovers. It has some great downloadable graphics and links to wonderful resources and activities. There are links to articles, art, tours, museums, references, and other things amounting to a gargantuan set of information. A great aid for a dinosaur unit.

## Global Change Ask Home Page

http://ask.gcdis.usgcrp.gov:8080/

> If you want to find out what's going on with the Earth's environment, come to this page managed by the U.S. government. A vast database of information is provided and the search engine is powerful and efficient. There is also a list of "canned queries" for instant information on dozens of common environmental topics.

## Gordon's Entomological Home Page

http://www.ex.ac.uk/~gjlramel/welcome.html

> If you want to learn about insects, or "mini-beasts" as Gordon calls them, visit this site in Britain designed for kids and schools. There's a nice mixture of information and humor about all things entomological. Check out the page called "Caring for Your Pet Invertebrates!" There are also links to subject areas this man finds interesting. So may you.

## Invention Dimension

http://web.mit.edu//invent/

The Invention Dimension highlights a different American inventor every week with a biographical sketch covering his or her accomplishments and impact on society. Subjects will range from historical figures such as Benjamin Franklin, the inventor of the lightning rod and Franklin stove, to living legends such as Steve Jobs and Steve Wozniak, the brains behind the original Apple computer. This site could be an entertaining resource for teachers attempting to instill in their students the tremendous importance of creative and innovative thinking. The people at this site couldn't help themselves and have added a few links of interest to kids of all ages, which they call "Sites for kids and the kid in all of us." They also provide information on copyrights, patents, and resources for inventors.

## The Mad Scientist Network!

http://pharmdec.wustl.edu/YSP/MAD.SCI/MAD.SCI.html

These scientific experts advertise themselves as the "collective crania of scientists worldwide," answering the science questions of students of all ages every day over the Web. Visitors can submit questions; the Network promises an answer in seven to ten days.

## The Nanoworld Home Page

http://www.uq.oz.au/nanoworld/nanohome.html

As the people at the University of Queensland, Australia, put it, "The Centre for Microscopy and Microanalysis is an interdisciplinary research and service facility dedicated to an understanding of the structure and composition of all materials at atomic, molecular, cellular, and macromolecular scales." In other words, you'll find some really, really close-up shots of diamonds, human hair, insects, etc., at this site dedicated to taking a closer look at the world. This is fascinating stuff and will be of interest to many, many people. The images are often of very high quality.

## The NASA Home Page

http://www.gsfc.nasa.gov/NASA_homepage.html

The National Aeronautics and Space Administration's Web site will let you learn all about this exciting agency's activities and projects on Earth and in space. There is a gallery of downloadable space photos, a questions-and-answers page where you can learn all about the science of flight, and a links page to various NASA centers across the nation. There are other areas to explore such as aeronautics, space science, NASA's Mission to Planet Earth, technology development, and more.

## The National Wildlife Federation

http://www.igc.apc.org/nwf/

This Web site, maintained by the nation's largest member-supported conservation group, provides information on issues and trends in conservation, lesson plans for teachers, an online library of reports and publications on the subject, online games and riddles for kids, and news of NWF's activities across the country.

## Sea World

http://www.bev.net/education/SeaWorld/homepage.html

Sea World and Busch Gardens offer this Web site full of facts and education aids for teaching about animals and aquatic life. There is information on the educational programs available at the various Sea World parks in California, Florida, Texas, and Ohio. Also available are teachers' guides on dolphins, orca, whales, manatees, gorillas, and walruses. For interested students, there is career information on zoology, marine mammal science, and oceanography.

## Sierra Club, One Earth, One Chance

http://www.sierraclub.org/

The site on the Web for the Sierra Club, the nonprofit, member-supported group which works toward conservation of the natural environment. Stay abreast of current threats to ecosystems and such.

There is an extensive page of links to other environmental resources on the Web.

## Tornadoes, by Cory Forsyth

http://cc.usu.edu/~kforsyth/tornadoframes.html

You can put together a nice little unit on tornadoes by visiting this site full of information on one of the United States' own peculiar and devastating weather phenomena. There are links to other sites about tornadoes and weather.

## The Weather Unit

http://faldo.atmos.uiuc.edu/WEATHER/weather.html

A series of lesson plans for various school grades, designed to teach about the weather. Lesson plans are available about weather as it pertains to math, social studies, science, geography, art, music, drama, and many other subjects, with ideas for field trips and classroom props.

## Welcome to Mount St. Helens

http://volcano.und.nodak.edu/vwdocs/msh/msh.html

This web site has over 1,490 still images of the volcano before, during, and after the eruption; it includes a living laboratory curriculum for the classroom. This could be a marvelous way of presenting volcanoes to students of all ages.

## Welcome to the Planets

http://stardust.jpl.nasa.gov:80/planets/

Here you'll find a collection of many of the best images from NASA's planetary exploration program, along with information on its famous space probes such as *Mariner*, *Voyager*, *Viking*, *Magellan*, *Galileo*, the Hubble space telescope, and the space shuttle. Along with the wonderful images, information on each planet is given. This is a great way to take your patrons or students on a guided tour of the solar system.

## Welcome to WebScience

http://marple.as.utexas.edu:80/~WebSci/

This very well-designed Web page, by Todd McDowell's sixth-grade class at Zavala Elementary School in Austin, Texas, for adventures in science could easily be a model for student Web projects. There are links to all kinds of science projects and resources. In addition, read the students' journals and pictures or have a real-time video chat with them using your CU-SeeME conferencing software.

## The Yuckiest Site on the Internet

http://www.nj.com/yucky/

The people at New Jersey Online challenge anyone to come up with a grosser, more disgusting collection than Cockroach World, which details more than you ever wanted to know about cockroaches. The site includes everything there is to know about everyone's least favorite—they say misunderstood—household guest. It's great science—and great fun.

# Government

## Government and Politics

http://galaxy.einet.net/galaxy/Government.html
http://gnn.com/gnn/wic/govt.toc.html

These are great sites from which to begin studies in government and politics.

## Library of Congress

http://lcweb.loc.gov/

The home page of the U.S. Library of Congress.

## Thomas: Legislative Information on the Internet

http://thomas.loc.gov/home/thomas.html
   This WWW page is a direct link to the activities of the U.S. Congress.

## U.S. Constitution

http://lcweb2.loc.gov:8080/constquery.html
http://www.hax.com/USConstitution.html
   Here are two sites for the study of the U.S. Constitution.

# Social Studies

## Index of Native American Resources on the Internet

http://hanksville.phast.umass.edu/misc/NAresources.html
   This Web page is a set of links to Native American culture, art, music, education, history, and archaeology, with links to other home pages for Native Americans. There is even a link to a Web site for Australian Aboriginal studies. This site has been rated ten out of ten by the Lynx of the Week List, and was rated four stars by Magellan.

## Lesson Plans and Resources for Social Studies Teachers

http://www.csun.edu/~hcedu013/
   Dr. Marty Levine, professor of Secondary Education, California State University, Northridge, has gathered lesson plans and resources from the Internet which social studies teachers will find useful. These materials are presented by sections. Select from the list to go directly to that section.

## NetNoir

http://www.netnoir.com/
   NetNoir describes its mission thusly: "The content/information is presented in such a way that anyone, from any walk of life, that

has any interest in Afrocentric culture, can participate in NNO. It is inviting, friendly, welcoming and global." They have a search engine that is dedicated to African-American interests; their "Spotlights" page is designed somewhat like a magazine; and their links page is well organized. NetNoir is an inclusive and intelligent site.

## Social Studies School Service

http://socialstudies.com/

Social Studies School Service searches out high-quality supplementary learning materials, including books, CD-ROMs, videos, laser discs, software, charts, and posters. This site provides links to social studies sites on the Web, free print catalogs, and free teacher's guides and write-ups about the service's products.

# Travel and Geography

## City.Net

http://www.city.net/

City.Net is a comprehensive guide to communities around the world. There are links to every aspect of culture for more than two cities and eight thousand locations online. Libraries and classrooms could use this site as a starting point for cultural, geographic, and language projects of all kinds.

## MapQuest! Interactive Atlas

http://www.mapquest.com/

With this interactive street guide, brought to you by GeoSystems Global Corporation, you get access to maps of anywhere in the world. You'll find such great cities of the world as Bangkok, Beijing, Belfast, Berlin, Buenos Aires, Cairo, Chicago, Dublin, Geneva, Honolulu, Johannesburg, London, Madrid, Mexico City, Moscow, New York, Oslo, Paris, Rio de Janeiro, Rome, San Francisco, Sydney,

Taipei, Vancouver, and more. Interactively click on a map to zoom in from a continental view to any of ten levels down to street view, or pan in any direction. I zoomed from a North American view down to my own street corner. Free membership allows you to add your own points of interests on maps and save them for future visits. Another feature is TripQuest!, which provides city-to-city driving directions in the continental United States, Canada, and Mexico.

## The Virtual Tourist

http://www.vtourist.com:80/webmap/
This site directs you to information of all kinds and links to WWW servers in countries and cities around the world. You can peruse train schedules, hotel and motel listings, local Web pages of interest, and anything in general which will provide you with a virtual tour of a locale or help you prepare for an actual trip.

## Welcome to *CIA World Factbook*

http://www.research.att.com/cgi-wald/dbaccess/411
This Web site offers access to the complete 1993 edition of the *CIA World Factbook*, a storehouse of information about the world and its countries. It provides a very efficient search engine. The depth of information available is impressive. This is geographic information only a few keystrokes and a second away.

## Foreign Language

## The Association des Bibliophiles Universels

http://web.cnam.fr/ABU/
This is a site for locating e-texts in the French language, with links to Project Gutenberg English e-texts as well.

## Le Coin des Francophones et Autres Grenouilles

http://web.cnam.fr/fr/

This is an award-winning site to be enjoyed by French speakers. You'll find practical information about France and other topics, including the arts, education, sports, French software, genealogy, and libraries in France.

## Ejercicios de gramática española

http://www.artsci.wustl.edu/~jrdearan/ejercicios.html

Juan Ramón de Arana, professor of Spanish at Washington University of St. Louis, developed these lessons for use in his courses and offers them to teachers and others interested in the Spanish language.

## German for Beginners

http://castle.UVic.CA/german/149/

This is an online introductory course on German, with exercises, materials, and dictionaries.

## Grammar of German

http://www.wm.edu/CAS/modlang/grammnu.html

Gary Smith of the College of William and Mary presents a resource to help you learn or review German grammar. Study on your own or, if you're a teacher, use this site to reinforce your teaching.

## Intercultural E-Mail Classroom Connections

http://www.stolaf.edu/network/iecc/

Would you like to hook up your foreign language class with keypals in another country? Here's the place to make the connection, whether it's for higher education or K–12 intercultural activities or projects. There are also discussion groups and mailing lists for student and teacher projects.

## Japanese Language Information

http://www.mickey.ai.kyutech.ac.jp/cgi-bin/japanese

This Japanese-language site, maintained in Kyushu, Japan, by Brazilian graduate student Rafael Santos, is a cornucopia of services and resources. There are online dictionaries, both English-Japanese and Japanese-English, as well as an online *kanji* (Chinese characters used in Japanese) server that allows interactive, configurable quizzing and reviewing of *kanji*, *hiragana* (syllabary for Japanese words and conjugations), and *katakana* (syllabary for foreign words and names). Among the scores of resources are links to Japanese-language software, reviews of books and dictionaries, and links to much Japanese information. A top-notch site for Japanese language and culture. Due to the maintainer's internationalism, you'll also find information and reviews of books for the study of Portuguese, French, Spanish, Italian, and German.

## The Language 3 Initiative at Penn State

http://mickey.la.psu.edu/lang3/welcome.htm

This foreign-language resource site has hundreds of links to resources for the study and appreciation of dozens and dozens of languages, from aboriginal languages to Yiddish.

## Web Spanish Lessons

http://www.willamette.edu/~tjones/Spanish/Spanish-main.html

Lessons in Mexican Spanish.

## Yamada Language Center Non-English Font Archive

http://babel.uoregon.edu/Yamada/fonts.html

Have you been looking for a font in Croatian, Japanese, or Morse code? Look no further. You'll find dozens of foreign-language fonts for Mac and Windows.

### You Too Can Learn French!

http://www.teleglobe.ca/~leo/french.html

This site, put together by a Frenchman in Montreal, Quebec, Canada, provides a Web course on French, neatly divided into well-organized lessons supported by wave audio files (digitally recorded real audio) to guide your pronunciation. The emphasis, of course, is on learning to read and write French. You are also provided with a link to The French Page at Appalachian State University (<http://www.acs.appstate.edu/~griffinw/website/french.html>), where you'll find many more resources to study French.

## Health

### Boston University Medical Center's Community Outreach Health Information System

http://web.bu.edu/COHIS/

Here you'll find a far-reaching site on health issues. Of special interest is the "Kids Corner," where children can pose questions to "Dr. Charlie" and learn more about health.

### KidsHealth.org

http://kidshealth.org/

This award-winning site is especially designed for children to access health information and learn more about their bodies and feelings. It is neatly divided into sections for kids, parents, and professionals. Kids will find the answers to many mystifying questions, and parents will welcome the wealth of information on the many health issues they face while raising a family. Professionals are equally rewarded with a host of resources concerning children's health.

## The Massachusetts Library and Information Network

http://www.mlin.lib.ma.us/

This Web page is a guide to the library resources of Massachusetts. Of great value is the Massachusetts Health Reference Institute page, which includes links to the following: national organizations and agencies, university-based health resources, association resources, commercial resources, electronic journals, and selected topical reference areas.

## Guidance/Career

### Claitor's Law Books and Publishing Division

http://www.claitors.com/

Bob Claitor presents Government Printing Office books and links to law books, law libraries, and a mixed bag of choices, including Louisiana Cajun cookbooks, travel books, retirement books, and others. Visit this unusual site to get hard-to-find GPO titles.

## Clip Art, Fonts, Graphics, and Desktop Publishing

### Barry's Clip Art Server

http://www4.clever.net/graphics/clip_art/clipart.html

Barry hopes to be your one-stop source for clip art of all kinds. There are some very interesting types here: clip art for chemistry, sports, cartoons, medicine, railroads, and more. You'll find color and black-and-white clip art. With the many, many links to other clip art sites on the Web, it seems Barry is not far from his goal. If it's clip art you want, you'll find it here.

### Classroom Connect's Clip Art Subdirectory

ftp://ftp.classroom.net/wentworth/Clip-Art/
Classroom Connect offers an A-to-Z set of clip art subdirectories at
its FTP site, plus a few choice graphics utilities for Windows and
Mac platforms, such as Paint Shop Pro and JPEGView.

### Clipart Collection Server

http://leviathan.tamu.edu:70/1s/clipart
An extensive collection of clip art in many areas valuable to education including science, maps, music, nutrition, agriculture, farm-
ing, food, etc. This is actually a set of links to different clip art sites.

### IncWell Clip Art Library

http://www.autobaun.com/~kbshaw/Dick/IncWellArt.html
This is a site operated by *Spectrum*, an online magazine. It features
very high-quality black-and-white clip art, downloadable in groups
as GIF files. This clip art can be used by anyone for any purpose
other than resale.

### San Francisco State University Multimedia & Clipart

http://itec.sfsu.edu/multimedia/multimedia.html
A great set of links to graphics, icons, clip art, sounds, QuickTime
video, music, art, and miscellaneous other stuff.

### Terry Gould's Graphics

http://www.netaccess.on.ca/~kestrel/list3.html
A broad selection of bullets, buttons, and icons reside on this graphics home page. A click of a mouse will take you to this site's pictures page, where you'll find scores of pictures in categories like
nature, music, fantasy and space, and cartoons and comics. Clicking on the button "Many Other Links" takes you to Terry Gould's
Image Strands, a set of links to fifty-one sites for GIFs, JPEGs, icons,
buttons, and clip art. This is a major graphic resource on the WWW.

## Yahoo! Computers and Internet: Multimedia: Pictures

http://www.yahoo.com/Computers/Multimedia/Pictures/

A combination search engine and menu of graphics of all kinds including animals, aviation, clip art, fine art, people, space and astronomy, icons, fractals, flags, and more. There are links upon links upon links. Watch out for "Supermodels" links; they lead to some pretty risqué graphics, so please supervise student access.

## Yahoo! Fonts Page

http://www.yahoo.com/Computers_and_Internet/
Desktop_Publishing/Fonts/

Yahoo! page for links to PC and Windows Type 1 and TrueType fonts, in English and other languages.

## Yamada Language Center Non-English Font Archive

http://babel.uoregon.edu/Yamada/fonts.html

Been looking for a font in Croatian, Japanese, or Morse code? Look no further. You'll find dozens of foreign language fonts for Mac and Windows.

# Books

## BBD Online

http://www.bdd.com/

The online service of Bantam-Doubleday-Dell.

## BookWire

http://www.bookwire.com

BookWire is a site dedicated to books. It boasts that it is "The first place to look for book information on the World Wide Web." It does have a wonderful set of resources for books including: *Computer*

*Book Review, Publishers Weekly, The Boston Book Review, The Hungry Mind Review, The Quarterly Black Review of Books*, book awards, and Mort Gerberg's Cartoon Gallery. You will also find an index of categorized listings for booksellers and publishers, plus the BookWire Reading Room, with direct links to electronic texts in the public domain. There are literally hundreds of books available for download. Additionally, there are links to a lot of information about goings-on in the book industry.

### The Boston Book Review

http://www.bookwire.com/bbr/bbr-home.html

In addition to a searchable database of book reviews organized by title, author, or reviewer, this online review of books offers articles, letters to the editor, and a "Who Wrote It?" quiz. Its pages are well organized into sections like Arts & Diversions, Fiction & Criticism, and Children's Corner. This is a rich resource for the literary world.

### Harcourt Brace & Company Home Page

http://www.harcourtbrace.com/

The company's home page has links to all the imprints in the family, including Holt Rinehart Winston, Academic Press, and W.B. Saunders.

### HarperCollins Publishers

http://www.harpercollins.com/

The home page for the publisher allows you to take an online tour of the publishing house and its various imprints, browse through its catalogs, or see full pages on many of its current titles. Here you can read news about forthcoming book tours, scan the bestsellers and new releases, and find complete ordering information about dozens of its products and services.

## The Internet Book Shop

http://www.bookshop.co.uk/

This Oxford, England, site claims to be the largest online bookshop in the world (with a searchable database of over seven hundred eighty thousand titles). It primarily features English-language books from European publishers such as Penguin, etc., but this may be a great way of locating titles of interest for your library or class. The site is nicely organized and easy to browse. If you like books, it's hard to get away. Books are listed by publisher or subject. You can order books from two English wholesalers, a Dutch bookshop, or directly from the publisher via this site. Complete ordering details are provided. Don't forget to take a virtual tour of Oxford while you're there!

## Yahoo!: Publishing

http://www.yahoo.com/Business_and_Economy/Companies/Publishing/

Yahoo! provides a search engine dedicated to publishers, plus a subject tree to narrow your search.

# Software

## Adobe Acrobat Reader Download Site

http://w1000.mv.us.adobe.com/Acrobat/readstep.html

Adobe Acrobat software lets you create electronic documents from a wide range of authoring tools to share across different computer platforms. Simply "print" files in the Adobe Portable Document Format (PDF). Now you can distribute your documents over the broadest selection of electronic media, including the World Wide Web, e-mail, Lotus Notes, corporate networks, CD-ROMs, and print-on-demand systems. Send a PDF file and a free copy of Acrobat Reader to Macintosh, Windows, DOS, or UNIX users, and they can view or print the document with the hardware and software they already have. There are versions available for every conceivable platform, including Windows, Mac, DOS, UNIX, etc. It is also available in eight languages.

## Microsoft

http://www.microsoft.com

The Web site of Microsoft offers information on products, online support, guides, and downloads of many free programs, updates, patches, and drivers. Among the important free software programs are the Internet Explorer Web browser and Internet Assistant, which turns Microsoft Word for Windows 6.0 into a Web page designer. There are many FAQ (Frequently Asked Questions) documents on a myriad of subjects. Use the search feature to find the product or information you desire.

## Netscape

http://home.netscape.com

Netscape, the leading producer of tools for browsing and utilizing the World Wide Web, has made its premier Web browser, Netscape Navigator for Windows/Windows 95 and Macintosh, available to students, educators, and librarians free of charge. Netscape Navigator brings Web exploration, e-mail, newsgroups, gopher, and FTP right to your fingertips with all the state-of-the-art refinements and capabilities together in one package. To take advantage of this generosity, visit Netscape's Web site and download the software directly.

## SoftKey International

http://www.softkey.com/

This excellent source of low-cost, quality CD-ROM products accurately says of itself: "SoftKey International ranks as the nation's number-one producer of CD-ROM software based on consumer purchases. Headquartered in Cambridge, Massachusetts, SoftKey serves its retail partners through five national and five international sales offices. More than half of its current product registry was developed in-house; additional titles are licensed or acquired through selective product-outsourcing programs. With leading-edge technologies, ground-breaking prices, and innovative merchandising programs, SoftKey International is the leading electronic publisher of consumer software worldwide." SoftKey's educational program has just been transferred to its new acquisition, The Learning Company, producers of well-known educational software such as *The Writing Center, Reader Rabbit, Math Rabbit,* and others. Programs are available for writing and publishing, math problem solving, reading and language arts, science problem solving, test preparation, and foreign languages. You can contact The Learning Company at <http://www.learningco.com/>.

## Welcome to QuickTimeVR

http://qtvr.quicktime.apple.com/

QuickTime VR allows you to experience virtual reality on your computer. You don't need an expensive, high-powered graphics workstation, and you don't have to wear goggles and gloves. You navigate with a mouse and keyboard. The program that allows you to experience this new form of graphics is downloadable free of charge for Macintosh and Windows. Also, sample scenes are available for download. Scenes are virtual reality spaces. You can look up and down, turn around, zoom in to see detail, or zoom out for a broader view. Come here to check out the future of computer graphics. (This is also a place to find the original QuickTime video player program for Macintosh and Windows.)

# Shareware and Freeware

### AntiVirus Resources

http://www.primenet.com/~mwest/av.htm

This Web home page by Mark West acts as a clearinghouse for antivirus information and software. It's a good site for keeping abreast of issues concerning computer safety and security. It has links to the major developers of antivirus software.

### The Association of Software Professionals

http://www.asp-shareware.org/

The ASP is a not-for-profit association of software producers, distributors, BBSs, and users formed with the goal of promoting the shareware concept of marketing software. Its home page has links to various members' and authors' home pages, links to catalogs of shareware, and links for direct downloads of members' shareware. This is some of the most reliable shareware available.

### c l net Resources Software Central

http://www.cnet.com/Resources/Software/index.html

Come here to access DOWNLOAD.COM and shareware.com, the new services from c l net: The Computer Network. Shareware.com replaces the Virtual Software Library (VSL) search engine previously offered by c l net. You can search for, browse, and download the best software—including freeware, shareware, corporate software, and more. This page is quite helpful to the shareware novice.

### CSUSM (California State University at San Marcos' Windows Shareware Archive)

http://coyote.csusm.edu/cwis/winworld/winworld.html

Another amazing site for Windows shareware. It has its own search engine; it also has HyperText links at the top of its home page for downloading PKZIP, the preeminent compression tool for unzipping compressed PC files that are found on the Internet, and the VBASIC files that are required by many Windows shareware programs in order to run; the home page also features a list of categories of various shareware to streamline your search.

## Disinfectant

ftp://ftp.acns.nwu.edu/pub/disinfectant/

This is the FTP site (accessible by most Web browsers) where you can download this top-rated freeware antiviral program for the Macintosh.

## Disinfectant and Gatekeeper

http://www.cc.umanitoba.ca/mrc/macvirus.html

This is the Web page where you can download either of these well-respected antiviral programs for the Macintosh.

## Educational Software Cooperative

http://www.execpc.com/~esc/

ESC (Educational Software Cooperative) is a nonprofit corporation bringing together developers, publishers, distributors, and users of educational software. This is a resource-rich set of dozens of links to DOS and Windows shareware vendors and providers. Some of the top names are represented here.

## F-PROT Professional Antivirus System

http://www.infoscandic.se/f-prot/

F-PROT Gatekeeper is a native device driver for Windows (.vxd), which uses the award-winning Secure Scan technology to scan all executed or copied files. F-PROT Gatekeeper works for both Windows and DOS applications. This is a highly recommended antiviral program and it is free for private users, with substantial discounts for educational and/or institutional use.

## Flix Productions

http://www.eden.com/~flixprod/

Come to this site to download some of the very best educational games for DOS. Flix is famous for its "animated" series, including Animated Word, Animated Clock, Animated Math, Animated Multiplication and Division, Animated Addition and Subtraction, Animated Money, Animated Shapes, and Animated Alphabet. With these programs, you can turn a bunch of obsolete PCs into a computer lab for K–4.

## ForeFront Group Inc.

http://www.ffg.com

This is the site for downloading WebWhacker and GrabNet, two very useful programs for making World Wide Web documents more accessible in the library and classroom environments. WebWacker allows you to "whack" single pages, groups of pages, or entire sites from the World Wide Web. Patrons and students can then browse these sites without maintaining an open Internet connection. GrabNet lets you grab information from the World Wide Web, including images, text, and URLs, for reuse, navigation, and organization within a customized collection of hierarchical folders on the local desktop, and surf from your local desktop without an Internet connection. These programs are available for Windows 3.1, Windows 95, and Macintosh.

## Harvest Broker, The Software Site

http://softsite.com/

A search-based clearinghouse for over thirty-five thousand PC shareware and freeware files, this site is proud that it "gives you complete program descriptions, program reviews, screen dumps, author information pages, and links to author home pages and e-mail addresses." It features Windows, DOS, and OS/2 shareware and freeware. It also provides links to other great shareware and freeware sites, including the ASP. Like many other sites, links lead to more specific category links, then (in this case) to a complete descriptive page which has a final link to download sites.

## I-Comm Web Browser

http://www.talentcom.com/icomm/icomm.htm

This is the Web site to obtain information on and/or download a Windows shareware Web browser that is inexpensive and versatile. I-Comm is a full-featured graphical WWW browser which does not require any kind of SLIP/PPP connection. If you have a PC with Windows, a modem, and an Internet Shell, VAX, or Freenet account, then you are ready to surf the Internet using I-Comm. No fancy setup is needed. I-Comm has a "Mosaic look and feel" interface and can display pages while downloading images in the background. I-Comm also has a built-in full-featured modem communication program which allows a user to switch between the communication program and the browser with just one button click. Price: $29.95. Talent Communications, Inc.

## The InfoMac Home Page

http://pacific.pht.com/info-mac/index.html

Info-Mac Network and Pacific HiTech have put together a Web site to truly represent Info-Mac, the largest known collection of Macintosh shareware. Come here to find good programs and stay current with this shareware archive.

## Jumbo!

http://www.jumbo.com

It claims to be "the biggest, most mind-boggling, most eye-popping, most death-defying conglomeration of freeware and shareware programs on the known Web!" It very well might be. Its home page contains the main categories of shareware, each of which is a series of links to ever-more focused areas of interest. This site features shareware of all types, including Windows, Amiga, DOS,

Linux, Macintosh, and OS/2. There is also a subpage at Jumbo! for educational and related shareware and freeware: <http://www.jumbo.com/home/>.

## MacTCP Unleashed

http://www.scescape.com/software/mac/

This site is maintained by SCESCAPE, an acronym for Southern Cities: Experiences, State/Local Government, Commerce, Arts/ Sports/Entertainment, People, and Education. It is dedicated to offering Mac Internet shareware and freeware. It offers five different Web browsers for the Mac; a variety of compression/extraction programs like StuffIt Expander; FTP programs like Anarchie and Fetch; a games section (non-educational); utilities for graphics, sounds, and QuickTime movies; eight different HTML editors for building Web pages; applications for Internet Relay Chat and netconferencing; three different mail readers including Eudora; and a link to download the Disinfectant antiviral program. This is a handy all-in-one Internet tools site.

## McAfee Antivirus software for DOS,
## Win, Win 95, OS/2 & Mac

http://www.mcafee.com/

ftp://mcafee.com/pub/antivirus/

Here are both the Web home page and FTP address for McAfee, the world-famous antiviral shareware producer. Top-rated, low-cost products for all platforms, these programs are constantly being updated to deal with evolving concerns. McAfee's products include programs for Web browsing, file downloading, protection against boot sector viruses, and network protection. McAfee also has high-quality products for backing up disk drives and network servers.

## Noware

http://www.infoweb.com.au/noware/

This company is offering a tool kit for putting JAVA applets on Web pages without needing to know anything about JAVA programming. The activator presents you with a palette of different applets and then walks you through to confirm and customize their operations. Allows you to preview their behavior and then writes the HTML code for you to copy and paste into your Web page. Download a fully functional beta copy of the software.

## Oakland University at Rochester, Michigan's Software Repository

http://www.acs.oakland.edu/oak.html

This can be accessed by FTP, but the WWW page may open other doors.

## Schedule Master

http://wuarchive.wustl.edu/edu/administrative/sched.zip

This is the Web site for downloading Schedule Master, the DOS course and instructor scheduling utility. It is described in the PC shareware section.

## Shareware

http://www.peinet.pe.ca/PEIhomepage/fyi/
sharewre/sharewre.html

This is a set of links to shareware sites, especially Mac shareware and freeware, and on and on and on—dozens more great links to shareware and freeware of all kinds.

## The Shareware Links

http://www.sdinter.net/%7Erbeck

This site may be a great way to search for shareware; indeed it may be the ultimate shareware source in the Windows/DOS arena. In addition to offering shareware and freeware by category, it has a seemingly endless set of links to shareware sites.

## SimTel Coast-to-Coast Software Repository

http://www.coast.net/SimTel/

Locate shareware and freeware of various types at one of the largest software sites in the country, with hundreds of education programs. The site is limited to the PC/Windows platform.

## Square Note 3.5 Cross-Referencing Application

http://sqn.com

Square Note is an index-card-style database program for DOS which can be very helpful for organizing, indexing, storing, and retrieving research, notes, clippings, and ideas. Store any kind of information in a very flexible database. Download directly from this site.

## University of Michigan Mac Archive

http://www-personal.umich.edu/~sdamask/umich-mirrors/

This comprehensive Macintosh shareware and freeware site offers mirrors (duplicates) of Mac FTP, gopher, and WWW sites around the world; search engines for finding Mac shareware; and dozens of links to Mac shareware archives here, there, and everywhere.

## Viable Software Alternatives

http://viablesoftware.com/

A set of links to various shareware sites on the Web.

## Washington University in St. Louis

http://wuarchive.wustl.edu/

This is the Web site where an enormous archive of shareware programs of every imaginable type resides, including many valuable programs for librarians, teachers, and administrators.

## WinSite

http://www.winsite.com

WinSite, which calls itself "the planet's largest software archive for Windows," offers thousands of downloadable shareware and freeware programs for Windows 3.1 and Windows 95. Use the search engine to locate programs or browse the archives in search of your needs.

## The Yellow Pages.com Shareware Programs Page

http://theyellowpages.com/shareware/default.htm

This is a Web site with links to many great shareware programs of all types. Of special interest are the many educational and Internet-related links. There are many great finds here.

# FTP Sites

Though the World Wide Web grabs much of the attention because of its resources and wonderful interactivity, most of the shareware and freeware, electronic texts, patches, fixes, and updates actually reside in FTP sites. The very best and most useful subdirectories at the major FTP sites such as <ftp://oak.oakland.edu> and <ftp.apple.com> are "mirrored" around the world. This means that an exact copy of all the files of a subdirectory or group of subdirectories is maintained and updated at scores of FTP sites around the globe in order to make program files of known value available to people in their own country or a neighboring one. As I've mentioned earlier, it also gives us an opportunity to select an FTP site with the least demand at any given hour of the day or night from which to download a file most efficiently. Below you'll find some of the most popular and valuable FTP sites on the Internet. Though the WWW is more friendly to most users, I suggest you become familiar with how to navigate FTP, finding files and indices of directory and subdirectory listings, in order to more directly harvest the fabulous resources that await you.

*Note*: Throughout most of this book, I've been trying to use the kind of FTP address that is used with Web browsers in the URL (universal resource locator) line. That format begins with "ftp://" as in <ftp://oak.oakland.edu/> and in most cases you should use it. However, sometimes it's best to enter a standard FTP address, such as <ftp.classroom.net/> into your URL; if you are using direct FTP through America Online, CompuServe, or programs like Fetch, you'll want to enter either just the FTP site name, such as <wuarchive.wustl.edu> or with the "ftp." in front of it, as in <ftp.wuarchive.wustl.edu>. Sometimes the "ftp." is needed and sometimes not. Why, I do not know. The addresses given below all work with any state-of-the-art Web browser, such as Netscape Navigator or Microsoft Internet Explorer.

Here's one last hot tip: Download the index file of a target FTP subdirectory at the beginning of your search. These index files often contain helpful program descriptions. You can then, if you wish, peruse them offline.

ftp.asp-shareware.org
> This site for the Association of Shareware Professionals has many of the best shareware programs.

ftp.cdrom.com/pub/
> Another popular mirror for many programs for all platforms.

ftp.classroom.net/
> Classroom Connect's site full of teachers' resources.

ftp.coast.net
> Here are mirrors of SimTel for Windows and DOS, and Info-Mac for the Macintosh platform. Go to the /SimTel/msdos/bbslist/

subdirectory to download ubbs137.zip, a list of over four thousand BBSs across the nation. Updated often.

ftp.coast.net/SimTel/win3/internet/
This FTP site and subdirectory will offer you one of the choice sets of Windows tools for the Internet. Go there and harvest to your heart's content.

ftp.hkstar.com/pub/simtelnet/msdos/teaching/
This is a subdirectory for teachers' aids—mirrored in many sites. Go back up the directory tree to discover many resources for all platforms.

ftp.marcam.com
Another mirror.

ftp://mirrors.apple.com
A comprehensive site for Macintosh shareware and freeware.

ftp://oak.oakland.edu/pub/
The main software directory of the FTP site at Oakland University at Rochester, Michigan. Here you'll find shareware and freeware for many platforms, including PC-Windows, Macintosh, OS/2, and UNIX.

ftp://oak.oakland.edu/pub/simtelnet/msdos/educate/
A great subdirectory full of DOS education shareware and freeware.

ftp://oak.oakland.edu/pub/simtelnet/msdos/teaching/
Principal subdirectory for teachers' aids.

ftp://oak.oakland.edu/pub/simtelnet/win3/
The subdirectory for finding Windows programs. Check its subdirectories for various programs, including educational ones.

ftp.orst.edu

Another mirror to use for downloading many great shareware programs.

ftp://sumex-aim.stanford.edu/

A very reliable mirror of Info-Mac, the large collection of Macintosh shareware and freeware.

ftp.uoknor.edu

Mirrors of sites for DOS, Windows, Mac, and Internet programs.

ftp.winsite.com

This is a site for Windows users. It has a lot of up-to-date stuff of all varieties, including many fine educational games. Look in the pub/ pc subdirectory.

ftp://wuarchive.wustl.edu

Washington University in St. Louis, Missouri maintains this archive site to hold much of its software collection. Look in systems/mac and systems/ibmpc for good programs. The SimTel/ subdirectory will have good DOS and Windows programs.

ftp://wuarchive.wustl.edu/systems/ibmpc/simtel/msdos/educatin/
Another mirror at Washington University for DOS teaching shareware.

ftp://wustl.edu

Washington University's principle FTP site. For the educational programs go to the /edu/math/software/msdos/ subdirectory. Their Aminet site (Aminet is also on the Web) is the best place on the Internet to find music module files.

# Index

## Software

## Macintosh Shareware and Freeware    90–135

# World Wide Web, Gopher, and FTP Sites

313

314

## ABOUT THE AUTHOR

**Calvin Ross** is a writer and educator. For the past five years he has tutored Japanese nationals in all subjects through his business, English Tutorial Services. A lifelong love of world travel brought Calvin to Tokyo, where he was faculty supervisor of Gakken White House English School. He has also taught for Napa Valley Unified School District and Napa County Schools. He is the author of the novel *The Aliens of Summer* and *Whiz Kid Starter Kit,* a parents' guide to computer-driven education. Before turning to teaching and writing, Calvin enjoyed twenty years as a musical performer and songwriter. He lives in the Napa Valley in California and is the father of two children—Will, six, and Annie, seventeen.

## EDITORIAL CONSULTANT

**Joyce Kasman Valenza** is the librarian at Wissahickon High School in Ambler, Pennsylvania. She has ten years' experience as a children's/young adult librarian for the Free Library of Philadelphia. Joyce writes a weekly column on technology in education for the *Philadelphia Inquirer* as well as a cybrarian's column for *Electronic Learning* and a database column for *Media and Methods.* She is a frequent contributor to *Technology Connection* and *Book Report* and is now at work on a forthcoming ALA Editions' book/disc resource for school media specialists.